Susan Mandel Glazer is a Doctor of Education from the University of Pennsylvania. She is a Professor of Education and Coordinator of the graduate program in Reading/Language Arts at Rider College in New Jersey. Dr. Glazer writes frequently for professional journals and is much sought-after as a speaker and consultant, sharing ideas about learning to read with parents and teachers throughout the United States and abroad. She is an elected officer of both the College Reading Association and the New Jersey Reading Association.

GETTING READY TO READ

CREATING READERS FROM BIRTH THROUGH SIX

Susan Mandel Glazer

A SPECTRUM BOOK

PRENTICE-HALL, INC., Englewood Cliffs, N.J. 07632

Library of Congress Cataloging in Publication Data

GLAZER, SUSAN M
    Getting ready to read.

    (A Spectrum Book)
    Includes bibliographical references and index.
    1. Reading readiness. 2. Reading (Preschool)
3. Reading (Primary) I. Title.
LB1140.5.R4G55   372.4   80-10442
ISBN 0-13-354787-6
ISBN 0-13-354779-5 pbk.

To my parents, Milton and Mary Mandel,
my husband, Richard Glazer,
and the many students who have shaped my teaching.

Editorial/production supervision by Donald Chanfrau
Manufacturing buyer: Cathie Lenard

© 1980 by Prentice-Hall, Inc., Englewood Cliffs, New Jersey 07632

Art on final of preface is © 1980 by Susan Mandel Glazer

A SPECTRUM BOOK

10 9 8 7 6 5 4 3 2 1

Printed in the United States of America

PRENTICE-HALL INTERNATIONAL, INC., *London*
PRENTICE-HALL OF AUSTRALIA PTY. LIMITED, *Sydney*
PRENTICE-HALL OF CANADA, LTD., *Toronto*
PRENTICE-HALL OF INDIA PRIVATE LIMITED, *New Delhi*
PRENTICE-HALL OF JAPAN, INC., *Tokyo*
PRENTICE-HALL OF SOUTHEAST ASIA PTE. LTD., *Singapore*
WHITEHALL BOOKS LIMITED, *Wellington, New Zealand*

CONTENTS

FOREWORDS

What do teachers want in the way of a professional text? The answer is loud and clear—ideas that are practical, applicable to many different classroom environments, clearly stated and easily understood, and exciting and fun for both teachers and students. *Getting Ready to Read: Creating Readers From Birth Through Six* meets all of the above criteria and is a valuable addition to any teacher's and administrator's professional library.

Susan Mandel Glazer is no ordinary teacher or writer. She is one who is genuinely concerned about children and how they develop as creative, resourceful, independent individuals. Her entire professional career has been filled with children, both as an elementary teacher in the Montclair, New Jersey public schools and in the laboratory school at Keene College and as a college professor at Rider College, where she has always been that exceptional educator who demonstrated her ideas rather than just lectured about them. The students in her experiences are at the core of this book. She knows the essential ingredients necessary in order to help learning take place.

The "activity" sections of this text sparkle with simple but extremely effective ideas for motivating students and for teaching them essential skills. Susan Glazer points out that commercially prepared kits, packages, machine programs, and worksheets can't match a teacher's own efforts and creative resourcefulness in developing games, skills activities, and lesson plans that are designed according to the special needs, interests, and abilities of students. Skills should not be taught in isolation; the literature being used—poems, stories, plays, newspaper articles, reference materials, varied subject matter materials, and so on—determines the skills that should be taught and mastered for immediate purposes. The author shows how practical and possible it is to transfer skills instruction to different kinds of reading assignments.

Another valuable component of this book is the emphasis on student involvement in the learning process. The more the students are involved and the more opportunities they have for expressing their own responses to reading, the more effective the instruction will be. Learning by doing and enjoying is a key concept few texts stress. It is important to note that this theoretical concept becomes much more than theory through the illustrations and examples provided in this book.

Professor Glazer demonstrates her own love of reading and storytelling. Any teacher who wants to inspire students to read needs to be an avid reader who can appreciate the impact that reading makes upon an individual. Reading is not a passive, fill-in-the-blanks, regurgitation series of events. The literature/reading experience is thrilling and personal, and it requires creative follow-up activities through which a student can explain the impact and learning that have taken place.

Finally, Professor Glazer has prepared an excellent professional bibliography that reflects the interdisciplinary processes involved in the study of reading behaviors. Professional scholars, such as Roma Gans, Nancy Larrick, Bruno Bettelheim, May Hill Arbuthnot, Frank Smith, James Moffett, Jean-Paul Sartre, Frank Jennings, Jean Piaget, and Viktor Lowenfeld, are cited as sources for ideas and for documentation for many of the excellent concepts presented in this book.

Although many professional texts will need to undergo constant revision in order to help keep teachers, curriculum specialists, parents, and administrators aware of the latest findings through research, this text will live on and on and on, defying a need for such revision, because a real teacher's mind, heart, and experiences are sensibly and sensitively revealed here.

M. Jerry Weiss
Distinguished Professor
Jersey City State College

Getting Ready to Read is a wonderful omnibus book about the reading and language development of children from birth through age six. In a single volume for parents and teachers it contains the answer to almost any question regarding the nature of the child at successive developmental levels and ways to enhance that development.

Susan Mandel Glazer was the right person to do such an encyclopedic work. She is, first and foremost, a gifted teacher of young children. I have had the pleasure of seeing her at work with them. She is a maestro. In addition, Dr. Glazer is one of the great workshop leaders in our field. Participants are always fully engaged: they read, they dance, and they sing. They interact. They go away feeling good and knowing more about how to bring language experiences to their children.

The organizing theme of *Getting Ready to Read* is the seven "Learning Places": a place each for listening, writing, acting, reading, playing, construction, and thinking. At each stage of the young child's development, Susan Mandel Glazer, with uncommon common sense and plain English, acquaints us with the child's view of the world and tells us how to create the Learning Places environment at home and at school.

Morton Botel
Professor of Education
Chairman, Language in Education
University of Pennsylvania

PREFACE

In this book, reading is associated with learning how to learn rather than being restricted to learning to read in school. Reading is an activity that embraces all communication respecting the total growth, personal values, attitudes, feelings, beliefs, and desires of each child. The book relies on the works of Roger Brown, Noam Chomsky, Arnold Gessell, Frances Ilg, Jean Piaget, Frank Smith and others, whose research into human development have served as guidelines for preparing the learning experiences that stimulate the growth of body and mind in this volume. Each of the six chapters in the text is devoted to an age, beginning at birth and moving through the sixth year of childhood. The expected growth patterns and behaviors appropriate to each age from the first day of life to the seventh birthday are described. The specific skills necessary for reading are discussed for each age, and activities that serve as stimuli for developing these skills are presented. These activities involve art, music, drama, and literature. Included are lists of appropriate books for children from ages 1 to 7. Suggestions for using these books at each age are offered.

The volume emphasizes the respect for the natural development of the child and offers ideas for preparing atmospheres that enhance growth. It is a book for professional educators and parents who want to work together in helping children become literate. It will serve as a guide for the professional interested in translating the theories of development into practical applications. It will serve as a guide for parents, grandparents, and paraprofessionals as well as for prospective teachers—for all those who have the desire to make the learning worlds of children become unified, where home and school become a team working together to help children read.

This book had its beginnings in my preschool years as my parents, Mary and Milton, read and reread stories and poems to me. It took shape as I learned from my great teachers, Morton Botel, M. Jerry Weiss, Charles Reasoner, Nancy Larrick, and from the late James A. Smith, who helped me form the book's structure. It became a reality with the support of my husband, Richard, my sisters, Lesley Morrow and Lynn Cohen, and my many good friends and Rider College colleagues who constantly cheered me on. The volume became a polished product with the help of Carol Nicolini, Patricia Sogzongni, Betty Nagy, Dolores Ulrich, and Louise Beste. It grew to fruition with the professional guidance of Ronald Hyman of Rutgers University, and Lynne Lumsden and Don Chanfrau of Prentice-Hall. The book would never have been started without the encouragement of Gail Garber Cohen and the rest of my students who said, "Write it down."

To those of you I have mentioned, and to those who know your friendship was so needed for this effort—THANK YOU!

Reading Is Lots Of Varied Experiences

INTRODUCTION

Teachers and parents, no matter how they differ, agree on one goal: that their children should read. They are vitally concerned with helping children become fluent readers in a society that takes literacy for granted. How can this best be accomplished? In searching for an answer, we must look back to our childhood years for clues as to how each of us learned to read. This is an almost impossible task, for the fascinating process of learning to read must be nurtured almost from life's beginning, and memories of daily events and activities cannot be consciously constructed in these early years.

recollections of learning to read

Jean-Paul Sartre, who learned to read before the "magic age of six," talks, in his biography *The Words*, of the books in his grandparents' home where he and his mother lived.[1] Both written and spoken language were valued in that household. Oral recitation was respected, and Sartre remembers making grown-up remarks and realizing later that these were far beyond his years. These remarks, poems, and short oracles had no meaning to him, yet he liked to "borrow whole sentences

[1]Jean-Paul Sartre, *The Words*, trans. Bernard Frechtman (New York: Braziller, 1964), pp. 9–135.

2

from grownups and repeat them."[2] He was praised for his imitations of adult language, which encouraged him to imitate the adults in his life even further. Sartre tells of his jealousy of his mother's ability to read. Imitating her, he sat down in a storeroom with a book entitled *Tribulations of a Chinese in China* and pretended to read the black squiggles on this adult manuscript. Much fuss was made by his family over this imitative behavior, and all decided that Jean-Paul was ready to learn the alphabet.[3] The magic of words and adult language, even without much understanding of the materials, built in Sartre an irresistible desire to read like his mother and grand-parents.

the literate environment: a major factor in learning to read

Children who grow up loving books have come from homes where books and language are respected and admired. In these homes, books are regularly read aloud to children. For centuries, mothers all over the world have read to children and shared wonderful stories and rhymes. E. B. Huey (1908) has referred to this naturalness of learning to read as the "growing into" reading process. The parents take their children on their knees and

So, almost as naturally as the sun shines, in these settings on the parent's knee, he comes to feel and to say the right parts of the story or rhyme as his eyes and fingers travel over the printed lines . . . [4]

Children adore hearing stories retold and seeing parents handle the book that holds the familiar words. As the parent reads the same story or poem over and over again, repetition teaches the child, and some children begin to follow the place in the book with their fingers. Children learn without formal instruction,

[2]Sartre, *The Words*, p. 31.
[3]Sartre, *The Words*, p. 48.
[4] E. B. Huey, *The Psychology and Pedagogy of Reading* (Cambridge, Mass.: M.I.T. Press, 1968) (originally published, 1908), p. 332.

without a step-by-step plan for teaching.[5] Of greatest importance is that the children learn that reading is print and language, part of a wonderful experience shared by those they love most.[6] They learn in an environment where there are books that hold the wonderful language. They learn when parents read labels on food cans or when they read instructions while assembling a new toy. Children who learn to read easily and successfully come from homes where reading is a valued behavior.[7] They see parents read and, like Sartre, they imitate and read, too. Children who become readers come from homes where adults are avid readers. In these homes, adults respond to children's desires for books by letting them explore and respond to books freely and by letting them use writing tools freely.[8] The home that facilitates this naturalness of reading and writing makes these activities an everyday experience. As children hear stories and ask questions and as parents answer in a casual fashion, children's natural curiosity about words and letters is satisfied. Parents' willingness to respond to children's questions about language says to the child, "I respect your curiosity, your questions, and your desire for books and words." This is the beginning of an early commitment to reading. Adults must create environments conducive to learning to read. To do this, they must make books jewels of the household, to cherish and treasure.

[5]F. J. Schonell, *The Psychology and Teaching of Reading*, 4th edition (New York: Philosophical Library, 1961), p. 87.

[6]J. B. Carroll, "Some Neglected Relationships in Reading and Language Learning," *Elementary English* 43 (1966), pp. 577–582.

[7]William H. Teale, "Positive Environments For Learning to Read: What Studies of Early Readers Tell Us," *Language Arts* 55: 8 (Nov./Dec., 1978), pp. 922–932.

[8]J. W. Torrey, "Learning to Read Without A Teacher: A Case Study," *Elementary English* 46 (1969), pp. 550–556, 658.

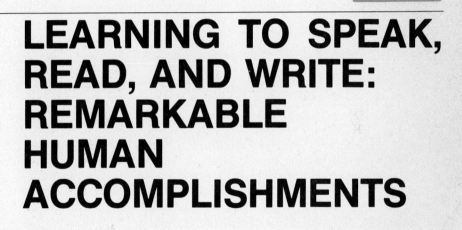

LEARNING TO SPEAK, READ, AND WRITE: REMARKABLE HUMAN ACCOMPLISHMENTS

learning to speak

Most adults take for granted that in the first three years of life the child will learn to use language to communicate.[1] Think of it—the child comes into the world helpless and within three years is able to communicate *without formal instruction.* How does this amazing phenomenon occur?

From birth, children grow and develop in accordance with their biological mechanisms, using all of the resources they can in order to grow and learn. As with other aspects of growth, language learning is part of that development. In an almost effortless manner, infants make lots of sounds, using these as they play with language in response to things that happen in their environments.[2] The baby uses almost all the sounds of infant language, becoming a tester of these

[1]Much of the theoretical background in this book is built upon the theories of scholars in the fields of linguistics, psycholinguistics, and reading. Many references might have been chosen for the following footnotes. Those selected are judged to be among the most significant and pertinent to each fact or finding in the research. The work of Frank Smith has had the greatest effect on the theoretical foundation laid in Chapter 1. Theorists and their words are cited in the bibliographical note section on page 306 of this book.

[2]Paula Menyuk, *Language and Maturation* (Boston, Mass.: M.I.T. Press, 1977), p. 33.

sounds.[3] In a sense, infants are truly linguists who are studying the language and how it works. By testing the use of language, they are trying to give meanings to these sounds in an active way.[4] The language learning process is an active one of testing, using, and discarding sounds, and it has one purpose—to convey meaning.

Infants have one purpose in sound production: to use it to convey meaning.[5] Often babies do not have words to convey ideas, so they just make up a word or borrow one from an adult word.[6] The meaning of these borrowed words may not be the same for the infant as for the adult, but the infant is copying mother or father, borrowing sounds of language from those who give love.[7] If the child uses the word and discovers that there is an inadequate or unexpected response from those around, that word will be discarded, and a new one with appropriate meaning will take its place.[8] The child learns early, almost intuitively, that language without meaning or purpose is unnecessary.

So, from the beginning of life, language is learned. The infant makes many, many sounds that have little or no meaning, but as time passes, meaningless sounds are rejected and meaningful language takes their place. The child has an intention when sounds are made—the intention to meet the needs and purposes of growth in the environment. Children begin to use language meaningfully from the time they are aware that sounds have particular purpose and meaning, but at the beginning of language production these sounds

[3]Frank Smith, *Comprehension and Learning* (New York: Holt, Rinehart and Winston, 1975), p. 126.

Philip Dale, *Language Development: Structure and Function*, 2nd ed. (New York: Holt, Rinehart and Winston, 1976), p. 16.

[4]Dale, *Language Development: Structure and Function*, p. 2.

[5]Smith, *Comprehension and Learning*, p. 170.

[6]Smith, *Comprehension and Learning*, p. 171.

[7]E. Clark, "What's in a Word? On the Child's Acquisition of Semantics in His First Language." In T. E. Moore (ed.), *Cognitive Development and the Acquisition of Language* (New York: Academic Press, 1973), pp. 65–100.

Dale, *Language Development: Structure and Function*, p. 9.

[8]Smith, *Comprehension and Learning*, p. 171.

are used in an unconventional way.[9] This unconventional grammar is controlled, in part, by the child's development, and as the child grows, the ability to use grammar will grow as well.

Children use single words to communicate a group of ideas at the beginning of language usage. When the child uses one word, in the beginning of language production, this word, for the baby, probably means the same as an entire sentence does to the adult.[10] We know that this is probably true because it is believed that children develop competence with language meaning before they are able to construct a grammatically correct sentence.[11] Most youngsters move through the following sequence of oral language production over a period of two years.

"Darren truck"
to *"This Darren truck"*
to *"This Darren truck?"*
to *"This is Darren truck"*
to *"This is Darren's truck."*[12]

As the child matures, words are added to the sentence ("This is Darren's *big* truck"). The child rearranges words ("The big truck is Darren's") and makes substitutions ("This is *my* truck").[13] The evolution of oral language is gradual and, interestingly, the

---

[9]Roger Brown, *A First Language: The Early Stages* (Cambridge, Mass.: Harvard University Press, 1973), p. 77.

[10]Dale, *Language Development: Structure and Function*, p. 13; R. Brown, "How Shall a Thing Be Called?" *Psychological Review* 65 (1958), pp. 14–21. Dan Slobin, *Psycholinguistics* (Glenview, Ill.: Scott, Foresman, 1971), pp. 40–41.

[11]Menyuk, *Language and Maturation*, p. 125.

[12]The following authors and researchers have provided information into the literature related to language development, specifically to syntactic structure. M. Braine, "The Ontogeny of English Phrase Structure: The First Phase," *Language* 39 (1963), pp. 1–13; R. Brown and C. Fraser, "The Acquisition of Syntax," in C. N. Cofer and B. S. Musgrave, eds., *Verbal Behavior and Learning: Problems and Processes* (New York: McGraw-Hill, 1963), pp. 158–197; R. Brown, *A First Language* (Cambridge, Mass.: Harvard University Press, 1974); Menyuk, *Language and Maturation* (Boston, Mass.: M.I.T. Press, 1977).

[13]Paula Menyuk, "Syntactic Structures in the Language of Children," *Child Development* 34 (1963), pp. 407–422.

same for almost all children.[14] The child stimulated in an environment filled with interesting sounds of language and wonderful things for experimental play does not learn language and understand it by sounding out words first, learning the meanings next, and finally memorizing grammatical rules last. The child does not learn the meaning of all language, either. Often the child learns part of a meaning, and at a future occasion, when that language is heard again and when there is a need to comprehend it, the child will take it in and understand it. Speaking is a way of giving part of one's self to others, a way of sharing ideas. It is essential that children learn to give freely, easily, and comfortably.

learning to read

Learning to read and learning to speak are related. Both are communication processes and involve the use of similar language structures. Speaking is a way one gives language to others and reading is a way to take in language.

Reading is partly a visual process because one sees the words with the eyes. But most reading activities happen in the brain. The brain is a marvelous instrument, in a sense, a computer that helps the child "make sense" of print on a page.[15] Many theorists have attempted to examine reading in order to explain what happens when we read. It is almost impossible to say exactly what occurs during the reading process, for we cannot look inside the human brain. So educators, psychologists, and researchers have developed theories based on observations of thousands of people reading.

The eyes begin the reading process when

[14]D. Slobin, "Universals of Grammatical Development in Children," in G. Flores d'Arcais and J. Levelt, eds., *Advances in Psycholinguistics* (Amsterdam: North Holland Publishing, 1970), pp. 174–186.

[15]The term "make sense" is used by Frank Smith to explain comprehension and understanding in his book, *Comprehension and Learning* (see note 3). It is an excellent phrase for explaining the "reading for meaning" concept.

10

a "flash" of print comes before them.[16] The eyes can see many flashes, but the brain can take in just a few of these at a time.[17] Basic psychological research tells us that approximately five to seven images or flashes can be taken in at one time. Any more will be discarded. So the brain uses only a small amount of the material fed to it through the eyes. The eyes take in the information without meaning, just as the child first makes sounds without giving these sounds meaning. As the information is flashed to the brain, the child begins to organize it. Let's imagine that the child has lived on a farm. The youngster remembers that the farm had a barn, some sheep, cows, a dog, and chickens. The child, when reading, gets the flash of the word "farm" fed to the brain through the eyes. The child searches his memory until he gets to the image of the word "farm" that has been stored away. Now the youngster has a clue to the information. The previous experiences of milking cows, running after sheep, scampering with the dog, and chasing chickens have helped the youngster to understand the squiggles that mean "farm." The brain has some knowledge of "farm," so the child can make the connection between information already in his or her memory with the new words and pictures.

Now, you ask, what happens if the child has never experienced anything concerning farms? Then nothing happens when the child sees the flash "farm." If the youngster knows the sounds the letters make, the word can be said, but the child will probably not make sense of the word. The brain cannot make the "farm" connection. When there is no resource, the new flash becomes excess information, and it is discarded.[18] Do we then read only words we know something about? Of course not! We let children come in contact with many, many words that at first might mean little or nothing to

[16]Work in the "flash before the eye" concept as it relates to learning to read was initially done by James McKeen Cattell, "Ueber die Zeit der Erkennung und Benennung von Schriftzeichen, Bildern und Farben," *Philosophische Studien*, 1855, 2, pp. 635–650; translated and reprinted in A.T. Poffenberger (ed.), *James McKeen Cattell, Man of Science, 1860–1944*, Vol. 1 (Lancaster, Pa.: Science Press, 1947).

[17]Frank Smith and Peter Carey, "Temporal Factors in Visual Information Processing," *Canadian Journal of Psychology* 20 (1966), pp. 337–342.

[18]Kenneth S. Goodman, *Reading: A Psycholinguistic Guessing Game*, International Reading Association Conference Papers (Theoretical Models and Processes of Reading), Vol. 14 (1970), pp. 259–272.

them. Who knows when the brain will get a flash that will make the connection that turns nonsense into sense and helps the child understand words in print. We can never be sure what children learn, and we can never make a judgment as to what is stored in memory.

what about the sounds
of language—better
known as phonics?

Phonics are the sounds of language represented by the squiggles on pages. These codes that carry the information are also nonsense without brain connections to flash meaning into them. Look at Figure 1–1:

Fig. 1–1

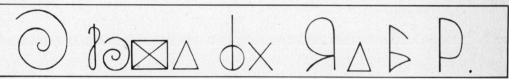

Can you read these squiggles? Of course not. You do not know the sounds signaled by the print, and there is nothing in your memory file to flash sense into this obvious nonsense. But if I were to present the symbols shown in Figure 1–2, the brain would change its behavior.

Fig. 1–2

Now there is some input. As an observer, you begin to compare the symbols you know to those you see for the first time. Then you see that there are repetitions, clumps of symbols, spaces between these clumps, and a punctuation mark. You know that clumps of letters make words. You know the words that are signaled by the symbols "I like to read," because this information is stored away. You can draw from it and connect the new symbols to the old data in order to make sense and to sound out these symbols. In a similar fashion, the child must make sense of the content as well as the alphabetic system that transmits this content. What an intricate, complicated job awaits the young reader.

learning to write

Writing, like speaking, is a mode of expression that permits humans to give of themselves and to share ideas. Two aspects of writing will be discussed: (1) mechanical writing—those aspects of writing that involve the muscle coordination necessary to make marks on pages and to create language in print, including penmanship, punctuation, capitalization, spelling, and others; and (2) composition—that aspect of written language resulting from the manipulation of ideas that are translated into printed form.

mechanical writing

Learning to manipulate one's hands and eyes is necessary for speaking and reading. The ability to coordinate the use of the eyes and hands together is developed, from the early years of life through drawing. Drawing skills proceed, in development, from haphazard experimentation (disorderly scribbles on pages) to deliberate written communication.[19] Writing begins as soon as the child can hold a writing tool and move the entire arm across a surface. At first, the movements are uncontrolled, and toddlers are unaware that they are creating the marks that appear under their hands and arms.[20] Just as first sounds vary with little or no meaningful

[19]Victor Lowenfeld, *Creative and Mental Growth*, 6th ed. (New York: Macmillan 1975), p. 123.
[20]Lowenfeld, *Creative and Mental Growth*, p. 123.

pattern, the first squiggles on paper have no intended pattern.[21] The child pounds and jabs and creates dots or trails. With growth, children move from simple lines to figures with intended detail. As the body grows and smaller muscles develop, children are able to control the hands and fingers and to make marks deliberately, aware that they are producing them.[22] With time, practice, and further physical growth, scribbles become lines, circles, and representations of ideas.

composing language through writing

Written composition is another form of language. Like learning to speak, learning to write is part of a child's natural development. Just as speech begins with single words and moves to complex sentences and just as reading begins with the recognition of one word and moves to many, so does writing proceed from simple squiggles to single words and then to complex sentence patterns. There is a distinct advantage to written composition that does not exist in spoken language. Writing is a way of making language permanent. It provides a vehicle for one to go back over ideas and rethink them.

Often an idea exists in one's mind, but in a vague sense. These ideas are only the beginnings of what happens once they are written down. The written ideas, supported by more vague ones, begin to come forth, to surface and bloom, as an author shapes thoughts when writing. Once the ideas are written, the writer works on them, manipulating them in order to build a picture through words. Almost like a fashion designer draping fabric on a mannequin, the writer drapes words on paper, adjusting, arranging, and rearranging them in a "fashionable" way, transmitting feelings, ideas, and trends as work proceeds. What begins one way will often result in a completely different product because of the adjusting and readjusting of ideas—taking out and putting in words and phrases that design the finished product. What was once a vague idea becomes an intricate weave of many ideas.

Writing may be equated with speaking, in that both of these communication vehicles are ways to give

---

[21]Lowenfeld, *Creative and Mental Growth*, p. 125.
[22]Lowenfeld, *Creative and Mental Growth*, p. 126.

ideas to the world. Both are avenues for saying, "This is what I think and feel, and this is how I go about my business." Children are permitted to experiment with spoken language from the time they make their first sounds. Children must also play with and manipulate written language so that they can become proficient sharers of ideas through composition. Written composition and spoken language are alike in that they permit humans to give a part of themselves to others. Writing must be learned as naturally as speech. Children need to be free to experiment without correction, as they did when they learned to express themselves and their needs through spoken language. Composition must become an integral part of children's total growth. Just as reading gives food for thought to the mind, writing (like speaking) releases the foods of thought to the world. Growth in writing should be treated as speaking and walking and running are. There must be time to play with words. Children must have natural practice in manipulating ideas in written form, just as naturally as they manipulate their bodies when learning to crawl, walk, and run. It takes time, patience, and practice. It is not an activity that begins with formal education but one that begins, like other developmental tasks, from birth.

adult participation in the development of the communication processes

Speaking, reading, and writing develop as naturally as other aspects of growth. The child's body and mind grow together, gaining ideas from the world and from the adults who interact with them.[23] Children are ready to learn to communicate from the time they take their first breaths. They take in ideas from their world, using these to stimulate mental growth, just as food is used to enhance physical development. They give ideas to others as they make noises and move writing tools on paper. It is the obligation of the adults in children's worlds to create environments that open the minds of children so that they may use their maximum potentials to learn to

[23]David Elkind, *A Systematic Understanding of the Child: Birth to Sixteen* (Boston, Mass.: Allyn & Bacon, 1974), p. 93.

speak, read, and write. Children's minds will open and take in ideas when there are opportunities to listen, touch, see, smell, and taste in their worlds. They need adults who will provide assistance to learning when it is needed but who will not interfere with children's manipulations of objects for the development of ideas. Children need freedom to give language. One gives language to others, either spoken or written, when one possesses confidence as a user of language. All humans build confidence when there is success, so children's language experiences during the early years of life must be successful. Children must use language with other children as well, learning for themselves which ideas and words can be manipulated in order to make their companions understand. Adults, children, and appropriate atmospheres filled with activities and materials geared toward successful communication create readers, speakers, and writers. Children must see the need to produce language and have a reason to share it. They must give and take language in atmospheres that encourage successful communication experiences. For the child, these atmospheres are everywhere. They are in the bedroom, in the bath, in the yard, and in the cellar. Places for language learning are where listening, writing, acting, reading, playing, constructing, and thinking occur. These activities provide the nourishment needed to create a firm foundation for helping children to become readers.

the learning places

Creating places for activities that stimulate language growth means providing materials and situations that help children build stepping stones to reading. Listening, writing, acting, playing, constructing, and thinking are these stepping stones. Each must be nurtured to the fullest in order to cement a firm foundation for successful reading. Each type of activity must have its own place for maximum development to occur.

Learning places are specific areas for independent learning or small group interactions. They can be places to store games and equipment. They can be places where things happen. They can be areas where deliberate instruction occurs. Each learning space has a specific purpose, thus attracting children who have different goals and interests that need to be satisfied. Learning places are like general stores; each houses activities that provide children with opportunities to respond to language, to create and compose with language, to select and reorganize ideas in literature and language, and to play with the grammatical structures of language. Learning must begin in infancy. At this age, activities must be brought into the infant's small world of the crib. The adult must provide materials that bring the learning activities to the baby. The infant selects and rejects stimuli provided by the materials based on physiological needs and goals. The child will collect experiences and build a storehouse of knowledge. Older children go to learning places. They learn to decide where to go, how to select materials and activities, when to move to a new place, and when to ask for assistance. Seven places for learning language are needed. Each is a stepping stone toward reading.

1. *The Listening Place*
2. *The Writing Place*
3. *The Acting Place*
4. *The Reading Place*
5. *The Playing Place*
6. *The Constructing Place*
7. *The Thinking Place*

Even small homes and classrooms can have seven places, for places are as much attitudes as they are physical spaces. These seven places provide the many kinds of experiences needed for maximum development in reading. The areas need not be permanent. They can be created in an instant by the activity in use. One can read in the same area used to play, write, or act. Materials change, specific goals change, but attitudes about learning remain the same. The freedom to manipulate and experiment with materials and ideas must be present at all times in all places. This freedom makes small places large and large ones small. The healthy atmospheres provide lots of varied experiences that create a love of reading for life.

the listening place

Listening, which provides the basis for literacy, is an art that must be learned. Children learn to select and respond to language when they learn to listen. Through listening come vocabulary skills and the attention skills necessary for learning to read. The youngest children learn most of what is needed by listening. In the nursery, the child listens to the sounds of mother's and father's voices. As the baby learns to crawl and walk, the child moves to places where listening to selected sounds of the world is convenient. Children need listening experiences that include music, literature, and other specially prepared materials.

the writing place

Making ideas and feelings permanent is the art of written language. Writing is putting things down forever. It is responding to the memories and summaries of experiences that have occurred from life's beginning. One composes through written language, responding to the world. Just as painting a picture is communicating by writing, composing a rhyme is communicating in written form. Children need to be authors so that they may appreciate the authorship of others. They need materials with which to write and a place to compose. They need activities that help them create ideas to write about. Children must have encouragement and positive feedback from adults in their worlds in order to build the confidence needed to communicate by writing.

the acting place

Acting and dramatic play are synonymous. When children act, they are playing the games of life. They are "feeling" situations, trying roles; in general, they are explaining the phenomena of daily living to themselves. Children must have time to play if they are to learn to read, write and spell, for play is the basis for intellectual development necessary for using letters and words in order to read.[24] Child

[24]Carl D. Glickman, "Problem: Declining Achievement Scores Solution: Let Them Play!" *Kappan* 60: 6 (Feb., 1979), pp. 454–455.

psychologists have much evidence which strongly suggests that without time and space to play at all ages of childhood, children will not be successful with letters, words, and the ability to compute.[25] When children read, they are expected to understand the many uses of letters. They must be aware of the fact that the letter "M," for example, is first a letter. It represents a particular sound, and it can be used in many different parts of words and sentences. Its sound can even be used alone and have meaning. Children are expected to take each letter and to use it and reuse it in many different ways when reading. Children cannot manipulate letters, however, until they learn to manipulate. Manipulation is a management skill that helps each person deal with objects, ideas, and situations. It makes sense, therefore, to assume that before children manage reading tasks, they must first learn to manage, to use, to organize, and to classify by tackling situations during play. Let's suppose that a preschooler is engaged in play activity with a toy truck. The truck has many uses, which means that it can be classified many different ways. First, it is a vehicle for transportation. The child can sit on it and be transported. It is also a vehicle upon which the child can transport things—a doll, other toys, and foods. So the child moves from being on the vehicle and moving to controlling the vehicle and moving other things. The truck can also become part of a large brigade of vehicles, a part of a parade where all are moving in unison. Here the truck is part of a larger group, not an object alone. So, just as the letter "M" stands alone, the truck is used by itself. Just as the letter has a sound of its own, so the truck has a purpose—to carry objects. Just as the letter is part of a larger unit—a word—the truck is part of a larger group—a parade.[26]

As children grow and mature, their play becomes deliberate. The child in the beginning school years

[25]David Elkind, "We Can Read Better," *Today's Education* (Nov./Dec., 1975), pp. 34–38.

[26]The entire paragraph describing play and its relationship to reading is based on Jean Piaget's explanation of the development of thought. Much can be gained by reading any of the books cited in the bibliographical section of this book. In addition, P. G. Richmond has written a simplified version of Piaget's theory. It can be found in P. G. Richmond, *An Introduction to Piaget* (New York: Basic Books, 1970), pp. 14–31.

will "play mechanic" and take the truck apart and put it back together again. The part will be placed in a different order and then reordered. This play is wonderful experience for using the "M" at the beginning of a word and then using it again in the middle or at the end of words. The organizing and reorganizing of the truck parts is equivalent in manipulation to organizing and reorganizing the "M's" position in different words.

It can be plainly seen that play is important to reading and writing. Play behavior at each standard age is related to children's intellectual growth.[27] Children who have not learned to play with objects, act out situations, and play with other children will most likely have trouble learning to read and write. It is, therefore, imperative to recognize acting and playing as facilitators of the intellectual development that is important for success in reading.[28] It is in the acting places that needed activities, materials, and space for play-acting are provided.

the reading place

The reading place is a place for all printed materials—books, papers, magazines, food labels, and more. It could be a corner in the child's room or the children's department of the public library. It is a place where children can interact with printed materials. It must be an inviting place where children can move about as they relate to the facts and fictions in the materials available. The reading place should have floors to lie upon; chairs to "cozy" into; and attractive posters, sounds, and toys that will entice children into books. The atmosphere must promote feelings of relaxation so that children will feel free to be comfortable with books. The atmosphere must invite children into the world of books by creating excitement that fosters self-selection. It must respect the physical development of children, their emotional concerns, and their intellectual requests.

[27]Sara Smilansky, *The Effects of Socio-Dramatic Play on Disadvantaged Pre-School Children* (New York: Wiley, 1968); Brian Sutton-Smith, *The Psychology of Play* (New York: Arno Press, 1976).
[28]Sylvia Kremin, *Three and Fours Go to School* (Englewood Cliffs, N.J.: Prentice-Hall, 1975).

the playing place:
building skills

In this book, "play" will refer to playing with games in order to develop specific skills. Game-playing involves manipulation—organizing objects, classifying ideas, describing details—in other words, using tools of thought. Children must use thinking tools, organizing ideas over and over again in order to learn reading skills. Each reading skill can be "played with" or practiced within the framework of a game. The child must play the game in order to learn the reading skill and must play to learn which skills they do not know. Two kinds of games, therefore, are needed for playing with reading skills: the game that helps the child learn the skill—the teaching game; and the game that helps the child learn where help is needed—the testing game. The place to play must, therefore, include games that teach a skill and companion games that test each skill.

CHARACTERISTICS OF TEACHING GAMES FOR THE PLAYING PLACE: Teaching games are designed to help children learn to use reading skills. These games are unique in that they are error free. Every response offered by the player is correct, and success is always inevitable. Figure 1–3 shows this error-free concept. The purpose of this success-oriented learning game is teaching the concept of compound words. The child will play with the game until the pieces fit. It is assumed that the youngster can easily work a puzzle, so success in puzzle construction is assured. When the child makes a word, the adult can say that word. Children will repeat the words over and over again as they work with the puzzle game. All of the pieces that can be added to the word "fire" will fit. There is no possibility of error.

CHARACTERISTICS OF TESTING GAMES FOR THE PLAYING PLACE: Testing games, which strengthen and reinforce that which has been learned, are checks on learning. There is usually a correct and an incorrect answer. Children test their ability to use a reading skill by playing the game and either winning or losing. Testing games often foster the competitive drive present

20

in most youngsters. The testing game shown in Figure 1–4 could be used after the concept of compound words has been taught in the playing place. The child must make a compound word by matching two cards. The cards have straight edges that offer no clue to correct responses. The player knows which is correct because instruction was given before the child was expected to use this testing material. Children will select testing games when they are sure that they know the information needed to play the game. Self-selection and rejection help to ensure success and to encourage the youngster.

The place to play is usually a place where children sit and manipulate games. Much pleasure accompanies learning when children use commercial and home-made materials independently and find success.

the constructing place

The place to construct is a place to manipulate materials in order to express ideas. Expressions, in this place, happen through the arts. The processes of drawing, painting, woodworking, sewing, and cooking help children bring together diverse elements of their experiences. In the process of creating, children give a part of themselves to the world. They

Fig. 1–3 and 1–4

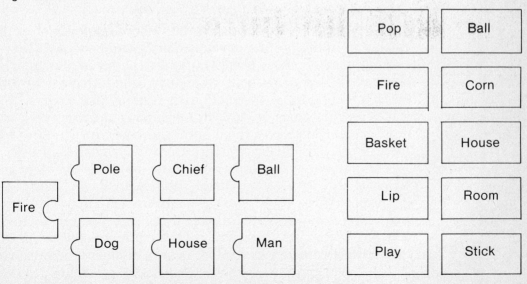

let the world know how they feel, how they think, and how they see. For children, constructing through artistic media is a unifying experience. Art pulls together, in a visual way, children's experiences. Teachers and parents can see how children interpret the world, their reactions and feelings about it.

the thinking place

The place to think is a place that provides the time for reflection, reaction, and organization of ideas. Part of learning is reflecting on experiences. Children need to be by themselves for periods of time in order to reflect, in privacy, on the ideas and feelings they collect from reading and writing. This place to think exists in all places, but it can be a special desk, a corner, or a large cardboard box that a child can crawl into. It needs to be a place where children can read, write, and think without interruption for sustained periods of time, free of adult comments, corrections, and interruptions. Places for private interactions with reading and writing make these activities become habits. The habit of reading permits thinking and dreaming about things that are read.

what occurs in these seven learning places?

The learning places are environments created to stimulate the development of children's abilities to communicate. In these places, children feel free to play in order to develop almost without realization the prerequisite skills necessary for formal instruction in reading and writing. The places provide props to play with whenever children wish, and they make available to them sufficient space in which to use these props without interference from the activities of others. As children grow, they are able to store materials in a systematic way and to preserve them for repeated use. Places for learning provide these storage facilities. Children play with materials alone or with others, using and reusing them in learning places. As they play, they become involved with the four critical experiences that are necessary for creating readers:

1. *Children respond to language they hear and read.*
2. *Children read, write, and listen to language for uninterrupted periods of time.*
3. *Children compose their own language in speaking, writing, acting, and constructing activities.*
4. *Children become aware of the grammatical structures of language by playing with language patterns as they talk, act, write, and read.*[29]

As children work in learning places, gaining experiences in the critical areas, they will develop their abilities to think. Thinking involves, among other factors, these fundamental activities:

COMPARING: observing similarities and differences between ideas, objects, and feelings.

SUMMARIZING: storing ideas in memory for future reference so that the child can connect something already in memory to a new flash presented in reading, writing, or listening.

OBSERVING: looking and watching, noting and perceiving, paying attention with a particular purpose in mind.

CLASSIFYING: sorting things according to some principle in one's mind.

CRITICIZING: making judgments based on information in order to think critically.

IMAGINING: creating new or original ideas from old information.

MAKING DECISIONS: helping to solve problems about ideas, feelings, and concepts encountered throughout life.[30]

Each learning place, its materials and activities, forces children to incorporate the four critical experiences necessary for developing readers into play. Each thinking

[29]Morton Botel, ''A Pennsylvania Comprehensive Reading/Communication Arts Plan'' (Harrisburg, Penn.: State Department of Education, 1978).

[30]Louis Edward Raths, Arthur Jonas, Selma Wassermann and Arnold M. Rothstein, *Teaching for Thinking: Theory and Application* (Columbus, Ohio: Merrill, 1967), pp. 5–16.

Table 1-1
critical experiences—places for interacting with children; how they foster thinking experiences

LEARNING PLACES CRITICAL EXPERIENCE	LISTENING	WRITING	ACTING
Responding to language experiences.	Collects data, classifies it, and stores experience for responding.	Imagines and classifies ideas about making decisions about what is heard and read by drawing and by writing language.	Organizes data collected by imagining about plots, experiences, places, or times by acting upon these with or without words.
Sustained reading, writing, and listening experiences.	Forces the development of attention skills, which establishes the reading habit. Permits the child to collect, organize, compare, and make decisions about materials for later use. Develops the aesthetic aspects of language.	Forces interactions for habit formation. Encourages the manipulation of data collections. Helps the decision-making process as students make their own decisions and select materials and ideas without outside interference.	Creates images for recalling information through drama. Develops the organization of ideas for the classification of body behaviors and behavior with language.
Composing in written, spoken, and body language.	Uses collected data for the development of imagination. Makes judgments by using collected data to judge self-development critically. Compares written and oral language productions.	Makes decisions about selections for writing and provides a medium through which to classify ideas. Collects data and uses the imagination to create new individual ideas from factual knowledge.	Provides an opportunity to exhibit compositions. Gives the child an opportunity to decide what to share. This is part of the decision making process. Encourages the growth of imagination by using the body for the release of ideas based on collections of data.
Becoming aware of the structure and meaning of language for more effective manipulation.	Home, school, and the world outside provide models so that children can select, judge, evaluate, and make decisions about language for effective use in communicating.	Copies patterns, and decides and judges how they are different or similar. Making decisions and classifying their use in written form develops language habits.	Uses colorful language collected by organizing and judging which actions and structures in language are most effective.

CRITICAL EXPERIENCE	READING	PLAYING	CONSTRUCTING	THINKING
Responding to language experience	Makes decisions for the selection of materials to *criticize, classify data, imagine,* and *observe.* Helps self-evaluation for making reading a habit.	Competitive games (board or card) require classification, recalling, organizing, and making decisions about activities with language.	Reproduction of objects is evidence of internalizing *collected data,* of using imagination, and of *classifying* and *criticizing decisions.*	Encourages the release of ideas by permitting the child to *imagine, interpret, make decisions,* and *observe* relationships in literature by responses based on inner feelings and emotions.
Sustained reading, writing, and listening experiences.	Learns to *make decisions* about choices based on personal *judgments, observations,* and *imagination.*	Interacts with plots, characters, and places in literature for periods of time by *organizing, imagining, observing,* and *making decisions* about materials for uninterrupted time periods.	Develops games to play by *imagining, organizing, comparing,* and *deciding* upon *data collected.*	Organizes, collects, imagines, and criticizes data collected.
Composing in written, spoken, and body language.	Provides a place to select, *make decisions, organize, compare,* and *collect* creations for others to read and hear. Builds self-confidence for making decisions and *judgments* about the work produced.	Develops games by *imagining,* by *comparing* existing games, by *deciding,* and by *organizing collected data* for game construction.	Self-selects and *organizes* creations developed through many art forms in order to unify experiences for self-*criticism* and self-*evaluation.*	*Imagines* and records in memory or in written form *classified data, collections, decision,* and *judgments,* using time and freedom to reflect upon experiences.
Becoming aware of the structure and meaning of language for more manipulation.	By reading in a place appropriate for language learning, children will come upon models of structure and interact with them in a free way.	Rules in games force children to *select* appropriate responses. Forces *organization, observation, comparison,* and *making judgments* about language structures.	Tests the child's ability to use language. When playing games, the child must *compare, classify, make judgments,* and *make decisions* about information used.	Time to contemplate forces the child to *decide* which structures feel and sound best. Makes *judgments* about structures and tests them silently for the development of decisions.

activity is used in conjunction with play experiences. The charts on the following pages illustrate the integration of the experiences and thinking activities as children move in and out of learning places.

relevance of the environment to life and learning to read, write, speak, and listen in order to communicate

The thinking operations, as seen in Table 1–1, are used in all activities in all learning places. As children move about, manipulating ideas through language and experiences, they are strengthening their abilities to manage ideas. As children take in experiences, they are experimenting with their management systems, refining them as they encounter all learning. The more highly developed children's thinking abilities become, the more able they will be to handle printed materials for reading. Organizing and arranging experiences that develop thinkers help to ensure the use of thinking activities. Creating childlike environments from birth means building positive feelings about language from the child's first day of life. Positive attitudes about language from birth are essential for laying a firm foundation for building the positive feelings needed in order to learn to read. The language necessary for reading is the same language used when parents hold and rock the infant and use colorful creative language that "sways with the rocking." Words used when feeding, during family trips, at family gatherings, and in preschools are words used in the language of books. It is essential that the adults who structure the first six years of children's lives fill those lives with enriched language in many forms. Children must hear language in poems and stories and songs. They must use language as they play indoors and out-of-doors. Children must interact with other children and with adults, using language to convey ideas and feelings. The language that expresses their ideas and feelings must be accepted and valued. These language experiences should take place in happy surroundings that respect children's growth processes. Each age and stage offers new and exciting accomplishments. The challenge for all adults in the lives of children is to first identify children's readiness for learning and then to create atmospheres filled with experiences appropriate to that stage. It is in learning places that children are successful with language. It is this success that builds the confidence as well as the skills necessary for becoming successful, thinking readers.

THE FIRST YEAR
OF LIFE: THE FIRST
YEAR OF READING

A child is born. The first year of life is a period of remarkable growth and development. So many miracles of nature happen in such a short period of time. Within a 12-month period, a babbling uncontrolled bundle turns into a toddler who communicates and waddles about, making a place in the world. In the world of the infant, the first growing places are imposed. The infant begins to sense the world in the womb, where development takes place. The child feels rhythm from the mother's heartbeat and receives feelings on the skin of its entire body as the infant floats in the liquid in the mother's womb.[1] This is the language of the child before birth. Through the senses, the infant learns about the world—thus far, a controlled environment. During the birth process, the child experiences pressures and sensations that involve other senses. The infant expresses feelings about these new sensations with the first cry. The child is saying, "I have arrived and I need attention." Thus, learning begins, and the child learns word meanings from the actions of the adults who take care of all his or her infant needs. The child makes many sounds. How nice it would be to know what these sounds mean, what the child is thinking! How exciting it would be to understand the bab-

[1]Lawrence K. Frank, "Tactile Communication" in *The Rhetoric of Non-Verbal Communication*, ed. Haig A. Bosmajian (Glenview, Ill.: Scott, Foresman, 1971), p. 34.

bling! But we cannot. We can only watch and listen to the behavior. It is difficult to know how aware the infant is of the sounds that are produced.[2] In order to learn to speak, children must produce an enormously large number of sounds so that they can select those they need in order to learn the language spoken in the home.[3] They intuitively imitate sounds and the beat of sounds. If you talk to children between 7 and 11 months of age, saying, "Lah-dee-dah-dee-dah-dee-dah," the child will attempt to imitate the sounds.[4] The child is not taught how to imitate. It just happens. When mother says "Um-pah," raising her voice in a sing-song way, the infant will imitate by making the same number of sounds. These sounds may be "Aaa-aaa or "Eee-eee," but the beat and the rise and fall of the child's voice will resemble the mother's voice.

The child learns to associate sounds of language with people and objects in the environment.[5] Seeing a lady appear each time the child intuitively says "Mama" will help that child say "Mama" deliberately in order to attract her attention. If Mommy smiles at Daddy each time she hears the child produce a noise that sounds like the word "Daddy," the child makes the association between the sound of the word and the person that the sound represents.

Most children, no matter where they live, learn to speak at approximately the same age without any difficulty.[6] The sounds and meanings of language all develop in coordination with the development of thought.[7] Children learn

[2]Karl Buhlar, *The Mental Development of the Child*, ed. and trans. Oscar Oeser (1930; reprinted. New York: Arno Press, 1975), p. 61.

[3]Roger Brown, *The First Language: The Early Stages* (Cambridge, Mass.: Harvard University Press, 1973), p. 97.

[4]R. Tonkova-Yampol'skaya, "Development of Speech Intonation In Infants During the First 2 Years of Life," translation in *Soviet Psychology* 7 (1969), pp. 48–54.

Noam Chomsky, *Topics in the Theory of Generative Grammar* (The Hague: Mouton, 1966).

[5]David Elkind, *A Systematic Understanding of The Child: Birth to Sixteen* (Boston, Mass.: Allyn & Bacon, 1974), p. 20.

[6]Philip S. Dale, *Language Development: Structure and Function*, 2nd ed., (New York: Holt, Rinehart and Winston, 1976), pp. 14–15.

[7]Janellen Huttenlocher, "Language and Thought," in George A. Miller, ed., *Communication, Language and Meaning: Psychological Perspectives* (New York: Basic Books, 1973), pp. 172–184.

to think in an atmosphere where they can play freely. As children play, they collect ideas through their five senses. Much of this information, which is then stored away, helps children to draw a picture of the world. These pictures are the children's way of "reading" the world, and they use them each time they encounter a new situation.

The need to learn and to think is as strong as the need for food.[8] The child's body, language and ability to think grow together. Children are very curious. They are flexible and are willing to investigate new materials and situations. They are willing to take risks and to discover new ideas. A 7-month-old, for example, will try to find out about a toy by looking, touching, smelling, feeling, and tasting it. The child will poke and prod and push and pull it in order to learn. A helpful adult can aid the child's curiosity by observing the play. As the child pushes the toy, the adult should say, "Push." As the child tastes it, the adult should say, "Taste." This helps the child to learn the language associated with the play. It helps the child to collect information about the actions. It is essential that children be allowed to learn in environments that respect their natural curiosity.[9] They must feel that their curious places belong to them. This feeling prevails if children are permitted to explore language in as many different ways as their immature minds will permit. Drawing an orange sky and referring to ice cream as the "bestest" are both explorations of language. Children explore language in order to learn to use it. They listen to many different sounds in order to become familiar with the language necessary to learn to read later on in childhood. These early language experiences are the child's first impressions of communication.

Happy times with language create happy attitudes for creating and listening to language. Creating fascinating language that pulls the child's attention to the sound-producing mechanism (your mouth, a record player, or a musical instrument) helps the infant build the desire to listen for more

[8]Elkind, *A Systematic Understanding of The Child: Birth to Sixteen*, p. 23.
[9]Burton White, *The First Three Years of Life* (Englewood Cliffs, N.J.: Prentice-Hall, 1975), p. 222.

language. Happy times with language create happy attitudes about learning to read.

the infant's atmosphere
for learning language

Learning places must come to the infant. The activities that facilitate growth must occur in an atmosphere that respects the infant's instinctive ability to grow. The infant selects and rejects the world based on the physiological needs of his or her body. Adults provide the infant with experiences from which to select and to build a storehouse of information.

The infant's tiny nervous system is not completely developed. Infants cannot always control their kicking feet and swinging arms. Their spontaneity can be observed when they crave food at unusual hours and at seemingly unnecessary times. Infants must have room and time to move when the instinctive urge compels them.

In the first days, the infant's schedule is dictated by bodily needs. It takes an infant about four weeks to adjust to the new environment. So, in a sense, babies are still behaving as if they were in the womb. Their activities are inconsistent and erratic. They jerk their heads, sneeze, choke, and sometimes vomit with little notice and for seemingly no reason. Their underdeveloped nervous systems are responsible for these spontaneous involuntary activities.

In order to create an environment to facilitate maximum growth in language and thought, the spontaneous behaviors of the infant must be respected. Infants need the opportunity to:

1. *Respond to the world through their senses.*
2. *Select from various stimuli—sounds, feelings, foods, odors, and sights.*
3. *Create their own sounds, movements, and expressions.*

The environment that respects the infant's needs must be structured around the infant's spontaneous activity.

the infant place

The infant place is unique. It is the child's only world. The infant remains in one place, usually a crib, for most of the time. This place should smell good, look good, and have good sounds and good things to feel. It must possess a potpourri of materials placed within the child's reach, view, and hearing range, so that the infant can reach for experiences when the spontaneous need requires. Answering "yes" to the following statements indicates that you have created an environment that stimulates language growth.

	YES	NO
There's a bright-colored object in line with the child's eyes.		
Objects are placed at a distance in line with the side from which a child looks at things and grabs things.		
There are nearby objects that hang within eye distance.		
The child's bed or playpen is moved once a week so that the youngster may have different views of the world.		
The child's place of rest is big enough for free body movement without constraints.		
Bumpers are colorful.		

adult behavior and
the environment

Strangely enough, the infant's mind and digestive system have a great deal in common. Phrases like "food for thought" or "absorbing an idea" are indications that we unconsciously recognize this relationship. Just as the first food a child eats is a factor in establishing good health, so the routine activities of the baby and the interactions between infant and family contribute in a special way to the development of intelligence.

The way adults satisfy the infant's cravings for food and the intense need for love influences the development of the child's personality and intelligence. The skill and tenderness of mother and father and their actual presence have great effects in bringing out the most complete mental development possible. Adults must talk to infants during their first year. Spending time with the infant when he or she is in the crib is important. Adults need to hold the child during feedings and talk to the infant when he or she is being changed. This helps language learning. Adults must listen to the infant. The child in the first year must explore the world in a large and roomy crib padded with brightly decorated bumpers. A mobile is important for the infant's exploration and curiosity. It might have a handle for pulling, a mirror for seeing, a bell for hearing, and a soft fluffy toy for feeling. The crib should have a few small toys scattered here and there for grabbing. A fluffy ball as big as an orange and a hard plastic rattle toy are attractive to the infant. A soft toy with a music box inside provides hearing and feel experience. These things should always be in the infant's crib so that the child can grab, pull or push when these spontaneous needs occur. These materials, the people in the child's life, and the child's place help the child to build images. Thinking initially takes place in the form of images or pictures which the child can associate with an earlier experience.[10]

Let the child play; let your baby know that you are there. If the child reaches for a rubber ball but finds that it is too far away to grab, push it within reach. Provide the material to satisfy curiosity, but let the infant solve the problem. This is working *with*, not *for* the child, providing indirect assistance. Pushing the ball within reach but not handing it to the child is the kind of indirect response that stimulates intellectual growth. The child is learning by exploring through play. The adult is providing the materials and creating the atmosphere that permits the infant to investigate in the way that comes naturally.

Adult behavior toward children, especially in the infant years, has a great influence on growth in intelligence and school success.[11] Adult behaviors are as impor-

---

[10]Elkind, *A Systematic Understanding of The Child: Birth to Sixteen*, p. 20.
[11]Ellis G. Olim, Robert D. Hess, and Virginia C. Shipman, "Roles of Mother's Language Styles in Mediating Their Pre-school Children's Cognitive Development," *The School Review* 75: 4 (Winter, 1967), pp. 414–424.

tant to the infant's intellectual growth as feeding is for proper nourishment. The appropriate adult behaviors for maximizing infant growth are suggested in the following checklist. Marking the "yes" column for each category is desired.

	YES	NO
I speak loudly with one activity and softly with another. I am consistent in the use of the tone of my voice.		
I whisper when trying to quiet the child.		
I use the same intonation in my voice each time I calm the child.		
I play music for the child at regular times each day (during rest time, or playing time, or fussing times).		
I know by the movement of the child's body what is liked or disliked, what gives pleasure, and what causes discomfort.		
I do not let the child cry excessively (excessive crying means discomfort).		
The child has the opportunity to smell different odors at the same times during each day (juice, milk, cereal, etc.).		
I know what kind of cry means, "I'm unhappy and want (or need) some attention" and which means "I'm hungry" or "Something hurts."		

preparation of the infant's place: activities and experiences

The infant's place must be prepared for spontaneous activity. The youngster learns by interacting at will, taking ideas in through the senses. The atmosphere has to include activities that are varied and pleasing to the infant. The following suggestions should help in preparing an environment that opens doors for maximum growth potential in language.

PROVIDE SIGHT EXPERIENCES PAINT THE LIGHT FIXTURE: The light is usually the first object that catches the child's eyes. The light pulls the eyes to the fixture. Painting a clown's face on a bulb-like fixture will help to stimulate the child's curiosity. A square fixture might be striped. If the fixture is rectangular in shape, it might be used as the body of a train (see Figures 2–1 and 2–2). The rest of the train could be painted onto the ceiling. If you use your imagination and lots of happy, colored paint to create unique light fixtures, you will provide stimulating visual excitement for the baby.

PROVIDE "WINDY" EXPERIENCES: Wind is movement. Movement is language. Movement from wind helps the child to feel and experience new sensations. These sensations help the infant to form images of pleasant experiences. When the days are warm, an open window and the breeze from the flowing leaves

Fig. 2–1 and 2–2

will create a soothing windy feeling against the child's tender skin. If there is no window in the child's room, a small fan placed on top of a counter and aimed in the child's direction will provide the same feelings. The wind should be gentle, easy moving, and relatively warm. If music is playing each time the wind blows against the child's skin, ideas about wind will be musical, rhythmic, and pleasant. A pleasant picture of windy movement will paint pictures in the mind of the child that will help printed symbols come alive when the child reads about them.

PROVIDE MUSICAL EXPERIENCES FOR THE CHILD: Hearing sound differences is important when the child learns to use phonics as an aid to reading. The child is learning likenesses and differences between one letter or word and another. Recognizing sound differences can begin in the cradle. Music is one medium through which the child learns to hear differences. There is soothing music for sleeping and resting. There is music to accompany kicking legs and arms. There is music that can go with windy feelings from the window or fan. Music can come from a radio or record player. It might come from a musical instrument. A piano, a flute, or even a toy kazoo can provide musical experiences. You don't have to be a musician to play a kazoo or a "hum-a-blow." You can make a "hum-a-blow" by placing a piece of wax paper over the teeth of a comb. Hold both ends of the comb, one with each hand. Place your mouth loosely over the fold of the paper and blow and hum your tune. If you are fortunate enough to play an instrument, find some songs that please the child. Play the same songs at the same time each day to accompany the activity that happens during the child's waking hours.

There should be times for listening to music and times for sleeping to music. Music played at consistent times (after feeding, before sleeping, during playing time) will help the child to associate sound with behavior. This is language learning. It is sound (auditory) discrimination. The singing voices of mother and dad will provide musical experiences that set the stage for the listening abilities necessary for success in reading.

Activities to stimulate growth in language and thought need to occur during consistent times each day. Feeding, wakening, sleeping, and playing times are all occasions for providing regular exciting activities for learning.

PROVIDE ACTIVITIES DURING FEEDING TIMES: Hard and loud cries probably mean, "I'm hungry." Hunger is probably the most uncomfortable feeling the infant experiences. Giving the child something to swallow will stop these uncomfortable feelings immediately. The feedings should be accompanied with language—happy, rhythmic, moving language. Language and feedings go together. When the child eats, soothing words should be spoken. Eating can be accompanied with cheek-rubbing. Touching is talking. It tells the child that we understand the painful discomfort and that we are trying to help relieve that pain. It says, "We love you and we care." It lets the child know that we are listening. The sucking sounds are heard. We listen to gurgles and burps. All cradle language is tied to physical needs. We help to satisfy the needs by soothing and patting and comforting with words. Poems, chants, and stories should be associated with the eating experience. The words recited to the child will seem to relieve the hunger, thus creating good feelings about language.

some poems
for feeding
time

PEASE PORRIDGE HOT
Pease porridge hot,
Pease porridge cold,
Pease porridge in the pot
Nine days old.
Some like it hot,
Some like it cold,
Some like it in the pot
Nine days old.

NURSERY RHYME[12]

[12]All Nursery Rhymes and Folk Ballads, not provided by the author, are from *The Oxford University Rhyme Book*, assembled by Iona and Peter Opie (1955). Reprinted by permission of Oxford University Press.

SUGGESTED USES: Say this briskly in time to sucking as the child drinks. Follow the child's rhythm as the baby sucks.

THE CUPBOARD
I know a little cupboard,
With a teeny tiny key,
And there's a jar of lollipops
For me, me, me.

It has a little shelf, my dear,
As dark as dark can be,
And there's a dish of Banbury Cakes
For me, me, me.

I have a small fat grandmama,
With a very slippery knee,
And she's Keeper of the Cupboard,
With the key, key, key.

And when I'm very good, my dear,
As good as good can be,
There's Banbury Cakes, and lollipops
For me, me, me.

WALTER DE LA MARE[13]

SUGGESTIONS FOR CHANTING: Chant with the beat of the poem. Do it in a singsong way. Repeat each time the child eats.

A SPOONFUL FOR YOU AND ONE FOR ME
Here's one for you—yum, yum,
And one for me—yum, yum,
And one for the man in your
little tummy.

S. M. GLAZER

SUGGESTIONS FOR USE: Use this when the child is ready for spoon feeding. Fill the spoon and say the poem as you feed the infant.

---

[13]Reprinted with permission of The Literary Trustees of Walter de la Mare and The Society of Authors as their representative.

Say "yum, yum" as the child tastes the food. Repeat this poem, matching the rhythm of the language to the rhythm of eating.

POETRY FOR SELF-FEEDING
Get some meat
Pick it up
Open your mouth
Eat it up.

Hold your cup
Hold it tight
Drink and drink—
*   Say—*
That's all right!
                    S. M. GLAZER

SUGGESTIONS FOR USE: Place the child's food in a bowl or on the highchair table. As the child grabs for it, repeat the poem, matching the infant's movements. Keep a constant and brisk beat to the language. Include the proper name of the food being eaten. Use happy, fluctuating intonational patterns when repeating this jingle. Emphasize "That's all right!"

PROVIDE LANGUAGE EXPERIENCES WHEN THE CHILD AWAKENS: Waking up happens many times during an infant's day. The world should be an inviting place to enter. Associating happy sounds and feelings with waking times helps to develop positive ideas and images about things the child sees and hears. The child needs to associate waking up with life and good feelings about the world. Making associations is an important part of reading instruction. New concepts and ideas presented to children in school are learned only through association with something they already know. If the child knows poems, songs, and stories from early childhood days and if that knowledge signals positive feelings, then those feelings will be present once the child learns more poems and stories in school. Mother's soothing voice repeating a poetic melody over and over helps the child to make a pleasant association between language and life.

After a nap or first thing in the morning, do the following: Walk into the child's room. As you walk, sing or chant one of the following selections. Walk in time to the beat of the language. As you enter the room, draw up the shade or open the curtain to let in the light of the outside world. Continue to sing or chant to the child as you care for his or her needs. You might touch baby's nose, forehead, or stomach in a warm way. Say the chants lightly and briskly, with an even beat. Repeat the chant often. The tempo has a most appealing ring. Move your head back and forth to the beat, tap the crib, or pat the child on a part of the body the child seems to like best.

CHANT 1
Stephie Morrow, Stephie Morrow, Stephie Morrow
(say your child's name)
Good Morning, Stephie Morrow,
It's a fine day.

S. M. GLAZER

CHANT 2
Mama has a baby, baby, baby,
Mama has a baby, baby, you.

S. M. GLAZER

CHANT 3
Where are you going to, my pretty maid?
I'm going a-milking, sir, she said,
Sir, she said, sir, she said,
I'm going a-milking, sir, she said.

May I go with you, my pretty maid?
You're kindly welcome, sir, she said,
Sir, she said, sir, she said,
You're kindly welcome, sir, she said.

NURSERY RHYME

PROVIDE GOING-TO-SLEEP ACTIVITIES: Communicating with an adult before going to sleep is important. It is a way to sum up experiences. This special time might be a time to sing a song that has been sung to the child during feeding time, playing time, or fussing time. This time can serve as a reviewing session to help the child hear the sounds of the environment. These reviews should be short. Some going-to-sleep poems and chants are important, too, in order to soothe the child. These chants will help the baby to make associations with language. After hearing these selections a number of times, the child will begin to relax, doze, and sleep in association with the poem or story.

GOOD NIGHT, MR. BEETLE
Good night, Mr. Beetle,
Good night, Mr. Fly,
Good night, Mrs. Ladybug,
The Moon's in the sky.
Good night, Mr. Rooster,
Good night, Mrs. Sheep,
Good night, Mr. Horse,
We must all go to sleep.
Good night, Miss Kitten,
Good night, Mr. Pup,
I'll see you in the morning
When the sun comes up.
                    LELAND B. JACOBS[14]

SUGGESTIONS FOR USE: Be happy and soft in voice quality. Be rhythmic. Move your head as you say the poem and rock your baby gently as you cuddle him or her.

Hush-a-Bye baby, on the tree top,
When the wind blows the cradle will rock;
When the bough breaks the cradle will fall,
Down will come baby, cradle and all.
                    A NURSERY RHYME

SUGGESTIONS FOR USE: Rock the baby in your arms or in the cradle

[14]From Bill Martin, Jr., in collaboration with Peggy Brogan, *Sounds of Home,* (New York, 1972), pp. 11–23, by permission of Holt, Rinehart, and Winston, Publishers.

as you sing or chant this old favorite. Rock your voice as well, so that your child will begin to make the association with this poem and sleeping time.

Sleep, sleep, sleep my baby,
Sleep, sleep, sleep a while,
Sleep, sleep, sleep my baby,
Awake with a very happy smile.

S. M. GLAZER

SUGGESTIONS FOR USE: Say this slowly, gently, with a smiling face.

Baby tired,
Baby rest,
Dreams of things,
You like the best.

S. M. GLAZER

SUGGESTIONS FOR USE: Repeat this tiredly, until the baby falls off to sleep.

Hush little baby, don't say a word,
Papa's going to buy you a mocking bird.

If that mocking bird won't sing,
Papa's going to buy you a diamond ring.

If that diamond ring turns to brass,
Papa's going to buy you a looking-glass.

If the looking-glass gets broke,
Papa's going to buy you a billy-goat.

If that billy-goat runs away,
Papa's going to buy you another today.

NURSERY RHYME

SUGGESTIONS FOR USE: Keep your voice soft. Sound sleepy. Raise your voice for the first line of each stanza. Lower it for second line. Your child will learn the chant and will say it with you in later years.

PROVIDE JUST-FOR-FUN TIMES: It is important for mother and others to spend private times with the infant. These one-to-one sessions, indeed, help to prepare the infant for better interactions with sounds, sights, and feelings. The following are only a few of the many stories and poems that can be shared with children. These are loved and remembered by children of all ages everywhere. It is important to learn these by rote and to tell them. Eye-to-eye contact is necessary.

ROUND IS A PANCAKE
Round is a pancake
Round is a plum,
Round is a doughnut,
Round is a drum.
Round is a puppy curled up on a rug,
Round are the spots on wee ladybug,
Look all around,
On the ground, in the air,
You will find round things
Everywhere.

JOAN SULLIVAN[15]

SUGGESTIONS FOR USE: Say the story-poem in a singing manner. Make your mouth round as you say the word round. Hold the word round, elongating the sounds of the vowel diphthong "ou." Rock the baby as you say it.

MOMMY AND DADDY
Mommy is here
Mommy is here
Mommy is here with her baby now.

Daddy is here
Daddy is here
Daddy is here
With his baby now.

S. M. GLAZER

[15]From Bill Martin, Jr., in collaboration with Peggy Brogan, *Sounds of Home,* (New York, 1972), pp. 30–36, by permission of Holt, Rinehart, and Winston, Publishers.

SUGGESTIONS FOR USE: Say in chanting-singing manner. Move with the language. Move the baby with the rhythm of the language.

1,2 BUCKLE MY SHOE
1,2 Buckle my shoe
3,4 Knock at the door
5,6 Pick up sticks
7,8 Lay them straight
9,10 A big fat hen.

A NURSERY RHYME

SUGGESTIONS FOR USE: Say the poem in a singsong fashion. Keep the tempo of the language of the poem. Rock the baby; move in a gentle way.

At another sitting, say the poem with other language. Say, for example, "Ah-ah la-day-dee-day." This is enhancing the rhythm of the language.

THE ALPHABET SONG (sung to the tune of "Baa-Baa, Black Sheep" or "Twinkle-Twinkle, Little Star")
A B C D E F G,
H I J K L M N O P,
Q R S T U and V,
W X Y and Z.
Oh, how happy I shall be
When I've learned my A B C!

NURSERY RHYME[16]

SUGGESTIONS FOR USE: Mark the beat by swaying your head or by moving the baby in your arms. This is the very best way to teach the alphabet. Keep doing this all during the preschool years. Your child will repeat by imitating and will learn.

A KNEE RIDE
This is the way the ladies ride,
Nim, nim, nim, nim.
This is the way the gentlemen ride,
Trim, trim, trim, trim.

[16]Used by permission of Morton Botel through Robert Botel-Sheppard.

This is the way the farmers ride,
Trot, trot, trot, trot.
This is the way the huntsman ride,
A-gallop, a-gallop, a-gallop, a gallop.
This is the way the ploughboys ride,
Hobble-dy-gee, hobble-dy-gee.

NURSERY RHYME

SUGGESTIONS FOR USE: A delightful chanting action should accompany this knee ride. Place the baby on your knee. Say the poem and bounce the baby each time you come to the action line of the poem. Line 2—bounce the baby gently. Line 3—bounce the baby a bit harder and raise your voice. Continue raising your voice, and bouncing the baby more vigorously with each line.

a concluding thought

Children who succeed in school have had positive, happy experiences with language during their infant years. Children who fail have had some unhappy language experiences. They have probably learned to distrust language because it has been harsh at times. A loud noise followed by a painful spanking results in bad language associations. Children who have had experiences like these fear and distrust school. They tend to withdraw, just as they did in the cradle, and fight the system. They sulk, dream, or cause discipline problems. Parents must realize that language experiences that imprint first impressions must be happy ones, for they are everlasting. The baby must learn to love the language that will be needed for reading. The infant must love the people who use the language and must have the desire to touch the books that hold the language. The baby must remember happy times with books and must recall being held against a warm breast and being rocked to the sounds of wonderful Mother Goose poems. The infant needs to explore by touching, tasting, smelling, hearing, and seeing the world in which the positive language activities are experienced. The infant body mechanism with all of its erratic realities must be respected. There is a certain fascination found in the knowledge that growth just happens. There is a wonderful feeling present when we know that we can guide that growth by respecting the infant's needs and drives. This is the only way the small new bundle of life will grow to be a mentally healthy child with a true desire to read.

3

CREATING READERS: ATMOSPHERES FOR THE TODDLER

The toddler is an amazing person. The child is uncoordinated and disorganized, and yet he or she cries and plays with sounds so that everyone around knows what is needed. The youngster accomplishes so much in such a short period of time: He or she learns to walk, responds to the world of people and things, and, amazingly, says his or her first words—all by the first birthday.

Many psychologists and physicians have looked at the development of children and have discovered that although each child grows at an individual pace, each follows a similar pattern. This pattern indicates that the child's body, mind, and language behaviors grow together. Although not a true indicator of growth, the Tables 3–1, 3–2, and 3–3 will help you to understand the expected growth patterns of the child at the ages of 1 year, 18 months, and 2 years.

how does language grow?

Before children say words, they use expressions. If a parent smiles, the infant will copy that smile. Children's first words are imitations of the language they hear. They begin to say one- or two-syllable words at approximately

Table 3-1
growth and implications for preparing environments for maximum development: 1 year old

PHYSICAL GROWTH		EMOTIONAL AND SOCIAL DEVELOPMENT		INTELLECTUAL GROWTH	
ABILITIES	IMPLICATIONS	ABILITIES	IMPLICATIONS	ABILITIES	IMPLICATIONS
Pulls his/her body up to stand.	Needs a place to support body weight.	Conscious of adult presence.	Likes to hear an adult voice.	Will search for hidden objects.	Likes to play hide-and-seek and peek-a-boo.
Drops objects.	Enjoys dropping objects repeatedly.	Will repeat actions to get adult attention.	Needs adult models for imitating behavior.	Imitates actions.	Likes to see an adult repeat behaviors so that he or she has a model for imitation. Likes, for example, "so-big," "up high," and so on, where body gestures are used to describe the language. This helps the child imitate the body movements and the words.
Can put objects in a line.	Likes to have a toy with many parts that are the same.	Has a wide range of emotions: rage, fear, love, and so on. Has some fear of strangers	Needs a time and place to release emotional feelings. Cries when a parent leaves. Needs touching and verbal language to help him or her through feelings.		

Tables depicting growth were developed from the works of Elkind, Gessell & Ilg, Stone & Church, White, Piaget, and others, all cited in the bibliographical note section at the end of this book.

Table 3-2
growth and implications for preparing environments for maximum development: 18 months old

MOTOR DEVELOPMENT		EMOTIONAL AND SOCIAL DEVELOPMENT		INTELLECTUAL DEVELOPMENT	
ABILITIES	IMPLICATIONS	ABILITIES	IMPLICATIONS	ABILITIES	IMPLICATIONS
Grows rapidly.	Needs roomy clothing.	Distinguishes between "you" and "me."	Likes to hear the word "you" and his name.	Knows where things are in space.	Likes to retrieve books and toys from regular storage spots.
Cuts teeth.	May be uncomfortable.				
Walks along quickly at a "flat-footed" pace.	Needs room where he or she can be safe—no obstacles present in case of a fall.	Shows distress easily through tantrums.	Needs a time and place to release emotions through tantrums.	Knows that actions and patterns have beginnings and endings.	Likes short poems and rhymes. Likes finger plays. Likes familiar songs.
Can aim backside when getting ready to sit.	Will look for a place that is at eye level.	Imitates adult behaviors.	Needs to hear related sounds. Needs to see repeated actions.		
Can turn the pages of a book.	Likes books. Needs durable books—ones that won't tear.				
Likes to climb.	Will try stairs.				

Table 3-3
growth and implications for preparing environments for maximum development: 2 years old

MOTOR DEVELOPMENT		EMOTIONAL AND SOCIAL DEVELOPMENT		INTELLECTUAL DEVELOPMENT	
ABILITIES	IMPLICATIONS	ABILITIES	IMPLICATIONS	ABILITIES	IMPLICATIONS
Walks and climbs without assistance.	Needs things to climb up and through.	Dependent on mother.	Role-plays, elaborating on mother–child relationship.	Examines objects and labels them.	Likes to have his or her own, familiar toys.
Likes to master a physical task.	Will repeat actions over and over until mastered.	Wants independence from adults. Beginning to establish individuality.	Objects to directions and demands to do things. Must do it alone.	Looks for hidden toys and seems to be able to recall where they were put.	Likes games that involve finding objects. Toys need their own places.
Kicks objects.	Will kick a ball.	Does not cooperate in play.	Prefers to play alone but likes to watch other children.	Can recall events that happened earlier in the day.	Likes to see and hear about toys and outings that he or she has just (immediately) had interactions with.
Pats, pokes, stacks, and strings.	Likes action toys, clay, blocks, and beads on a string.	Must possess his or her own things.	Does not share. Cannot share.		
Pushes and pulls.	Likes simple puzzles. Likes toys on a string.				
Can rotate his or her forearm.	Opens doors and fills empty containers.				
Walks and can coordinate body.	Climbs stairs, jumps, unbuttons coats, jackets, and other clothing, begins to toilet train himself/herself, can follow musical beat.				

10 months of age.[1] These words, however, do not always have meaning for the child. The child hears sounds and repeats them. Often children cannot make the sounds the same way adults do because their mouths have not developed sufficiently so that they can pronounce words correctly. For example, the word "bottle" will often be repeated as "baba," and the word elephant will be reproduced as "eh-ah-ent." Pronunciation may not be adult, but the number of sounds or syllables will be the same. Children repeat the sounds as they are able to make them with the same number of syllables that they hear.

As children grow, they collect words. Parents sometimes serve as models for the collection of language.[2] In the early years, it is best if language sounds the same and has the same meaning. "Up," for example, might be used to mean "I'll pick you up." If the word up is used for "look up," "pick me up," and "I see you up there," the meaning of the word "up," when used by itself, might be confusing.

Some children learn to understand many words before they are able to say them.[3] They will, in fact, understand a whole sentence or paragraph, and yet they may not make a sound. When the toddler finally says a word, that word might mean many things.[4] If, for example, the child says "mama" or "dada," these words might be used to mean all females or all males. The television repair man and the checkout man at the supermarket may both be "dada." The child is making a generalization about all the people and is identifying one male with another. Likewise, "ball" may mean anything that is round. An apple may be a ball, as may a radish or a stone. This is also true with sounds. A bell may mean the sound of a clock, a telephone, or a doorbell. Children make this "transfer of learning" when they taste and smell. "Good" may

[1]Burton White, *The First Three Years of Life* (Englewood Cliffs, N.J.: Prentice-Hall, 1975), pp. 84–85.
[2]Michael Howe, *Learning in Infants and Young Children* (Stanford, Calif.: Stanford University Press, 1976), pp. 111–112.
[3]F. Antinucci and D. Parisi, "Early Language Acquisition: A Model and Some Data," in C. A. Ferguson and D. I. Slobin, eds., *Studies of Child Language Development* (New York: Holt, Rinehart and Winston, 1973), pp. 607–619.
[4]Philip S. Dale, *Language Development: Structure and Function* (New York: Holt, Rinehart and Winston, 1976), p. 13.

mean sweet for lollipop, ice cream, marshmallow, or jello. So it might be said that, for young children, individual words mean many things. Children learn words and often use the same words to represent more than one idea.

The meanings of words change as the child grows and learns new things. As new words are learned, they take the place of old ones.[5] Growth and experiences play a great part in the development of language. As the child's body changes with growth, so does language and the ability to use it. As with other aspects of growth, certain language behaviors occur at approximately the same time for each year of development. Table 3–4 indicates these behaviors, but the guidelines must be used with caution. Generalizing the time table to all children can be dangerous. The age profile can be used as a sort of "way-station" at which to wait for the next developmental happening.

helping children's language to grow

It is important for adults to realize that success in reading is dependent upon the development of language. Language development can be maximized through activities that parents do with their children before they come to school. Certain kinds of activities help language to grow. The more language the child has, the easier it will be to learn to read. The more activities the child experiences before school, the better able the child will be to learn the many and varied things related to reading. Each age and stage of growth has its own needs. These needs must be satisfied through the experiences provided by the parents at home. Home is the child's first classroom, and parents are the first teachers. Parents, therefore, are the first and most important teachers of reading. Preparing the home by creating the environment for the greatest development in language is essential for reading. Language experiences must occur in warm, friendly places. These places for language learning are all around the child. When children touch, taste, smell, see, and hear, they are experiencing the world.

[5]Dale, *Language Development: Structure and Function*, p. 175.

Table 3–4
chronological review of language growth: age 1 and 2
implications for instruction

CHRONOLOGICAL AGE	ABILITIES	IMPLICATIONS
Around Age 1	1. Language is in a transitional state.	1. Tries to make sounds.
	2. Imitates sounds.	2. Needs models to imitate: adults, children, recordings, and so forth.
	3. Selects sounds to make.	3. Needs a wide variety of sounds to hear from which to select.
	4. Has large listening vocabulary.	4. Likes to hear stories, songs, and poems. Likes to chat with adults and children.
	5. Uses language to get attention.	5. Needs people who will respond to language and give him or her appropriate attention.
	6. Uses physical actions to accompany somewhat incomprehensible speech.	6. Needs an adult who will try to find out what behavior and language means. This reinforces the desire to learn more language.
Around 18 Months	1. Begins to use language to express needs.	1. Likes to tell about his or her needs; needs a listener who responds.
	2. Listening vocabulary increases at a rapid rate.	2. Needs lots of things to listen to.
	3. Uses actions to accompany language.	3. Likes to shake head "no" rather than saying the word. Needs adult models that provide actions to accompany words. This helps to develop word meaning.
	4. Seems to understand complex sentence structures.	4. Will understand, for example, "Open the jar of peanut butter." Likes to receive commands in sentence form.
2 Years Old	1. Constructs grammatical forms, some of which the child has never heard before. Says, for example, "I go-ed" or "I went-ed."	1. These are intelligent generalizations. Needs accepting encouragement for playing with language.
	2. Uses pronouns "I," "me," and "myself" for talking about him- or herself.	2. Needs a listener who models but who does not punitively correct.

CHRONOLOGICAL AGE (cont.)	ABILITIES (cont.)	IMPLICATIONS (cont.)
	3. Uses possessives.	3. Needs personal belongings and his or her own place.
	4. Begins to put two words together.	4. Needs a model to expand a construction, Such as "Darren's ball."
	5. Sentences, such as "'Brian up," have many meanings. The sentence may mean one of the following: (1) pick me up, (2) I want what's up there, or (3) I want to pick up the object that is over on the table. Will use body language, such as raising arms, to go with speech.	5. Needs an adult observer to understand language and meanings.
	6. Says "catchy" language phrases.	6. Likes language with tempo, interesting tones, and repetitious phrases. Likes rhythm. (Story content is not as important as interesting language for listening.)

Based on the works of Buhler, N. & C. Chomsky, Dale, Elkind, Menyuk, F. Smith & Miller, Weir, and others. All references are cited in the Bibliography.

These experiences provide ideas for children that need to be described with language. Many different language experiences are needed in order to help children learn language.

Children learn as they mingle with people and things in the home. They will enjoy their own special place, however. This place needs sections to store materials, based on their use. Areas (whether a small box, a laundry basket, a space under a bed, or a large room) need to be designated according to the activities that occur in them. Organizing the child's place according to materials and their functions serves to help the child organize ideas and play habits. The child's room needs to be filled with seven kinds of experiences necessary to language learning: listening, writing, acting, reading, playing, constructing, and thinking. Adults must clearly define which of these experiences the child is having. Each activity should have its own place for learning. Small apartments as well as big homes can have seven places for seven kinds of experiences. Materials help to set atmospheres that create learning places in an instant. A child can read a book in the same place where he or she acts out a story. The children construct a paper plane or listen to a record in the same place as well. As materials change, specific goals change. But with each experience comes a new idea and new language needed for reading.

the child's place

This checklist should help in preparing the toddler's place to encourage maximum growth for language learning.

	YES	NO
There are objects to push and pull.		
There is a chair to sit in that is "just the right size."		
There is a place to jump and run.		
There is a place for large toys and small toys.		
There is a place for books and papers.		
There is a place where the child can comfortably release emotions (crying, kicking, yelling, etc.).		
There is a place for clothing and other necessary items.		
There is a place to eat and drink.		
There is a place to listen and chat.		
There is a place to create and compose with crayons.		
The child spends a similar amount of time in each place each day on a regular schedule.		

places and activities that create readers: the child at 1 and 2

the listening place

The toddler learns almost everything he or she needs by listening. Listening provides the child with a speaking vocabulary. The child listens to adults and copies the sounds of language in order to speak. The more language children hear, the more they will produce.

For the toddler, the listening place is everywhere. It might be the bathtub or the area where diapers are changed. It might be a rocking chair in the nursery or a comfortable chair in the living room where the child can cuddle up on Mother's or Dad's lap. Here, the child and the adult become trusting companions. Adults chat with the child, showing that they care. Knowing that Mom, Dad, Grandmom, Grandpop, or a babysitter show interest produces in the child the desire to please, and to the child, pleasing adults means imitating them. Thus, the child copies language.

GUIDELINES FOR LISTENING AND CHATTING: These consistent behaviors will help to encourage language:

1. *Chat at the same time each day.* This helps the child to build a schedule for expected events, thus adding a secure dimension to the new world of language.

2. *Observe your child for clues of discomfort.* Does the toddler fidget? Does the child hold both hands over the ears or turn the head as if not to listen? Does the child look or move away? If the child shows signs of discomfort or loss of interest, *stop* chatting. Continuing unpleasant behavior will "turn the child off" to chatting and, therefore, to language.

3. *Discover what the child likes to chat about.* When you make sounds of language, say sentences or sing songs, observing to see which kinds of language experiences the child likes best. Continue that language behavior until you notice an interest. Always try new poems or chants. Preferences will change as the child's listening repertoire and ability to use language grow.

4. *Chat as long as your child is happy.* If the child can chat for two minutes, then do so. If the toddler continues to chat for ten minutes, this is also fine. Do not persist and insist that the child chat if there is no desire for the interactions.

5. *Chat at special times.* Chatting should be done under comfortable circumstances. It seems reasonable to suggest, therefore, that chatting be carried on at one or two of the following times:

    a. After feeding and burping time.

    b. During and after diaper-change time.

    c. During bath time.

    d. At waking-up time after his or her nap in the middle of the day.

chatting activities

Activities for chatting should be planned in order to provide models of speech for imitation and of actions to accompany spoken language.

1. *Wave "bye-bye" as you say the words.*
2. *Ask, "How big is (child's name)?"[11] and raise the child's arms as you hold onto the word "So-o-o-o-o" to teach that extended sounds can mean bigness.*
3. *Bounce the child on your knee and say, "Bounce-bounce-bounce." The child will continue, in some instances, the action even after you stop the activity and the language.*
4. *Hold your baby on your lap facing you. Hold the child's head and neck in the palms of your hands and lower the baby to a lying position, saying, "Down." Then bring the child back to a sitting position, saying "Up." Repeat the action and the words, saying, "down and up and down and up," until you stop the activity.*
5. *As you hand your child a "cup" or "bottle," say either word, and as he drinks, say, "Darren drinks." Use the child's name. Repeat the word "cup" or "bottle" when the child puts it down.*

the writing place

Recording ideas and experiences permanently is the art of written language. Painting a picture is communication, as is making a shopping list or composing a novel. Children need to be authors in order to build an appreciation for the authorships of others. They must experience the joys of marking paper and seeing their productions. A place for writing for the toddler is as important as the eating place. As food is the material for eating, so writing is the raw substance for reading. "Nourishing" the mind by writing things down in the writing place is, in a sense, the beginning of formal reading.

APPROPRIATE MATERIALS FOR THE CHILD OF 1 AND 2: Children need materials that they can control. These might include (1) a long, thick felt-tipped marking pen; (2) large, fat pieces of chalk about an inch in diameter; (3) big, dark-colored crayons that are unwrapped. Paint, for example, is not suitable for a child during these first two years of life. It will run and flow uncontrollably from the child's brush. The child needs a table or an easel with a hard surface free of obstacles (nails, partitions). Paper for writing can include old newsprint or old wrapping paper—any kind of paper that is large and will lie flat on a writing surface.

Materials need to be stored together in the place where writing occurs. This way, children will be able to classify writing behaviors in terms of writing tools. Borrow the radio or record player from another part of the house. This will provide music to work by.

GUIDELINES FOR WRITING: THE CHILD OF 1 AND 2: At age 1, the toddler can use a crayon, but in a rather primitive way. The toddler will use the whole arm and bang the crayon or scratch it. If the child raises the hand high, the crayon will usually miss the paper and mark the table instead of the paper. The child does not yet have the ability to aim the eye and hand together. This coordination of eyes and hands develops at a much later time. At this age the child can skillfully grasp and manipulate long slender objects, such as spoons or rods, with his or her fingertips. The child cannot, however, use these objects to poke, tap, or brush, as in painting.

At about 18 months, the child can grasp the crayon and hold it firmly. A child uses his or her shoulder and entire arm to draw a line across a piece of paper. Children bang and make marks on paper. For the first time, the child will make strokes on paper in an almost deliberate fashion. This indicates that there is an awareness of the difference between scribbling and stroking.

By the age of 2, the child can often pick up a crayon and adjust it for writing. The child is usually ready at this age to find pleasure in written activities. Pleasure will occur only when the child has control over the writing tools.

Scribbling and art work for the child ages 18 months through 2 years are vital activities in establishing learning patterns, attitudes, and sense of self as a worthwhile human being. Writing "art" contributes a tremendous amount to the child's development. Writing has begun earlier, however, in a less formal way. The child's sensory activities—the touching, smelling, seeing, tasting, listening, and manipulating—earlier in life have written for the child, in memory, the groundwork for the production of written expression. First marks on paper are important steps in developing the beginning of self-expression necessary for writing words. A look at Table 3–5 offers some insight into the developmental stages of written expression for the child through age 2.

ADULT BEHAVIORS AND EARLY WRITINGS: The adult reactions to a child's first marks on paper are important for developing good attitudes about written language.

Typically, most adults ask, "What is it?" when they look at a child's scribbling picture. They try to find something in the early scribbles that they can recognize. A well-meaning grandparent will often draw an object in an attempt to provide a model from which the child can copy. It is impossible for a child who scribbles in a disordered fashion to make something. Trying to get the child to draw an object is like trying to get the child to say the pledge to the flag during the babbling stage. Forcing a child to draw objects is harmful to his or her future success with reading and writing. As with language development, scribbling occurs in all children at approximately the same age, no matter where they live in the world. It is a natural part of development. Children must scribble in a disordered fashion before they can deliberately draw. Just as spoken words begin with babbles, so written expression begins with scribbles. Adults should encourage scribbling behaviors in the following ways:

1. *Be sure that the tools available for writing are suitable for the child. The child should not experience frustration. This is indicat-*

Table 3–5
growth of written expression and suggestions for preparing the
writing place

AGE	BEHAVIOR	IMPLICATIONS AND SUGGESTIONS
1 Year	Grasps and manipulates long, slender objects.	Needs long spoons and durable plastic straws.
	Moves his or her full arm in rotation when holding long objects.	Needs a large, soft brush with a handle for grabbing.
18 Months	Will grasp a writing tool.	Can begin to use fat crayons and fat felt-tipped pens (nontoxic).
	Writes with shoulder movements.	Child needs a large area and paper to cover writing area.
	Bangs with a writing tool.	Surface for writing needs to be hard (avoid carpet).
	Is aware of marks being made, but there is no order in the drawing.	Needs materials, time, and a space that permits the movement of tools for writing.
	A large child tends to draw large scribbles, and a small child draws small scribbles.	Materials should be provided that fit the child's physical growth.
2 Years	Scribbles are often based on physical and emotional development.	The child does not draw with the intention of producing some representational image (a thing).
	No visual control over scribbling.	Indicates that the child is not ready to perform tasks that require small muscle control (he or she cannot eat neatly, button buttons, or follow directions). Lack of visual control indicates lack of ability to control other activities.
	Often finds a writing tool more interesting than writing.	Will taste, look at, or feel a writing tool rather than scribble or pound with it.

This table and others concerned with growth of written expression are based on the works of Linstrom, Lownfeld, and Smith cited in the Bibliography.

ed by behaviors that show lack of interest: throwing a crayon down or moving away from the area.

2. Encourage the child to continue the pleasure of scribbling by providing materials in a place that is conducive to development. While drawing, the child should be able to stand, lie down, or sit. Comfort is most important. A hard surface on which to write is essential for early writing experiences.

3. *Let the child use writing tools freely.*

4. *Do* **not** *draw on the child's paper. Do* **not** *correct or improve on the scribbling. Do* **not** *ask, "What is it?" or look for objects in the drawing. Say, "Tell me something about your picture" or "How do you feel about your painting?"*

WRITING ACTIVITIES FOR AGES 1 AND 2:

activity 1

Tape a large piece of paper—newspaper, wallpaper, or wrapping paper (at least 12 × 18 inches, but preferably 18 × 24 inches)—to the top of a smooth-surfaced table. Use masking tape. Place a large dark-colored crayon on the table. Leave it there for the child to use at will.

activity 2

Tape a piece of paper to a table top. Alternate the type of paper and the size used from day to day. Place a round piece of fat chalk on the table. Be sure that a light piece of chalk is matched with a dark piece of paper.

activity 3

Tape a piece of paper to a table top or on the side of the refrigerator at the child's eye level. Leave a large felt-tip pen for the child to discover, and scribbling will happen naturally. Be sure that you begin to display all of the child's work. Hang it around the child's room and around the house. Do not judge the child's creations. Hang all paintings, one at a time, in a given place in the house, perhaps in the child's room. Let the child watch you hang these creative expressions.

activity 4

If your child owns a large chalkboard, do the following: Place a brush and a container half full of water next to the chalkboard. The child will discover that the brush can be dipped into the water. The child will use the brush and write on the chalkboard. This is an exciting experience.

A WORD ABOUT HANDEDNESS: Most children show a preference for using one hand, foot, and eye over the other. Often, even at birth, the child will lean toward one side. Some children will use their right hands for writing, eating, painting, and throwing a ball, and others will use their left hands. Forcing a change from left to right increases the possibility of creating a learning problem that could show up during reading instruction in school.

The preference for using one hand appears sometimes during the second half-year of life. Using the left or right hand consistently appears more frequently at about 2½ years of age. It is important that adults *not* try to change a child's handedness. Forcing the use of one over the other is a problem-causing behavior.

the acting place

Acting for the child is a means of expression in the development of the imagination. Imagining helps children build language. It helps them to feel the pains, pleasures, loves, and hates of others. By acting in an informal, unplanned way, children learn about the complexities of the world.

The acting place for the toddler must be separated from other places. It is in this place that the child can release emotions in privacy. This place must have room for the toddler to interact with objects such as stuffed animals, for the animal may represent a whole host of associations. The child might recall Grandma bringing the toy or the trip to the zoo where the animal lives. Playing and acting with the toy helps the child to remember and relive the experience. Acting helps the toddlers to identify people and their roles in the world. It helps them to understand who they are in relation to others. Children can use their entire bodies to exercise feelings and emotions in the acting place.

MATERIALS: The acting place should include the following materials:

1. *A rug to lie on or fall down on. The rug should have a rubber liner for protection against hard falls and slipping.*
2. *A place to put clothing for dressing up: hats, necklaces, earrings, neckties, bracelets, boots, and wigs. Plastic bins are marvelous.*
3. *A mirror for looking at oneself.*
4. *Tables free from harmful pointed corners.*
5. *A chair to sit in that is just the right size for the youngster.*

6. *A record player for music.*
7. *Dolls and doll furniture for both boys and girls.*
8. *Stuffed toys and other favorite toys and objects that have a special meaning to the child.*
9. *Puppets.*
10. *Old magazines and newspapers for tearing and pounding and ripping.*

Activities for acting can be classified into two kinds of behaviors: those that are controlled greatly by emotions and those that involve other memories and associations with experiences.

EMOTIONALLY CONTROLLED BEHAVIORS: It is normal for the child of 1 and 2 to cry and throw tantrums by kicking, screaming, and swinging his or her legs and arms wildly. The child does not know how to use language well enough to let adults know about feelings. So the child acts in order to tell us, and we read the behavior. Adults must let the child know that they understand this need to release. The child needs direction in understanding that it is O.K. to act out but that this behavior must occur in the acting place.

When children begin to show signs of distress, instruct them to go to the acting place. Say something like the following:

1. *"I think you are unhappy, Darren. Why don't you go and be with yourself during this time."*
2. *"If your feelings are hurt, you can act them out over in the special acting place (pointing to that place)."*
3. *"If you like, I'll sit with you until your sadness goes away."*
4. *"You can tear the newspaper in the acting place."*

Each parent must find his and her own way of directing the child to the acting place for emotion releasing. Directions, such as "Get over there, and be quiet" or "Move quickly, you're disturbing everyone," are usually destructive. The child will develop negative feelings about behaviors, and problems about language and learning may occur.

ACTING MEMORIES AND EXPERIENCES: Memories are the results of experiences that have been summarized in the child's mind. The child does not know that ideas result from interactions with things and events. The child does not know, too, that others cannot hear these memories. All thoughts, silent and spoken, are heard and seen by all outside—so the child thinks. This is interesting, for often we see a child act and cannot understand why, for example, the child feels ashamed or distraught, for there is no obvious reason to warrant these feelings. Yet the child might be thinking, "I hate my Mommy" or "I want to spill my milk all over her." These thoughts, for the child, are as if they were said aloud to the adult in the child's world.

Objects that go back to early days should be placed together in a section of the acting place. The child will delight in selecting a doll, a music box, or a mobile that is remembered fondly, but not quite consciously, from earlier days.

activity 1

Play a record that has a book to accompany it. Place the book within the child's vision. Open the book to a page that you are sure your child likes. Do not put the book into the child's hands. Permit the child to take the book voluntarily. If the child *does* select the book while the recording is playing, say the poem or story as the child turns the pages. Be sure to say the lines with the record.

activity 2

Record, in your voice, a poem or story that has been repeated over and over to your child from early childhood days. These might include "Pease Porridge Hot," "Good Night, Mr. Beetle," "Round Is a Pancake," "1, 2, Buckle My Shoe," and "The Alphabet Song." Put the recording in the acting place. This is best done with a cassette player. Let the tape run during a play period.

activity 3

Using the taped selection, make a book for your child. You may select the following poem:

SLEEP
Sleep, sleep, sleep my baby

Sleep, sleep, sleep a while
Sleep, sleep, sleep my baby,
Awake with a very happy smile.
S. M. GLAZER

Here's how to make a book with four pages (See Figure 3–1).

1. *Select hard tagboard or cloth so that the pages are durable.*
2. *Write one line on each page.*
3. *Make a cover with the title of the poem on it, in this case,* **Sleep.**
4. *Find old photos of your child in the infant years. Collect some new sleeping photos. Paste one photo on each page.*

Place the book next to the tape recording. Turn on the tape. Open the book to the first page. If the child goes to the book, read it with your own taped recording. Read only that which the child looks at. Do not correct the child if the page and the tape are at different places. You follow the child.

activities with old toys & objects from earlier days

Old toys, dolls, mobiles, push toys, music boxes, and the like need to have a special spot in the acting place. This spot helps the child to classify the objects with another time of his or her life. The child does not need a purpose or direction for play. The toddler has manipulated these objects before and has stored lots of memories. Therefore, a certain knowledge has been accumulated from acting with these. Books that were in the life of the child earlier should also be included in this special place.

MUSIC IN THE ACTING PLACE—NEW EXPERIENCES: Music is a form of language; therefore, it is a form of reading. Children can learn language by listening to music. They can learn to follow instructions given by the language in a song. It is important to have lots of songs and stories for children to hear.

finger plays

Finger plays tell stories and make the language come alive. They have been part of children's literature for years. In fact, they have often been the child's introduction to language. Almost everyone recalls "This Little Pig Went to Market" or

"Here is the Church, Here is the Steeple." The repetition, rhythm, and dramatic actions in these rhymes entrance the child. Finger plays permit children to make a picture of the actions for themselves. These pictures build meanings for the words. The finger plays that follow are only a few of the many known by both children and parents.

First finger plays should be personal. Children's body parts are important to them. Hands are the first body parts that are of concern to toddlers. They see their hands first; they usually know how to use them consciously before any other body part; and they like to look at them in their spare time. Following are finger plays about children's hands. Memorize and use these with your child.

See my thumb dance,
See my thumb sing,
Dance and sing my little thumb
Dance, dance and sing.

See my pointer dance,
See my pointer sing,
Dance and sing my pointer man
Dance, dance and sing.

See my longfinger dance,
See my longfinger sing,
Dance and sing my longfinger
Dance, dance and sing.

See my ring finger dance,
See my ring finger sing,
Dance and sing my ring finger,
Dance, dance and sing.

See my little finger dance,
See my little finger sing,
Dance and sing my little finger,
Dance, dance and sing.

ADAPTED FROM A NURSERY RHYME

BY S. M. GLAZER

SUGGESTIONS FOR USE: Extend each finger and wiggle it as you say the rhyme. Keep all fingers moving as they are mentioned in the rhyme. Have them dance until the jingle ends. Use when the child is on the way to the kitchen for eating, when you are walking in the out-of-doors, or whenever you think the child will enjoy the finger actions.

I'M POINTING
I'm pointing to your nose, nose, nose,
I'm pointing to your eye
I'm pointing to your little mouth
I'm pointing to your thigh—

I'm pointing to your little mouth,
I'm pointing to your chin—
And now I'll start all over—
So let's begin again.

S. M. GLAZER

SUGGESTIONS FOR USE: Follow the actions as suggested, and repeat the poem for as long as your child delights in the language. Use as your child lies in bed. Say the rhyme and point to a body part. Repeat the rhyme at least once. If you still have the child's attention, repeat the rhyme and hold the child's hand to help the child point to the body part mentioned. This is fun during diaper-changing times.

CLAP YOUR HANDS
Clap, clap, clap your hands.
Clap them just like me.

Touch, touch, touch your head,
Touch your head like me.

Tap, tap, tap your nose,
Tap your nose like me.

Touch, touch, touch your chest,
Touch your chest like me.

Clap, clap, clap your hands,
Clap your hands like me.

S. M. GLAZER

SUGGESTIONS FOR USE: Do the action indicated by the rhyme as you repeat it. Children will enjoy this play when they begin to enjoy imitation. Notice when they copy your actions in daily situations. Then use this poem. It teaches the names and locations of body parts. It is marvelous for helping children with eye–hand relationships. Develop your own play using the names of other body parts.

A BALL FOR YOU
A very little ball
(clap hands tightly together)
A little ball
(clasp hand loosely, in shape of a ball)
A medium-size ball for you
(clasp hands at knuckles, forming a circle)
Now I have a big ball
(touch fingertips rounding hands in a ball-like position)
What about you?

S. M. GLAZER

SUGGESTIONS FOR USE: Encourage the child to imitate your hand actions; repeat jingle. Use during bathing or during rest time. As you say the finger play, raise your voice as the ball gets larger. This small and large voice will help the child to learn about these concepts.

I SEE
I see one
I see two
I see three little fingers;
I see four
I see five
I see six little fingers;
I see seven
I see eight
I see nine little fingers;
Ten little fingers I see.

S. M. GLAZER

SUGGESTIONS FOR USE: Make fists with both hands. Then extend each finger as you say each line of the poem. Use this play when the child is interested in hand movements. Make your voice singsongish. Nod your head back and forth as your fingers are extended upward.

PUPPETS AND DRAMA: Puppets make language come alive for the child. Puppets that belong to stories, television shows, and family outing experiences are meaningful to the child of 1 and 2. The talk, with an adult's help, serves as a model of language behavior for children to imitate. What an exciting event: A new friend can come into the child's life at will and disappear when the time is right.

Old socks, old dolls, and old rags can serve as bases for making puppets appropriate for the young child of 1 and 2. Included are some simple instructions for puppet making. Use your imagination and create a character that your child will love, will want to talk with, and will never forget.

Puppets can be made in an instant, permitting adults to meet the language needs of the child immediately. No elaborate preparations are needed for the construction of these puppets. A hand, a handkerchief, and a marking instrument are all that is required.

a thumb puppet

MATERIALS: Ball-point or felt-tip pen, and a head scarf.

DIRECTIONS: Make a face on your thumb or index finger. Wrap the head scarf around the base of the finger as shown in Figure 3–2. Pull the scarf completely around the base of the finger to cover your hand.

Fig. 3–1 and 3–2

a winking hand puppet

MATERIALS: Ball-point or felt-tip pen and your hand.

DIRECTIONS: Find the top fold in the palm of your hand. It is directly under the little finger. Draw the rest of a face. Curl your little finger down and make your hand puppet wink (see Figures 3–3 and 3–4).

puppet-in-hand

MATERIALS: Ball-point or felt-tip pen and your hand.

DIRECTIONS: Draw a face on the top side of your hand as shown in Figure 3–5. Use a lipstick to color the lower half of the first finger and the upper part of your thumb. Now, make a fist (see Figure 3–6). Your finger becomes the upper part of the mouth and your thumb the lower part. Move both fingers and the puppet will move its mouth.

Fig. 3–3, 3–4, 3–5, and 3–6

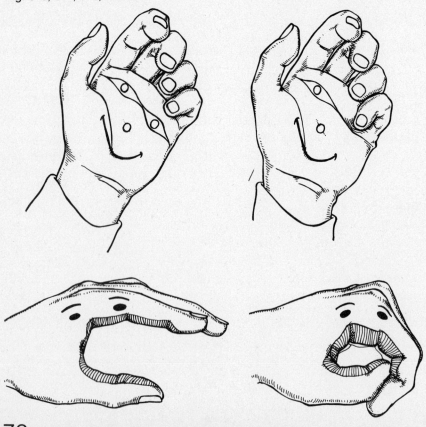

food puppets Young children learn best through play. Use this natural learning system for language development by making a puppet from vegetables. Licking the puppet's face tastes good and, therefore, reinforces the language experience.

claudia carrot MATERIALS: One carrot, food coloring, a carrot slicer, and one large handkerchief.
DIRECTIONS: Clean the carrot. With the carrot slicer, shave the top of the carrot to make hair. Let the shavings hang on the top of the carrot. Paint facial features onto the carrot with food coloring. Drape the handkerchief, as shown in Figure 3–7, around the carrot for a body.

When the child is in the kitchen, clean a bunch of carrots. Create the carrot puppet as you work. Let the child see you creating the character. Say the following as you create:

I am making a puppet
Just for you,
Watch me do it
One, two.

Repeat the rhyme until the puppet is complete. Use the puppet to say the poem. Let the child have it. The youngster will grab for Claudia Carrot.

mr. squash elephant MATERIALS: One squash with a curled-up end, food coloring, two small carrot sticks cut like large toothpicks, two slices of carrots cut like ears, a knife, and an apple corer.
DIRECTIONS: Bore a hole in the bottom side of the squash with an apple corer. Slit each side of the turned-up trunk-like part with a knife. Make a slit on each side of the top of the elephant for ears. Make a slit for the carrot ears. Paint eyes with food coloring (see Figure 3–8).

Find stories or poems about elephants. Circus books are also fun. Create the puppet while your child is watching. Put the puppet onto your finger and say,

I have made an elephant for my
(use your child's first name)

73

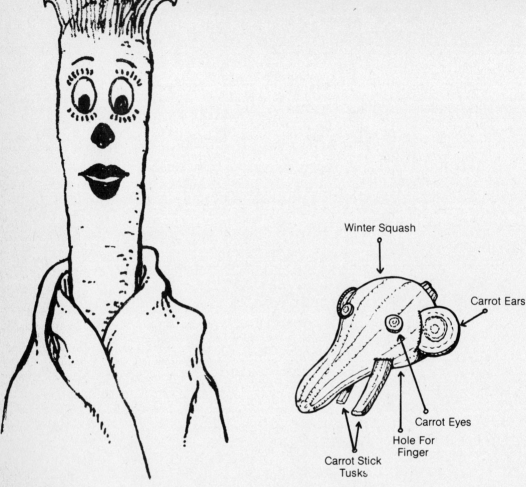

Winter Squash

Carrot Ears

Carrot Eyes

Hole For Finger

Carrot Stick Tusks

Fig. 3–7 and 3–8

The elephant has a long trunk
And lots of spunk.
He bounces, and bobs, and loves to know
That my (name) loves him so.

S. M. GLAZER

Move your finger along with the actions described in the poem.

a final word about puppets

Puppets and the people who make them come alive have a warm way of sharing language, thoughts, and feelings with the child. They can appear and disappear upon request. Buy them or make them! Put puppets into the play of your child's early years. They will help children experience deep feelings necessary for growth in language. If children are given opportunities to respond to language in their small world, later they will respond to the language of literature.

the reading place

A joyful zest about books is created in the child's first environment—the home. Parents have always played a great role in children's reading success. Mothers, through the ages, have recited rhymes and poems. They told folktales to their young children. They sang lullabyes as they rocked them to sleep. They showed pictures and told stories about them as they fed, held, and cuddled their babies. This is all, in a sense, reading to the young child. Many parents routinely read to their children before bedtime. Reading to children at consistent times each day helps to develop language and also affects children's interest in reading.[6] Reading literature to the young in a systematic fashion in their early years affects children's later achievement in reading.[7] Children who hear stories at home in the very early years will grow into children who read stories later on. When books are a natural part of daily living, reading becomes a natural lifetime experience.

Early experiences with books make language come alive. If young children hear language, they will repeat it. A 3- or 4-year-old, for example, will refer to a snowman outside a window as a "smiling snowman" if the child has heard an adult read Ezra Jack Keats's *The Snowy Day* (Penguin). This language pattern is in this wonderful book. Youngsters will fill with joy if they hear about familiar places in the books that are read to them. If grandmother is going to Miami for a vacation and if the child has heard Dr. Seuss's *Horton Hatches the Egg* (Random House), Miami will be a familiar spot because Mazie, the lazy bird, flew there. What a marvelous thing—identifying life through literature!

Parents must read to children so that they can build the desire, interest, and vocabulary necessary for

[6]O. Irwin, "Infant Speech: Effect Of Systematic Reading Of Stories" *Journal of Speech and Hearing Research* 3 (1960), pp. 187–190.
[7]D. Durkin, *Children Who Read Early* (New York: Teacher's College Press, Columbia University, 1966), p. 136.

reading achievement. The love and need for books can be built most effectively in the early years. Places for reading should be all around the child. They should be in the bathroom, where books are kept in a basket. They should be in the kitchen, where the cookbooks are used. They should be in the bedroom, where a book sits next to a bed waiting to be read.

The joy of ownership is important if books are to be loved by children. A special place just for the child's books is important for developing the habits of caring for, handling, and reading books. It is a place where the child can come to play with old friends—those books that are loved and desired over and over again. It is a place where mother, father, and child can spend time together with books—reading, looking, and chatting about things on the pages. The child should feel free to find books and to curl up with them. A list of characteristics for the Reading Place follows:

1. *Comfortable and well lit.*
2. *Familiar.*
3. *Just the right temperature for comfort (not too warm and not too cool).*
4. *Clean and clear of distraction (noises, many toys, messy papers, leftover food, and so forth).*
5. *Colorful, clean, and sweet smelling.*

MATERIALS: Materials for the reading place are books, books, and more books. Young children must have books that are right for them. This means that they need to be (1) durable, (2) tastable, (3) colorful, (4) large enough to hold on the child's lap so that he or she can turn the pages, (5) full of pictures, (6) filled with single words that label objects in pictures, (7) packed with lots of rhymes and jingles, (8) filled with fascinating language that makes interesting sounds. Books can be made of cloth, wood, and hard tagboard.

A little bit of time, some old scraps, and willing hands can produce a book made of cloth. What a lovely way to give language to a child!

doll books   MATERIALS: An old sock that does not stretch, buttons for eyes, yarn for hair, felt for facial features and clothing, fabric scraps for clothing and text, scissors, a needle and thread, and cotton batting or old nylon stockings.

Stuff the sock with old nylon stockings or cotton batting. Make the arms with felt. Sew fabric scraps together to make a book. The book should be as big as the bottom half of the sockdoll. Sew the book to the doll's middle (see Figure 3–9). Put appropriate pictures in the book. Words are not needed to tell a story to your child. Turn the pages and hold the doll.

cloth books

MATERIALS: Old T-shirts with pictures on them, any fabric with vivid, nontoxic pictures printed on it, a needle and thread, rickrack or stiffening tape, and a black nontoxic marking pen (broad tip).

DIRECTIONS: Cut pictures from fabric, making sure that each piece is the same size. These may be square, rectangular, round, or triangular in shape. All pictures, however, should be the same shape. Sew rickrack or stiffening around the edge of each fabric picture. Label each picture with one identifying word. Write that word on the picture. Bind the pictures by sewing all of them together so that the pictures open like a book (see Figure 3–10).

When you are buying toys, look for dolls or stuffed toys that represent stories. Find the book in the library. Read the book to your child while the child plays with the toy, which will seem to come alive as the words make the puppet and words a living–reading experience.

making feel books for children

Words and touching go together. In the first year of life, the youngster learns through the senses. Children like to say a word and feel the object that the word represents. There is no better way to encourage the growth of meaningful language than by creating something that the child can feel.

Surfaces that are rough, smooth, furry, soft, hard, and prickly are exciting. Making a book with exciting surfaces to touch will provide language experiences for the child.

MATERIALS: A piece of sandpaper (something rough), a piece of cloth that feels like fur (something furry), a piece of cellophane paper (something smooth), a Brillo pad (something prickly), a small sponge (something soft), some cloth that can be used for the pages of the book, a nontoxic marker, a needle and thread, and 4 × 4 inch pieces of cloth, one for each page.

DIRECTIONS: Paste each piece of material to be felt on separate pieces of cloth that have been cut into 4 × 4 inch pieces. Label the cloth pages with the feeling that the special fabric offers. Bind the book by sewing all the pages together.

Fig. 3–9 and 3–10

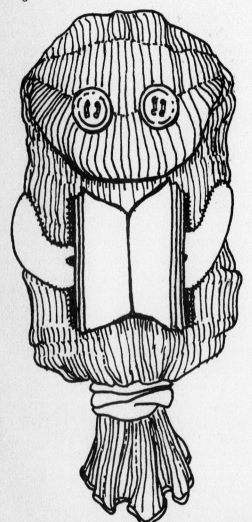

SELECTING BOOKS: Although there are many books to select, you should be cautious when choosing books for toddlers. Just as there are "junk" foods, so too there are junk books. Books for the very young are books to look at and books to listen to. Good children's books are always good. They never age. Books to look at should be washable and tastable. Books to listen to should be full of exciting language and vivid pictures. The language must be simple, catchy, and appealing. Catchy language is language that (1) rhymes, (2) repeats, (3) has consistent patterns of words and phrases, and (4) has interesting words that feel good to say and that are delightful to hear. There are catchy poems and catchy stories. Wanda Gag, in her very wonderful book, written in 1928 and called *Millions of Cats*,[8] repeats a section of rhyme over and over again each time that language is pertinent to the story's plot:

Cats here, cats there
Cats and kittens everywhere.
Hundreds of cats
Thousands of cats
Millions and billions and trillions of cats.

WANDA GAG

What marvelous language to anticipate when seeing the book on the shelf! How wonderful for the 2-year-old to tap out the language with both feet while mother or father reads it.

Language need not be poetry in order to be catchy. Ann McGovern, in her delightful book, *Who Has a Secret?* (1964), has repeated one sentence pattern throughout the text. She begins with the question, "Who has a secret?" She answers the questions, changing only the secret holder. One sentence accompanies each delightfully illustrated page. The question is answered with such sentences as "The earth has a secret" or "The pond has a secret."

---

[8]Reprinted by permission of Coward, McCann & Geoghegan from *Millions of Cats* by Wanda Gag. Copyright © 1928 by Coward-McCann, Inc.; renewed © 1956 by Robert Janssen.

Language that is unusual is interesting. The sounds of the language please the ear. Language like "your prancing dancing pony," from a Japanese nursery rhyme, and phrases, such as "screeching monkies and braying donkeys," from Uri Shulevitz's delightfully illustrated book, *Oh What a Noise!*, entice children into books. Books for the toddler need no plot or story, just lovely language that is fun to hear.

Use the following selection guide when buying books for toddlers:

	YES	NO
The book is durable. It can be tasted, washed, and twisted (for the very young toddler).		
The book has vivid pictures.		
The book has no plot or story.		
Only one of the following needs to be present in a book:		
The book has rhymes.		
The book has catchy language (interesting words that sound and feel good to say).		
The book has repeated sentence patterns (I like mice, I like hay, I like tomatoes, etc.).		
If there are words on the page, the words go with the picture.		
The book is short so that the child can pay attention to the words and the language.		
Some books are small enough for the child's hands.		
Some books are large—for grabbing and hugging.		

Owning a book is like owning a part of language—it belongs to the child, and it is to be treasured. The child can sleep with it, eat with it, play with it, and identify things about it. What a wonderful way to begin to read!

READING ACTIVITIES TO GROW ON:

activity 1 (For the child who can only hold a book.) Place a cloth or a doll book near the child. Be sure that it is within the child's view and reach. As the child grabs it, say "Book." Be sure that your voice is pleasant, with happy voice intonations.

activity 2 (For the child who can hold and turn pages.) Read something yourself as the youngster spends personal quiet times. Be sure that the child sees you relaxing and smiling as you read. Read books, newspapers, and magazines. Just read. This provides a framework for the development of feelings about the reading process. If the adult enjoys it, it must be fun.

activity 3 (For the child who can hold the book and sit with it.) Put books in the play area. As the child picks one up to look at it, give positive reinforcement by recognizing this behavior. Smile, shake your head yes, and say, "Book." Give recognition to the book selection only if the child seeks it. When playtime is over and you put the book in place, say "Book" when picking it up.

activity 4 Hold a book when you hold your child. Turn the pages in the book and say the names of the pictures printed on each page. Let the child turn the pages. If the child turns, do *not* put your hand in to interfere. The child can turn lots of pages or just one. As pages are turned, say the names of the objects printed on each page.

activity 5 The even flow of the voice and the soothing intonational patterns provide an environment for relaxation and a desire to use the language and the information being shared. It is important that children feel that mother or father are interested in the books and poems. Read to your child in the following way:

1. *Hold the child on your lap. Put your arms around your baby and hold the book.*
2. *Point to the pictures and the words as you say them. Identify each object on the page in this manner.*
3. *Stop reading when the child loses interest.*

4. *When reading poetry, say it flowingly, happily, and with lots of voice inflections.*

5. *If reading a story book, be sure that the words are catchy and that the selection is short.*

6. *Give the child a choice of books. Give limited alternatives. Say, "Pick one of these two."*

7. *Read the same story over and over and over again. Children like to hear familiar language. Remember: Language is more important than the story.*

activity 6

Use books with catchy language. Picture books with catchy language become a unique experience for the youngster. The language offers pleasure, enlightenment, and a creative aesthetic adventure. The book provides not only a literary experience but also attention from an adult. Sincere adult interactions help children to value books with treasured language. Interactions with books should represent joy, warmth, and security. The rhymes, repetitions, and consistent language patterns in these books provide an element of familiar friendship that children will seek and request over and over again. It is important that these wonderful books be used in such a way that they facilitate an acceptance of language and books. Use the following guide for enticing children into books that hold the language so important for reading.

1. *Memorize the catchy language sections in favorite books.*

2. *Be sure to read the book to the child at least three times.*

3. *Begin to use language sections from the book(s) during feeding time, when you are playing with the child, or during bath time.*

4. *Use the language to match physical movements:*
   a. *When the child crawls, say a rhyme in time with the crawling.*
   b. *When the child waddles at the beginning of his or her first waddling days, repeat the language that follows the gait. Clap along with the language.*

5. *Say language as you do your chores around the house, when the child is around. Tap your foot or your finger to the language.*

6. *Say a catchy language section of one of the books as you do your work, and then substitute other language sounds for the language in the book. For example:*
   If you have been saying, "Hundreds of cats, Thousands of cats,

Millions and billions and trillions of cats," you might say, *"Tah-tah-tah-tah, Tah-,tah-, tah-tah-tah-tah-tah-tah-tah-tah."*

7. *Casually pick up a book that contains some of the catchy language you have repeated and look at it a moment yourself. Do not involve the child directly. Just give the child the opportunity to see you reading some valued language in its treasured place—the book.*

A CONCLUDING REMARK FOR THE READING PLACE: First experiences last forever. Therefore, first experiences with books must be positive, enticing, and exciting. Value books and the child will too. Resort to books at happy times and go to them with the child in times of stress. Read stories at consistent times during the day. A book habit in the very early days of life becomes a habit for life—one that we want to create and preserve forever. The following suggested books for toddlers are only a few of the many books available. Look for other books written by these authors.

BOOKS FOR TODDLERS:

wooden tagboard books

These are found in most toy stores, are durable, and are easy for the toddler to hold onto. They are toys that are also books.

Porter, Cyrus. *If I Had a Dog.* Grosset & Dunlap, 1974.
———. *If I Had a House.* Grosset & Dunlap, 1974.
———. *If I Had a Bus.* Grosset & Dunlap, 1974.
———. *If I Say A, B, C.* Grosset & Dunlap, 1975.

cloth books

These, too, are found in most toy stores. They are "doing" books. Toddlers touch, push, pull, and feel interesting things on the pages of these Golden books.

Kunhardt, Dorothy. *The Touch Me Book.* Golden Press, 1961.
———. *Pat the Bunny.* Golden Press, 1962.
———. *The Telephone Book.* Golden Press, 1975.

books with catchy language

Brown, Margaret Wise. *Four Fur Feet.* Addison-Wesley, 1961. A story repeated in a poem-like fashion.
Burningham, John. *Mr. Gumpy's Outing.* Holt, Rinehart and

Winston, 1971. Repeated language patterns are included with good illustrations.

Gag, Wanda. *Millions of Cats.* Coward, McCann, & Geoghegan, 1938. The story has a simple plot and repeated rhyming passages.

Ginsburg, Mirra. *The Chick and the Duckling.* Macmillan, 1972.

Miles, Miska. *Apricot ABC.* Little, Brown, 1969. This is an unusual ABC book with a plot.

Ness, Evaline. *Old Mother Hubbard and Her Dog.* Holt, Rinehart and Winston, 1972. This paperback nursery rhyme book has much repetition of language.

NicLeodhas, Scorche. *Always Room for One More.* Holt, Rinehart and Winston, 1965. This old Scottish song has marvelously flowing language, repetition, and rhyme (paperback edition).

Raskin, Ellen. *Twenty-two, Twenty-three.* Atheneum, 1976. Silly pictures and catchy language. Interesting words and rhymes make this a delightful book.

Ringi, Kjell. *The Parade.* Franklin Watts, 1975. This includes beautiful illustrating and *marvelous* catchy language.

Scheer, Julian. *Rain Makes Apple Sauce.* Holiday House, 1964. Nonsense in rhymes of repetition makes this book marvelous for intonational vocal expression.

Shulevitz, Ori. *Oh What a Noise!* Macmillan, 1971. Interesting language and colorful pictures will stimulate the imagination.

Tudor, Tasha. *A Is for Anne Belle.* Henry Z. Walck, 1954. This is an alphabet book with catchy language, rhymes, and repetition.

Walcott, Patty. *Pickle, Pickle, Pickle Juice.* Addison-Wesley, 1975. A silly book of rhyming language that repeats and provides listening fun for the toddler.

play and construction places   Play is the child's work. Children express ideas in play by construction. They curiously inspect and organize objects through trial and error, with no purpose but to play, thus satisfying their natural desire to learn.

Children at 1 and 2 need to construct with materials that smell good, sound interesting, feel exciting, and taste delicious. Materials that appeal to the senses excite the child and help to create an interest in play.

Two kinds of materials are necessary for learning: materials that teach and materials that test. Materials that teach help children to learn. Every manipulation is error free, thus providing success. Figure 3–11 shows an appropriate game for a toddler who needs to classify objects. All of the pieces are the same color, shape, and size, and all fit into the container provided. Because the container is the same color as the pieces, it indicates to the toddler that everything belongs together. The toddler puts the blocks in the container, empties it, and begins again. This sorting of materials helps the child learn to classify in an orderly fashion.

Testing materials are needed to strengthen and drill that which is learned. Materials that test have correct and incorrect responses. Children test themselves by playing a game and by winning or losing, based on their own manipulations. The testing game shown in Figure 3–12 can be used to check children's abilities to classify shapes.

Children are expected to select the block that fits into the opening of the same shape. They have learned about the properties of the shapes from the teaching materials and have constructed an image of this shape in their minds. If they can classify and identify, then they will place the proper block in the appropriate opening.

All materials should be manipulated by children without adult assistance. If children struggle, then the materials are not appropriate for their use.

A special time can be set aside each day when the child can work. The child should be permitted to self-select toys. The child should have a place to play with the toy freely—a place where punching, pinching, twisting, or smushing can happen, depending on the nature of the material. The adult needs to watch from a short distance away to see whether the child needs help in securing the materials. The child should be permitted to use materials freely without adult interference. When the child has completed the play period, both parent and child should help to put the material back into its proper place.

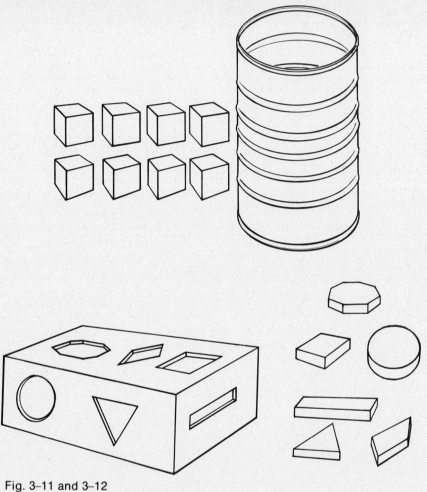

Fig. 3–11 and 3–12

When the child is under 2, much help will be needed in organizing the places for learning. As children grow, they will know where things belong, how to put them away, and how to secure them.

MATERIALS FOR PLAY AND CONSTRUCTION: Toys for the child at 1 and 2 are toys that should have the following characteristics:

1. *Some toys should have multiple pieces.* Children need to repeat behaviors in order to learn. Toys with many pieces provide opportunities for repetition. Children need to repeat behaviors because repetition permits them to feel comfortable with an activity and builds confidence for learning. They learn to see that materials can be used in alternative ways. Blocks and beads are only a few of the toys with similar parts.

2. *Some toys should make sounds.* Sound toys include books that help adults to convey the sounds of the world to children. These are important for later success in reading, for it is essential that children differentiate between sounds. This is important for hearing differences in the sounds of letters and words. It is important, too, that children associate different sounds with different situations. This helps children to understand the world through their ears. Understanding through sound and remembering these sounds helps children to visualize objects and sounds when they read. There are many books with sounds in them. Margaret Wise Brown is only one of the many authors who has written stories using sounds. Some of her books include:

Brown, Margaret Wise. *The Noisy Book.* Harper & Row, 1939, paperback.
———. *The Indoor Noisy Book.* Harper & Row, 1942, paperback.
———. *The Winter Noisy Book.* Harper & Row, 1947, paperback.

3. *Some toys should be for pushing and pulling.* Toys that push and pull make simple sounds. A pull toy with a bell attached will help a child associate the bell sound with the physical pushing and pulling behaviors. The child is, in essence, creating the sound when pulling. The pull toy with a built-in sound device will permit the child to exercise the need to pull or push. This helps to develop the large and small muscles that are important for the coordination necessary for writing. Pull and push toys help to develop sound associations. They provide experiences that give the child a repertoire for classifying differences in sounds. There are many toys

available that encourage pushing and pulling exercises. Only a few of these are included below:

Baby rattles
Baby bells
Play phone
Mother Goose in music box
*Toys that make sounds when you push a
    button or pull a cord*
Baby balls to clutch onto
Toys to push and pull
Music boxes that you can see into

4. *Some toys should be for constructing and pounding.* Toddlers need to pound. Children of 1 and 2 need to create by constructing. Manipulating materials in the beginning years is similar to manipulating words and phrases when children read and write. It is a form of self-expression when children use their large and small muscles in accordance with their needs. The constructing place must have things that can be pounded and beaten. There must be opportunities for twisting and turning and for children to use their fingers and muscles in different ways. Materials are needed that involve fingers, fists, and elbows.

creating playing materials for the toddler— toys with multiple pieces

All you need are some containers and many of the following: bottle tops, large buttons, large beads for stringing, small blocks, and thread spools. Collect a large group of one of these types of items. Put them into a plastic container with a lid that snaps on. The child will play with this freely, easily, and with much delight.

Sound toys are toys that shake, play music, or have a surface on which sounds can be produced. These can be easily constructed.

toys to shake

MATERIALS: A hard plastic unbreakable container (or wooden box), buttons or beans or rice, and epoxy glue.

DIRECTIONS: Fill the container half full with rice, beans, or buttons. Place the top over the container and secure with glue. Let dry for the period of time specified by the directions on the adhesive material. Toys to shake should be small so that small hands can hold them, but they should be large enough so that they can't be swallowed.

Toys that create sounds can be hit, banged, or rubbed.

toys to hit

MATERIALS: A coffee can, a plastic top or some rubber book-binding tape

DIRECTIONS: Place the plastic top over the coffee can opening or stretch rubber over the coffee can. Secure the covering with book-binding tape (see Figure 3–13). The child should instinctively hit the homemade drum and compose sounds.

toys to rub

MATERIALS: A piece of wood, sanded smooth, approximately 6 × 3 inches × 2 inches, a piece of sandpaper, a stick, and some epoxy glue.

DIRECTIONS: Paste the sandpaper on top of the wood block. Be sure that it covers the surface (see Figure 3–14). Rub the sandpaper woodblock with the stick. Give it to the child, and the youngster will make music by rubbing, too.

An old pot with a lid is marvelous for banging and making sounds. It provides the child with many experiences for pushing and pulling as well as those for opening and closing.

A large soup spoon and a tin plate can also serve as an excellent noise-making device. Youngsters love to bang.

A door, an ottoman, a carriage, or a very large stuffed animal are all good for the pushing and pulling that children need to do in order to develop large muscles. Let children push you and pull you as well. Let them pull your arms and your legs. Give them a bit of a struggle when they pull, but after a bit of a challenge, let them succeed. This is fun and meaningful for children. They are using muscles and, at the same time, getting attention from the most important teacher in their lives—a parent.

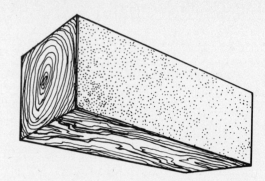

Fig. 3–13 and 3–14

materials for construction: clay

Clay is marvelous for the development of small hand muscles in the child of about 2, who thinks by touching materials. Children's actions are usually expressions of their thoughts. Clay provides the medium through which youngsters can create the picture or idea that is in their minds. The best clay for youngest children is homemade. This permits them to watch mother make the materials and gives them a sense of being important. Homemade materials are also edible. Since youngsters taste almost everything that they use, clay, too, can be sampled. Some recipes for homemade clay (play dough) follow:

NONHARDENING NO-COOK PLAY DOUGH
2 cups of self-rising flour
2 tablespoons of alum
2 tablespoons of salt
2 tablespoons of cooking oil
1 cup, plus 2 tablespoons of boiling water

Mix together and knead.

COOKED PLAY DOUGH
1 cup flour
½ cup salt
1 cup water
1 tablespoon vegetable oil
2 teaspoons cream of tartar

Heat in a saucepan until the ingredients form a ball. Add food coloring.

90

POTTER'S CLAY
½ cup flour
½ cup cornstarch
1 cup salt, dissolved in 3 ¾ cups of boiling water

Blend the flour and cornstarch with enough water to make a paste. Boil the water and salt. Add to the cornstarch mix and cook until clear. Cool overnight. Then add 6 to 8 cups of flour and knead until you have the right consistency.

HARDENING HOMEMADE CLAY (PLAY DOUGH)
2 cups of flour
1 cup of salt
Water—just enough to make into molding material
Assorted food colorings

Put the flour and salt into a container. Add water and knead the material until it has a clay consistency. Roll in a bag of flour if it is too moist. For color, add a few drops of food coloring. Clay should be about the size of a grapefruit for small hands. To store: Wrap clay in a moist towel and place in a plastic bag. Close the bag.

rubber foam

Rubber foam is flexible, soft enough for little hands to grab, and hard enough to make grabbing it a challenge. Foam rubber materials can be purchased, but finding a furniture store owner or fabric store proprietor who has samples makes the material very inexpensive to acquire. Some foam rubber is cut into flat pieces like sheeting. Other kinds are cut in long pieces and still others are round or square.

Use a pair of large scissors to cut pieces of foam rubber into sizes big enough for the child to handle and small enough to grab without difficulty. Some suggestions for shaping foam rubber follow:

1. *Cut rubber foam with a pair of scissors into the shape of a car, a fruit, a toy, or any object (see Figure 3–15).*
2. *Cut foam rubber into a ball about as big as a grapefruit.*
3. *Cut foam rubber so that there are at least 10 pieces that are the same size and shape. Place these in a container. Label the container by cutting an extra foam rubber piece and gluing it to the outside.*
4. *Cut foam into ring shapes about 6 inches in diameter. Cut out the*

Fig. 3-15

middle, like a doughnut, leaving a ring about 3½ inches in circumference. Cut about 6 of these and put them onto a long stick about a foot long. This stick can be made of rubber foam, styrofoam, wood, or plastic.

sponges

Sponges satisfy the child's desire to twist and turn, to pinch and punch. These can be any color or size. Food markets, general stores, and flea markets are the best places to purchase sponges. These can be cut into shapes. They are also usable for bath play. Store these in a box and label it with a sponge for identification. This helps children to classify their ideas and to imagine what is inside. Organizing thoughts is important for reading. This kind of organization—storing according to some rule—is important in establishing the ability to organize.

CHANTS FOR CONSTRUCTION: Adults can help the children and encourage play and construction by providing colorful language as they pound, pinch, twist, and turn materials. Following are some poems and phrases that can be chanted as children work. They will begin to learn these and chant to themselves as they work. The chanting helps to develop children's intonational patterns. It helps youngsters feel the rhythm of language, which is so important for expressive, meaningful, reading experiences. The more language accompanies physical behavior, the more descriptive language children will acquire. This increases vocabulary, which is a prerequisite for high-achieving readers.

ONE, TWO, THREE, FOUR
1, 2, 3, 4
Pound, and pound, and pound some more;

5, 6, 7, 8
Roll the clay and twist it straight;
9, 10, 11, 12
Watch it change as you pound and delve.

ADAPTED FROM A NURSERY RHYME

BY S. M. GLAZER

SUGGESTIONS FOR USE: As the child pounds, say the chant in time to the pounding. After repeating the poem, use other sounds and keep the same chant tempo. Say, for example:

Lah-lah,
Lah- day-dee-dah, and so on.

BOW-WOW
Bow-wow, says the dog,
Mew-mew, says the cat,
Grunt, grunt, goes the hog
And Squeak goes the rat
Whu-whu, says the owl,
Caw-caw, says the crow,
Quack, quack, says the duck,
And what cuckoos do you know.

NURSERY RHYME

SUGGESTIONS FOR USE: Emphasize the second syllable of each animal sound, and the second single sound (squeak) in lines without animal noises. As the child pinches, raise your voice on the sound of the animal noise.

You may want to chant the child's name as the youngster pounds. This makes it rhythmic and happy. Children will begin to say their names as they pound.

SUGGESTED MAKE-UP CHANT
Pound and pound and pound, my boy,
Pound and pound and pound your toy.
Pound it hard
Pound it fast
Pound it 'til you're done at last.

S. M. GLAZER

IN THE KITCHEN: Constructing in the kitchen means helping mother. There are many things to do that permit the child to construct and learn language at the same time. The following activities occur in the kitchen while the child is working and constructing in adult ways.

activity 1

When baking, give the child a small piece of dough to knead. Use language like this:

Knead the dough, pound it strong,
We will have a pie
Before long.

activity 2

A child loves to put hands in jam, jelly, honey, and the like. Let the child experiment with these. As his or her hands go in, say something like this:

Sticky, icky, mushy jam (or honey, or sweets, etc.)
All over your face and hands.

activity 3

When beating eggs or mixing a batter, it is fun to let the child beat and pound as you do this. You can teach the child the concept of fast and slow as you mix the substance. As you turn the spoon, say the following:

Beat it fast (speed up your beating),
Beat it slow (slow down on the movements).
Faster, faster, faster, faster (speed up actions and permit voice
to get louder and quicker in pace),
Slower, slower, slower, slower (slow down pace, and slow
down the movement of the language, lowering your tone of
voice).

ADULT BEHAVIORS WHEN CHILDREN PLAY: Children, in the toddler years, need time to play and construct by themselves. Solitary activities encourage the investigation and exploration of materials. Adults must observe the play and provide assistance when the child requests it. Assistance during personal play periods means being around, but not in the middle of the play activity, and providing appropriate materials that nourish the physical, social, emotional, and intellectual growth of the child. It is important to observe the difference between challenge, which will help children grow, and frustration, which will encourage them to withdraw from the behavior that causes this uncomfortable feeling.

Adult assistance is important in building confidence for later learning. Observing children but keeping "hands off" tells them that they have your confidence and love. The atmosphere you set will let them know that you like their investigations, explorations, and manipulations of materials. Your patience and warm smiles demonstrate your respect for their private play times. Becoming astute observers of children's behavior is important. Once adults learn the signals children send out about their growth needs, the easier it will be to supply them with the essentials necessary for developing thinking readers.

Use the guide shown in Table 3–6 when observing children. It will help you to respond helpfully to the toddler during construction and play.

the thinking place

Even the very young child needs time alone to sift the events of the day. Children need to reflect in order to organize the ideas that have come into their lives. The place to think, for youngsters of 1 and 2, can be any place where they are comfortable. It can be their crib, their place to play, or their place to read. What is important is that the adults respect the privacy of children. Children enjoy playing by themselves at particular times during each day. Observing children to find out when, where, and how each thinks by themselves is important. Important, too, is an observation of the time each of the children likes to spend alone. This will help each adult plan around that time. Adults in the lives of children must help them respect the time it takes to think by permitting thinking to occur early in life. Then children will understand, for they will have had experiences working things through as they organize, classify, reject, and accept ideas from the world about them.

Table 3–6

observing the toddler at play: a behavior guide

CHILD BEHAVIOR	APPROPRIATE ADULT BEHAVIOR WHEN THE CHILD PLAYS AND CONSTRUCTS
1. If the child waits for an adult to hand him a toy . . .	1. Do not hand the toy to the child. Place it where the child can see it. Let the child get it. Put it just within reach but far enough away so that the child must solve the problem of getting to the object. This helps the child become an independent learner, one who will self-select his own books to read later on.
2. If the child gets the toy from the place where it is stored . . .	2. Hurray! Leave the child alone. The older child will do this more readily than the younger one.
3. The child cries and throws tantrums until someone gives the toy(s) to the child.	3. This is expected behavior for the child around 18 months of age. Observe the older and younger child. Provide times to let the child cry, but help by giving limited alternatives. Put two toys within the child's reach. Let the child select with guidance.
4. The child uses language to try to tell what is desired.	4. Using language is marvelous. Encourage the language behavior. Say what you think the child is trying to describe, and point to objects as you say their names. The child will imitate your language behavior. Give the youngster time to try to talk.
5. If the child uses body language, hands, feet, and arms to describe a desired toy . . .	5. Encourage body language. Use it to help the child to describe the toy. The child will imitate and will become an expressive speaker of his language.
6. If the child makes an object . . .	6. Do not label it. Do not name it or ask, "What is it?" The construction, not the product, is important to the child.
7. When the child begins to name constructions (calls a lump of clay a plane or a car) . . .	7. The child is ready for a different kind of experience (see Chapter 4).

96

adult behavior

The major job for all adults is to provide materials, atmospheres, and supportive assistance that will help children learn. Adults need to watch toddlers, permitting them to investigate for themselves. It is difficult to watch a youngster try and try again to zip a zipper or snap a snap. But children must be permitted to try with all the persistence they possess. Interfering with the process will interfere with the learning. Knowing when independence ends and frustration begins is hard to learn. Parents must observe children for signs of contentment and oncoming frustration in order to make this judgment.

The checklist below should be posted on the refrigerator door, in the child's place, or wherever it serves as a constant reminder for effective adult behavior. Marking "yes" for each statement is the desired response.

YES   NO

1. I stand back and observe the child at play.

2. I let the child investigate an object without sticking my hand, nose, foot, feelings, into the play area.

3. I say the name of an object each time the child grabs for it. I repeat its name only when the child looks up at me. I point to the object as I say its name.

4. I make rules the child can understand. I am consistent when carrying out these rules.

*5. I step back and let the child release emotions in a personal way, without letting the child face harm. I do **not** use physical punishment except to restrain the child for safety reasons. I tell the child to go to the place where crying, kicking, and stomping can happen.*

6. I eliminate materials if I see frustration (crying, loss of attention, impatience) occur.

97

7. I remind the child, during the second year, of past experiences. We repeat parts of those experiences by doing them again, acting them out, and talking them through.

8. I watch the child's physical movements as language is used in order to try to find out what meanings the child has given to words and phrases.

9. I show signs of approval (smiling, patting on the head, appropriate comments) when the child tries to use language in original ways.

10. I say things clearly so that the child can imitate my language. I do not say, "You are saying it wrong." I provide a model for imitation.

11. I let the child sit on my lap when I read and sing and talk to him or her. We do things at special times during each waking day.

summary

Children in their first and second years learn language, begin to use it, and can communicate. They imitate in order to learn. They need models of behavior. They need the time and place to learn and think. Adults must provide models and materials to guide learning in atmospheres that permit children to experiment using the language they will be expected to read.

THE CHILD IN THE PRESCHOOL: AGES THREE AND FOUR

"Why do you have that crayon?" "Why is there cereal in my bowl?" "Why did the car stop?" Nonstop questions characterize the child of 3 and 4.[1] Children, at this age, ask some questions because they really want to know the answers and others simply because they want attention. Still other questions are asked because children wish someone would ask them that question—they know the answer and want a chance to show off. Threes and fours love language and want to use it. They can now manipulate language to make the world work for them. This is the time of life when adults must take special care to help develop a love of language and books. It is during this period that interests, images, and a love of learning become part of the youngster's scheme of the world.

Language develops fast during these two years. Physically, youngsters have matured so that they can control their bodies when they run, skip, or walk. They can balance while walking on a straight line down the edge of a sidewalk. For the first time, they will begin to string beads or pile blocks successfully. They will cut, paste, and begin to talk about their creations. When they write, they will tell about their productions. They will act dramatically to find out more about the roles they will play in the world. They will use

[1] A. Gesell and F. Ilg, *Child Development* (New York: Harper & Row, 1949), pp. 224–225.

language to help themselves understand the roles of mother, father, policeman, or teacher. They will distinguish between sounds, and most importantly, they will begin to converse with adults and children, relating experiences and feelings. Physically, at the end of the fourth year, a child should be able to:

1. *Run, balance on a sidewalk's edge, climb, and begin to skip.*
2. *Use crayons and pencils for scribbling and drawing.*
3. *Use scissors and paste.*
4. *Fold paper and fasten buttons, hooks, zippers, and snaps.*
5. *Turn pages.*
6. *String large beads.*

Language skills have now developed to a point where children begin to understand differences through language. They will, for example, be able to realize the difference between big and small things by hearing oral language descriptions. These will be demonstrated when they are building with blocks or drawing with crayons.

Growth is continuous and gradual; varied experiences produce the greatest growth. Adults do not have to go far to find many and varied experiences to help develop a love of language. These experiences are all around: at home, in the food market, down the street, on T.V. Atmospheres where children feel free to express themselves in their own way are important for total growth. Tables 4–1, 4–2, and 4–3 offer a general summary of the physical, mental, intellectual, social, and language abilities typical for most children ages 3 and 4.

creating atmospheres that make a difference

Atmospheres for growth in language must reflect the curious nature of the 3- and 4-year-old. Places to learn language should be prepared so the child may move freely from one activity to another. The child should be free to imitate adult language in an informal, nonpressured situation. Places that help the child's language growth can be anywhere. Create them, using the following checklist as a guide.

Table 4–1
growth and implications for preparing environments for maximum development: 3 years old

MOTOR DEVELOPMENT		EMOTIONAL AND SOCIAL DEVELOPMENT		INTELLECTUAL DEVELOPMENT	
ABILITIES	IMPLICATIONS	ABILITIES	IMPLICATIONS	ABILITIES	IMPLICATIONS
Balances erect.	A fall may break a tooth, holding a sharp object might be harmful.	Shows self-control: a sense of self.	Can rest for short periods of time (10 minutes). Can wait; can take turns.	Can count to at least 3. Always counts beginning at 1.	Will build a three-block bridge. Points out three objects in a picture—says "one, two, three."
Can alternate feet. Stands on one foot.	Can climb, hop, and jump.	Is learning to share. Will play beside another child.	Will share toys, but *cannot yet* share work space.	Can take part in planning future events.	Talks about a proposed trip.
Is developing coordination.	Can jump; walks and runs with music; can button or unbutton; can zip; rolls a ball, can throw underhanded; can toilet self during the day; can use writing tools deliberately.	Proud of what he or she makes. Develops independence. Is sensitive to people.	Likes to show off. Can leave mother for periods of time; plays by him- or herself. Tries to please. Tries to conform. Feels sympathic. Likes simple guessing games. Likes to dress up and role-play.	Can sort objects with one idea in mind.	Will put things together, usually according to color or size.
				Sees things as they appear now, not as how they looked previously or as how they will appear later.	Will say ten (10) blocks are more than ten (10) pennies or balloons because they consume more area.

ABILITIES	IMPLICATIONS
Uses shoulder and arm to throw.	Needs objects that have some weight for throwing.
Boys are usually superior to girls in ease of throwing and in accuracy of direction.	Boys especially enjoy throwing and aiming activities.

ABILITIES	IMPLICATIONS
Things happen because they are "supposed to" or "are needed."	Believes the car is there to give him a ride or that rain comes to water the grass.
Has special awareness of activities occurring in the environment.	Uses terms such as "down," "up," "off," "gone," "go," "here," "these," etc.

Table 4–2
growth and implications for preparing environments for maximum development: 4 years old

MOTOR DEVELOPMENT		EMOTIONAL AND SOCIAL DEVELOPMENT		INTELLECTUAL DEVELOPMENT	
ABILITIES	IMPLICATIONS	ABILITIES	IMPLICATIONS	ABILITIES	IMPLICATIONS
Likes to climb; does it easily.	Can climb a fireman's pole or trees.	Goes overboard when explaining or discussing a topic.	Likes to brag and show off. Likes freehand drawing (not coloring books).	Assumes that thoughts and observations are obvious to everyone.	Cannot reason to change his mind; will act as if you know all about something you have never discussed with the child.
Can make running or standing jumps.	Can do stunts on a tricycle.	Is learning limits.	Likes to go on excursions. Runs ahead but will wait at a corner. Interested in rules. Can plan ahead with adults; will act silly when tired.	Likes to imagine.	Does much acting out. Learns the difference between real and fancy through acting behaviors.
Has more motor control.	Can throw overhanded; will attempt to catch a ball.				
Uses a preferred hand.	Will throw a ball, more often with one hand than the other.	Will play with other children.	Exchanges materials; takes turns; plays with a small group and can take others into the group.	Has fluid thoughts (ideas and interests change easily).	Interested in death; will change titles of drawing as he or she draws.

ABILITIES	IMPLICATIONS
Is often agressive in play.	Will disrupt an activity or push or shove another child.
Is sensitive to people.	Quotes parents as authorities. Does not like being taken out of a group.
Likes birthday parties.	Likes to dress up. Talks about invitations (not anyone specifically).

ABILITIES	IMPLICATIONS
Still sees things as they appear (fooled by "looks").	Thinks a bowl of cereal—because it is spread out—has more in it than an entire box.
Things happen as they are seen.	A leaf floats because it is light; a ship floats because it is wood, a chair sinks because it is wood.
Has an understanding of distance.	Knows an object is far away but is not aware that an object is behind, beside, or in front of him or her.
Begins to know about past and future.	Uses the past tense words; says "for a long time," "next time." Confuses terms—will say, "next tomorrow," or "I will take a nap yesterday."

Table 4–3
language growth and implications for creating environments for
maximum development: ages 3 and 4

	ABILITIES	IMPLICATIONS
Around Age 3	Is attentive to words.	Responds to adult suggestions; likes to talk about adults; can listen to stories told or read. Enjoys praise; likes simple humor.
	Sentences are longer in length (children use more words to express an idea than at age 2).	Uses language more dramatically—takes lots of words to describe one idea or object.
	Uses "-ing" and "-ed" endings more frequently than before.	Is beginning to realize when things happen and can express it with language. Will say, "I making a pie" or "I goed yesterday" or "I wanted the toy then."
	Uses negatives more easily. (These include "no," "not," "didn't," "nothing," etc.)	Will say, "I no want it" or "I am not a boy" or "I didn't did it."
	Begins to ask question but does not necessarily understand what they mean when they use them or are asked a question.	Will say, "Who that?", "Ball go?", "Why you sad?", "What you does?," "Why not me go?"
	Can use plurals but will often make mistakes.	Will say, "Who that?", "Ball go?", "Me like the fishes."
Around Age 4	Experiments with words.	Makes up words. Likes to rhyme. Likes to hear and use new words. Likes big words. Listens to stories for longer periods of time.
	Asks lots of "why" and "how" questions.	Likes explanations. Will run a topic "to the ground." Does not necessarily understand questions when they are asked. Responses to the following questions might be: Question: What did you do? Response: You do what? Question: Where is the toy? Response: The toy———? Question: Why are you eating? Response: You eating.
	Likes to describe things with lots of language. Will continue a sentence and go on and on and on.	Will say, for example: "Mary has a dog and a ball, and she is going to the park and play with the boys, and then I am going to school."

Based on the works of Buhler, N. & C. Chomsky, Dale, Elkind, Menyuk, F. Smith & Miller, Weir, and others. All references are cited in the Bibliography.

*YES**NO*

There is adequate space for jumping, walking, and hopping.

There is space in or around the home for running, rolling, and throwing.

There are places to rest and work quietly.

There is space where the child can work alone.

There are costumes, old clothing, and other props available for acting out and dressing up.

There are special places and times to show adults what has been accomplished.

There is room for other children to visit and play.

There are materials for listening to recordings that go with books.

There is a place to display the child's own creations.

The child knows that each place is used in a routine way during regular times each day.

Each place has its own rules that are easy for the child to learn and follow.

There are many books with simple plots, colorful pictures, and rhyming words.

There is a place where the child can listen.

There is a place where someone listens to the child.

There are places that provide the child with opportunities to use language expressively.

There is a place and a special time just to play with words and language.

There is a place for the whole family to read together routinely.

There is a place where the family routinely shares reading or writing creations.

the listening place

The listening place, where youngsters respond to language, needs to be filled with experiences that draw attention to the sounds. Literature filled with interesting words that represent sounds, such as water, egg beaters, crinkling paper, and more, pull the child's attention toward listening. Guiding children to listen for special sounds helps children to select the language that best describes their world.

MATERIALS FOR LISTENING: The following materials will help to create activities for listening indoors:

Records and books that tell the same story
A cassette recorder that can be used by the child
A radio
A television set
Some rhythm instruments
Books with short stories and rhymes

Some disposable materials used to make sounds at home, which include:
Food and related kitchen objects
Macaroni
Rice
Liquids—juice, milk, water, and so on
Nuts
Beans (dried)
Breakfast cereals
Crisp toast or crackers
Hard candies
Wrappers from food products
Empty food containers—cereal boxes, tin cans, plastic jars, cottage cheese containers, sour cream containers, and so on.

outdoor materials

The following objects are good for outdoor listening experiences:

The car
Rakes

108

Water hose
Bicycle
Tricycle
Birds

Construction materials
(when men are using them)
Buses
Wind
Rain
Pets (dog, cats)

GUIDELINES FOR BEHAVIOR IN LISTENING PLACES:
1. *Help children listen for likenesses and differences in the sounds of their language.*
2. *Let children listen with an adult for periods of time.*
3. Provide consistent quiet times for listening together. *Listen to the children when they make sounds.* Children need to know that they have a listener who is interested and sincere. Listening to children helps them to develop the desire to produce more language.
4. *Praise children when they produce sounds of language.* Children who are learning to use language may make everything plural or may say lots of adjectives, such as "sticky" and "icky." Do not stop this language, and do not correct constructions that sound unusual. Children are probably testing the language to see if it fits into what they already know about the sounds of their world. They will use and disregard those words that do not have real meaning in their world. Praise is necessary for further growth.
5. *Permit children to repeat.* Three- and 4-year-olds tend to repeat words over and over again. This language behavior often sounds like stuttering. It is probably not stuttering but the repetition of sounds that please the child's ear. This is normal language behavior for many preschool children.
6. *Give children the opportunity to hear the same sounds of language over and over again.* Children

love to hear familiar language and like to produce familiar sounds. Re-read stories and poems to children. This helps them to build confidence for language production and to remember language patterns, so that they can recite the poem or story. This helps children to see the relationship between spoken language and the language written in books.

LISTENING ACTIVITIES FOR INDOORS: The kitchen, the bath, the bedroom, and the playroom are all good indoor places for listening activities. Use each of the suggested activities as examples for developing more activities in the same framework.

activity 1: a guessing game

While you are putting knives and forks or dinner dishes back into the cabinet after washing them, say the following:

"Let's play a game. You hide your eyes, and see if you can guess what I am putting away."

If the response is incorrect, say, "Guess again." Continue the guessing until the child finds success. Give some clues if there seems to be a problem. Say, for example, "We put food on this when we want to eat it."

activity 2: another guessing game

When cooking, say to the child, "Hide your eyes, and guess what I am pouring into the pot." You may pour rice, noodles, or water. Give the child time to listen. Let the child open his or her eyes and discover what was poured after one or two guesses. Repeat the activity at another time.

activity 3: a baking activity

When you are beating eggs, tap the beats with your foot and repeat "La, la, la, la" each time you swish the beater. Let the child join you in the language. Permit the youngster to beat the eggs and encourage the accompanying language behavior.

activity 4: comparing sounds

Pour two kinds of foods and ask, "Which is the cereal?"

Say, "Listen again, which sounds louder?"
Say, "Listen again, which sounds softer?"

activity 5: comparing sounds	Let the tap water run. Ask, "What do you think that sound is?" When the child responds, say, "What else sounds like water running?" The child may have some difficulty comparing sounds like this at first. It is a good activity for a 4-year-old.
activity 6: keeping the beat	Fill an empty metal food container with nuts or dried beans. Cover and seal the lid. It is now a rattle. As you beat batter or eggs or mix food, have your child shake the rattle in time with the beat. Say the following poem to help keep the beat:

Shake your rattle, baby dear,
Shake it hard, shake it near
Your head
Your nose
Your ears
Your toes,
Shake your rattle, baby dear.

Shake your hands, baby dear,
Shake them high
Shake them low,
Shake them fast
Shake them slow,
Shake your hands, baby dear.

S. M. GLAZER

Say the poem in time with the beating. Use your voice and body to enhance the language. When you say the word "shake" make a shaking movement with your body. Carry this kind of language expression throughout the poem.

After saying the poem many times to beating activities, just say the following to the beat of the poem: "La, la, la, la, la, la, la," and so on.

The child, after beating and listening many times, will say the poem as you beat it on the drum.

activity 7: a listening game	Put indoor sounds on a cassette tape. Use the following familiar sounds for recording:

Water running from a tap
A shower
A telephone
A doorbell ringing
A toilet flushing

Play the following game. Run one sound on the tape and say to the child: "In what part of the house does this sound belong? What is the sound?" You are helping the child to classify and identify the sound.

activity 8: leaving listening notes

Record a message with things to do on a cassette tape. Leave it for your child to listen to. Be sure that the directions are simple, short, and to the point. If, for example, you want your child to be sure that there is fruit in the refrigerator, say the following:

"Open the refrigerator door." (pause)
"Look in the fruit bin." (pause)
"Is there fruit in the bin?" (pause)
"Do you think we need to buy some more?"

Notice that each sentence is simple, direct, and has only one thought. These kinds of directions help to give instructions clearly. They also help the child to become an alert listener who can learn to follow directions. This is very important for reading in school.

The following are some activities for the bath:

activity 1: comparing sounds

As you run the water in the bath, say, "Where else in the house can you hear this sound?" Say, "Try to make that sound."

activity 2: developing the "beat of the language"

Learn the following poem:

THE WONDER OF WONDERS
I saw a peacock with a fiery tail
I saw a blazing comet drop down hail
I saw a cloud with ivy curled around

I saw a sturdy oak creep on the ground
I saw an ant swallow up a whale
I saw a raging sea brim full of ale
I saw a Venice glass sixteen foot deep
I saw a well full of men's tears that weep
I saw their eyes all in a flame of fire
I saw a house high as the moon and higher
I saw the sun at twelve o'clock at night
I saw the man who saw this wondrous sight.

NURSERY RHYME

Use a small bathtub sailboat. Say the poem and sail the boat with your hand to the beat of the poem. At another bathtime, put the boat in your child's hand and say the poem. Hold onto your child's hand and help the child to keep the beat of the poem. You are helping the youngster to get the feel of the rhythm of language for reading. If you see that the child has used one hand more often than the other—for painting, or drawing, or eating—place the boat in the hand that is used more often for these activities.

activity 3: pouring water

COMPARING SOUNDS. Secure two containers that hold water, one with a large open top and the other with a small opening or a sprinkler top. When the child is in the bath, fill each with water. Say to the child, "Close your eyes." Pour water from one of the containers and ask, "What do you hear?" Give the child time to answer. Accept all responses. Then pour the water from the second container. Ask, "Now what do you hear?" Again give the child time to answer. Do not supply the words for the child. Encourage the youngster to say whatever comes to mind. Use words like, "What do you think you hear?" or "What do you suppose it is?" Then fill each container half full of water. Say, "Close your eyes." Pour water from one container to the other and ask, "How are the sounds of pouring different?"

activity 4: dropping objects into water

Select objects that can drop into water. At different times, drop the object into the water and say, "How does it sound?" At a later time, say to the child, "Close your eyes—how does this sound to you?" Encourage the child to use descriptive language.

Say, "What else sounds like that?" or "How do you think it looks?" "How would you feel if it were dropped on your toe?" "Why would you feel that way?" These kinds of questions will encourage the child to use descriptive words like "heavy," "light," "wet," "cold," and so on.

Use a cassette tape recorder and record the following poems for your child to listen to at will in his or her private moments.

activity 1

The following poem is a counting rhyme. It is poetic and repetitive and helps children learn to count while listening to delightful catchy language.

ONE, TWO, THREE, FOUR, FIVE
One, Two, Three, Four, Five,
Once I caught a fish alive.
Six, Seven, Eight, Nine, Ten,
Then I let it go again.
Why did you let it go?
Because it bit my finger so.
Which finger did it bite?
The little finger on the right.

NURSERY RHYME

SUGGESTED USES: Read the rhyme and record it on a cassette tape. Read it slowly, using lots of intonational voice patterns. Put the recorder in your child's place. If possible, buy a book with this rhyme in it. You might also make your own book, one that includes this poem. Place the book next to the tape recorder. Before rest time, read the poem to the child. Then run the tape and read the poem along with the recording. Leave the book next to the recorder. Permit the child to go to it at leisure. Do not instruct or teach directly. The tape and the book itself will do the teaching.

What will happen? The child will probably learn the poem by rote and create an original version.

activity 2:
a radio alarm
activity

Use a clock radio to awaken your child from nap time. Be sure that the radio is set at the same station and at the same time each day. This helps the child to predict what will happen.

After one or two weeks, change the station. The child will notice the difference in the sounds. When the child comments about them, ask one of the following questions:

1. *What was different?*
2. *Make the sounds that you heard.*
3. *Why do you suppose they are different?*
4. *Which sounds do you like best?*

LISTENING ACTIVITIES FOR THE OUT-OF-DOORS:

activity 1: walking and listening

Take a walk with your child. Ask the child to listen to all the sounds as you both walk together for two minutes. Stop and ask, "What did you hear?" Tell the child what you heard.
          Repeat this walking and listening activity many times in different places at different times of the year. It is wonderful for vocabulary development, descriptive language, and the coordination between listening and speaking.

activity 2: listen and writing

During the latter part of the fourth year, begin to write down descriptive words. If your child says, "I heard a tweeting noise," write the word "tweeting." Write in manuscript form (print the word as shown in Figure 5–1 p. 168) Write only single words and use a bold, dark marker or crayon. Post it.

activity 3: building descriptive language

When raking the garden or sweeping the pavement, ask the child to listen to the sounds of the rake or broom. Say, "Try to make that sound." Ask, "What else makes a sound like that?" Ask only one question at a time.

activity 4: car activity

While riding in the car, close your eyes and listen. Say "What outside sounds do you hear?"

SONGS AND CHANTS THAT ENCOURAGE LISTENING

A FARMYARD SONG
I had a cat and the cat pleased me,
I fed my cat by yonder tree;
Cat goes fiddle-i-fee.

I had a hen and the hen pleased me,
I fed my hen by yonder tree;
Hen goes chimmy-chuck, chimmy-chuck,
Cat goes fiddle-i-fee.

I had a duck and the duck pleased me,
I fed my duck by yonder tree;
Duck goes quack, quack,
Hen goes chimmy-chuck, chimmy-chuck,
Cat goes fiddle-i-fee.

I had a goose and the goose pleased me,
I fed my goose by yonder tree;
Goose goes swishy, swashy,
Duck goes quack, quack,
Hen goes chimmy-chuck, chimmy-chuck,
Cat goes fiddle-i-fee.

I had a sheep and the sheep pleased me,
I fed my sheep by yonder tree;
Sheep goes baa, baa,
Goose goes swishy, swashy,
Duck goes quack, quack,
Hen goes chimmy-chuck, chimmy-chuck,
Cat goes fiddle-i-fee.

I had a pig and the pig pleased me,
I fed my pig by yonder tree;
Pig goes griffy, gruffy,
Sheep goes baa, baa,
Goose goes swishy, swashy,
Duck goes quack, quack,
Hen goes chimmy-chuck, chimmy-chuck,
Cat goes fiddle-i-fee.

I had a cow and the cow pleased me,
I fed my cow by yonder tree;
Cow goes moo, moo,
Pig goes griffy, gruffy,
Sheep goes, baa, baa,
Goose goes swishy, swashy,
Duck goes quack, quack,

Hen goes chimmy-chuck, chimmy-chuck,
Cat goes fiddle-i-fee.

I had a horse and the horse pleased me,
I fed my horse by yonder tree;
Horse goes neigh, neigh,
Cow goes moo, moo,
Pig goes griffy, gruffy,
Sheep goes baa, baa,
Goose goes swishy, swashy,
Duck goes quack, quack,
Hen goes chimmy-chuck, chimmy chuck,
Cat goes fiddle-i-fee.

I had a dog and the dog pleased me,
I fed my dog by yonder tree;
Dog goes bow-wow, bow-wow,
Horse goes neigh, neigh,
Cow goes moo, moo,
Pig goes griffy, gruffy,
Sheep goes baa, baa,
Goose goes swishy, swashy,
Duck goes quack, quack,
Hen goes chimmy-chuck, chimmy-chuck,
Cat goes fiddle-i-fee.

A FOLK BALLAD

SUGGESTIONS FOR USE: Say the poem, moving your head and arms with the beat of the language. Repeat the poem often. This will teach the child the language and will help the child to remember the different animal sounds in the poem. The repeated animal sounds help the child to develop the ability to remember things in sequential order.

MICHAEL ROW THE BOAT ASHORE
Michael row the boat ashore, Hallelujah,
Michael row the boat ashore, Hallelujah.

Brother, lend a helping hand, Hallelujah,
Brother, lend a helping hand, Hallelujah.

A BLACK SPIRITUAL

Substitute the child's name for the ones in the poem and put in action words that relate to the child's world; for example, "Brook put the toy away, hallelujah, Brook put the toy away, hallelujah," and so on. For the tune, see Denes Agay's *Best Loved Songs of the American People* (Doubleday, 1975).

Use other songs that have repetitious language and simple rhyme. This helps to develop vocabulary and awareness of sentence structure.

SELECTING RECORDINGS TO ENCOURAGE LISTENING: Listening to records is a wonderful way to encourage listening behavior. When selecting recordings for children, be sure to include the following:

Songs with repeated language phrases.
Songs that rhyme.
Songs that have silly words.
Songs about the family and things around the home.
Songs that tell familiar stories.

LISTENING WITH TELEVISION: Like sunburn and tooth decay, television also needs prevention from overexposure. We know that television plays an important role in the lives of children. Its influence is powerful. Concerns about television center around (1) its ability to create passive lookers and listeners and (2) the enormous amount of violence and sexual activity shown on some programs. Youngsters at 3, 4, and 5 cannot reject these visual activities. Their limited experiences often do not include a device that says, "These aggressive acts are bad." The child cannot rethink, rework, or re-evaluate a television "shoot-em-up" or an arsonist's malicious house-burning. So children imitate violent activity seen on television and these actions become a form of self-expression.

Youngsters in these preschool years are puzzled by the television picture. They do not understand how it appears in front of them. Children will look inside or behind a television set for an explanation of the image, but they cannot solve this problem.

THE CHILD IN THE PRESCHOOL: AGES THREE AND FOUR

With all of these concerns, like it or not, television is here to stay. Our job is to provide children with guidance for viewing television constructively. With guided television viewing and listening, children can use this medium as an aid for developing the listening skills necessary for reading.

The first step is to make a list of those programs that you think are acceptable for children. Programs that are acceptable for children should have the following characteristics:

1. *Simple plots that are presented in short periods of time.*
2. *Programs should be realistic in nature, using experiences familiar to children, such as neighborhood or family relationships.*
3. *Programs should promote children's interests—role-playing, painting, eating, playing with other children, and so forth.*

GUIDELINES FOR ADULT BEHAVIOR:
1. *Watch Television With Your Child.* Watching with your child helps to build common experiences. After watching the same programs, both of you will have something in common to talk about. This talking helps to build vocabulary. You will be able to relate to the ideas expressed by your child's knowledge about his or her observations, because you have seen the same information.
2. *Sit And Talk About Television Viewing With The Child.* Discuss times for watching. This is a must! Guides are necessary for developing the ability to be self-selective. Self-selecting programs is like self-selecting books.
3. *Set Goals For Television Watching.* Setting goals gives the child a purpose for watching. The child, in essence, is skimming the viewing in order to gain the information that is to be sought. Viewing with a purpose is like reading with a purpose. The child is purposefully viewing in order to find the answer to some problem that has been posed.

activity 1: television and listening

After the child has watched a television show, ask some of the following questions, one at a time:

What sounds did you hear?

Make some of the sounds (you may be specific after the response to your first question).

Where else, besides on that television program, can you hear that sound(s)?

activity 2: television looking and real life

Watch television with your child. Set one goal from the following list.

1. *Watch to see if there is a pet like yours on the program.*
2. *Watch to see how the children run. Run with them in this room as you watch.*
3. *Watch to see how many times something is yellow on the television show.*

activity 3: guided listening

When you and the child watch television, listen for the following:

1. *Sounds you hear in the kitchen.*
2. *Sounds you hear in the bath.*
3. *Sounds that are heard in a park.*
4. *Sounds that are heard in the food store.*

Make up more of your own. Ask the child to reproduce the sounds.

activity 4: the t.v. set

After a field trip—a walk in the park, a trip to the food store—watch television and listen for the sounds heard on that trip.

activity 5: listening to t.v. without words

When you and the child are watching television, turn on the picture without the sound. Watch the program for a period of ten minutes. Ask, "What do you think they were talking about?"

activity 6: listening without viewing

Turn on a favorite television program. Tune in the sound but not the picture. Listen to the program and then say to the child, "What do you suppose they were doing?" Let the child tell it, write it, draw it, or act it out.

the writing place

The writing place for children of 3 and 4 is a place for social experiences. Children at this age like not only to work alone but also to work near others. They find it relaxing to scribble when friends are there. It does not matter what is produced, it's the doing that counts.

WRITING MATERIALS: Materials must reflect the child's need to become involved with creating rather than with the material itself. In fact, too many things may stand in the way of the child's ability to express feelings through art. Materials need to be simple and easily available. They need to be the kinds of materials that are controlled by the child. Writing instruments should include (1) large, unwrapped crayons in bright colors; (2) felt-tipped markers; (3) large pencils; (4) fat pieces of colored chalk; (5) thickly prepared paints and novel items for painting, such as string, potatoes, straws, and toothbrushes. Paper needs to be large (about 18 by 24 inches). Newsprint is a good choice for painting at 3 and 4.

GROWTH IN WRITTEN EXPRESSION, SOME GUIDELINES: Expression in written form grows in conjunction with the total child. The child's physical, emotional, social, intellectual, and language growth are all part of the writing creations. Feelings are expressed through art. If, for example, a child has a medical problem, it will affect his or her drawings. An upset family will also have an effect on the child's productions. Any chronological sketch of development of expression through art must be read with caution, for it is only a general guide (see Table 4–4). Individuality in expression is of greatest importance.

ADULT BEHAVIORS AND EARLY WRITINGS: It is extremely important for adults in the lives of 3- and 4-year-olds to respect children's writing and scribbling, for the marks are more than squiggles on pages. They are self-expressions of children's thoughts. Adults often step into children's artistic experiences. They might help children to use the "correct" forms or colors. Some interject with such comments as "An arm doesn't look like that," or "Look at your picture: You only have a head and legs; where is the rest of you?" These discrepancies between adult taste and children's expressions may prevent children from using artistic media as a means of self-expression. Children who have had too much interference often say, "I can't draw" or "I'll make a picture for you if you help me do it." The

Table 4–4
growth of written expression and implications for preparing the environment

AGE	BEHAVIOR	IMPLICATIONS
3 years	Begins to name his or her scribbling but has no preconceived notion about what will evolve when the picture is finished.	Communicating with self—scribbles are an important means of communication in making sense of things in his or her world.
	Often uses only one color when scribbling.	Interested in the movements of writing, so colors distract him or her.
	Begins to use colors when naming scribbles.	Indicates that the child needs choices of colors in order to give meaning to each scribble.
	Experiments with finger and whole hand movements.	Likes to try finger painting. Has some feeling for design.
4 years	Children are conscious of forms they create. Marks and scribbles begin to lose their relationship to the children's body movements.	Begins to realize that the child can communicate by "putting it down."
	When drawing, has the intention of creating a particular object.	Begins to show ideas in deliberate ways.
	Can hold a writing tool in an adult-like manner.	Needs large brushes, pencils, and pens.
	May work on one written project for a long period of time.	Has an active imagination; will often shift ideas in the midst of a project.
	Increases verbal description of creations.	Needs someone to listen sincerely and accept comments.
	Begins to make crude letters.	Indicates an awareness of written language.
	Size or space relationships are barely evident.	The most important details, to the child, are the largest objects.
	Begins self-criticism of products.	Is asking for adult acceptance. Values his or her own creations and needs to take them home.

following checklist should serve as a guide for adult behavior when children are engaged in written expression. "Yes" is the desired response for freeing children to write.

                                                        YES   NO

I show an interest in the child's products. I listen and look while the child talks about them. I notice and nod acceptingly as the

*youngster demonstrates and talks about the
product.*

*I do not put my hand on the drawings to
correct lines, letters, colors, or forms.*

*I look at the child's creations as an
expression of growth.*

*I do not say, "That isn't nice," or "Oh, you
can do better," when seeing the child's work.*

*I permit the child to select materials and the
time needed to create.*

I play music in the writing place.

*I do not give the child patterns, coloring
books, and tracing materials. This stifles the
creative thinking powers of the child.*

WRITING ACTIVITIES:

activity 1:
a painting
activity

Make your own paint *with* the child. The recipe that follows is
fun, easy, and exciting.

SOAP FLAKE PAINT
1½ cups soap flakes
1 cup hot or warm water
A few drops of food coloring

*Whip with an egg beater until stiff. Put the paint in containers
and leave these on a table next to some paper for the child to
use.*

activity 2:
a writing
activity (for
the fourth
year)

Schedule a time when you and the child sit and write with a
pencil or crayon for a period of 1 to 3 minutes. This should be
a quiet time with no interruptions. The activity should become
a daily experience for all in the family. Adults and children
should have their own private note pads. Sharing is *only* voluntary.

activity 3

Children in the beginning of their fourth year can begin to
produce art and writing products for loved ones. When Grandmother, for example, sends a gift, this provides the opportunity
to write or draw a note of thanks. Encourage the child to draw

something—anything—to send to Grandmother. When the child is finished, ask, "What would you like to tell Grandmother?" Write the response on the paper.

activity 4: music and painting

Play a record when your child paints or draws. Sway with the music. The child may see you, imitate your actions, and paint or draw to the beat of the music.

the acting place

Children tell you about themselves when they act. They show their emotional and social concerns. A death in the family may result in a child "playing dead." A child who is experiencing confusion will act out to unravel problems. If, for example, mother is off to the hospital to have a baby, youngsters will often play "Mommy going off to the hospital to get my baby." Instant drama is a way of trying out the different roles of the people in the child's world. A preschool child might play Grandpa fixing the back screen door or Mom shopping at the market. The child can instantly become a fireman, policeman, or physician. Children tell what they remember by acting. A child will re-enact a circus trip by being a tight-rope walker or a tiger jumping through a flaming hoop.

Social and emotional development, role identification, and memory training are important tasks directly related to reading. When they read words, children are expected to distinguish between ideas. The child who put on Grandpop's hat when fixing the screen door or the fireman's hat to play firechief is comparing objects to ideas and is making distinctions. Becoming aware of these everyday differences by acting is preparation for seeing differences between letters such as "c," "d," "o," and "a." Visually comparing objects for acting is directly related to seeing differences between letters, words, and sentences. Recalling facts about the circus forces the child to use the mental abilities necessary to recall facts when reading. Children act in sequence to recall events and teach themselves how to remember. If facts are wrong, if they don't feel right to children, they re-act the event, teaching themselves the logical ordering of events. The small muscles that coordinate the eyes and hands for acting are those that help children focus to find a word or phrase on a page of print.

Acting helps the child use the words needed for reading. Often youngsters can act an idea but have not discovered the language that describes events. By acting, children are able to translate actions into oral expression.

Acting is a must for all 3- and 4-year-olds for (1) emotional and social growth, (2) role identification, (3) memory training, and (4) the development of muscles that help children make visual distinctions. Acting guides children into (5) ordering events and ideas and (6) translating these ideas from physical activity into words, phrases, and, often, long oral dissertations. Adults must create atmospheres for acting by providing materials that encourage the release of ideas.

MATERIALS FOR ACTING: The following list of acting materials is based on the child's need for growth.

1. *Things to climb (small ladders, step stools, library steps, large blocks).*
2. *A mat or cot for resting.*
3. *Room to show off and move about.*
4. *Old clothing representative of community workers (fireman's hat, policeman's badge, nurse's uniform, doctor's operating room suit, etc.).*
5. *Appropriate size furniture (small tables and chairs).*
6. *Dolls and dolls' clothing.*
7. *A mirror hung in a permanent spot.*
8. *Pictures and photos of important people and events in the child's life.*

GUIDELINES FOR ACTING: Children need to act in order to learn roles, remember ideas and events, and express feelings. When the child acts, adults must observe and restrain from interfering. These are two kinds of adult behaviors desirable when children are involved in acting: (1) adult acting that children look at and "read" and (2) observing behavior, where adults watch as children act for themselves.

The checklist that follows should serve as a guide for adult behavior when children are involved in acting activities. The desired response for each is "yes."

YES   *NO*

I do not tell the child how to play-act.

I provide specific time for acting experiences.

I do not interrupt when the youngster acts.

I offer no opinion concerning the child's instant drama activity.

I do not comment upon the acting events at a later time.

I do not question the child about acting behavior.

I do notice the child's interests.

I periodically place new materials and books, based on observations of the child's interests, in the acting place.

When I dramatize for children, I act without words and encourage children to tell about the drama. This encourages growth in oral expression.

I provide words that the child can translate into behaviors.

I accept all of the child's responses to my actions.

ACTING ACTIVITIES:

activity 1:
puppets and
role playing

Leave the puppets from earlier years in a special place. Create an instant puppet stage using a small table covered with a sheet or large bath towel. Children will use this as a playhouse as well.

You can also make a stage from an old cardboard carton using the following materials:

MATERIALS: A carton that enclosed a large television set, refrigerator, or dishwasher, tempera paint, and broad felt-tipped markers.

Cut the cartons as illustrated in Figure 4-1. Paint the cartons with a bright color nontoxic tempera paint. Write "Stage for Puppets" on the front of the carton.

Put puppets on the floor of the stage or underneath the table covering. Use puppets that represent community service workers and old favorites from previous years. A policeman's hat sewn onto the head of an animal puppet delights the child.

activity 2: encouraging vocabulary growth

Beat a toy drum or the lid of a pot with a spoon. Look at your child as you beat the drum. Encourage the child with your eyes and smiling face to get up and move to the drum beat. At the end of the activity, ask the child the following:

1. *How do you feel when you jump to the drum beat?*
2. *Show with your hands and face how you feel when you jump.*

When you do this, you are teaching your child to coordinate sound with movement.

activity 3: imaging to encourage vocabulary and the power to remember

You will need the following:
MATERIALS: Space to move about and a drum-like instrument. Beat the drum as in Activity 2. As your child moves to the drum beat, say, "Make believe that you are walking in your bare feet." "Now make believe that you are taking off your shoes and socks." "Walk in the grass." Allow the child ample time to move.

Fig. 4–1

You are teaching the meaning of the word "bare" by saying, "Now take off your shoes and socks." It is important to note that this is the way you teach word meaning. You use the word and then follow up with directions that explain the activity. The behavior helps the child to learn the word's meaning. Do the following at later times:

1. *Imagine that the grass is wet.*
2. *Imagine that there are lots of grasshoppers in the grass.*
3. *Imagine that there is ice under your feet.*
4. *Imagine that you are walking on a hot pavement or hot sand without your shoes and that it is in the middle of the summertime.*
5. *Imagine that you are stepping over puddles.*
6. *Imagine that you are walking in very high snow.*
7. *Imagine that you are throwing a very heavy ball.*
8. *Imagine that you are jumping rope (riding a bike, playing catch, playing hopscotch, etc.). (These are suggestions for many different times. Only one should be exercised at a time.)*

This activity can also be used for vocabulary building. After one of the activities, ask, "How do you feel after you step in high snow?" Repeat the words your child says. Let the child say them on recording tape. When the youngster is 4½, begin to write the feelings down on paper as the child says them. Do not teach. Just write. The child will ask you what you are doing. Say, "I am writing down your words."

activity 4: developing language from memories

Act out the following, one at a time, for as long as your child enjoys your acting. Things to act out might include the following:

1. *Washing the dishes.*
2. *Running.*
3. *Watching television.*
4. *Going to the bathroom.*
5. *Cooking a particular food.*
6. *Paying a bill at the supermarket.*

As you act, encourage your child to guess what you are doing.

This acting behavior encourages language growth. It also helps the child to read an activity visually and translate it into oral language. This develops vocabulary and memory abilities.

activity 5: acting the sequencing—leaving out parts

Act out an event in detail. Leave out one part. The event can be one of the following:

1. *Purchasing some food.*
2. *Taking a bath.*
3. *Washing windows.*
4. *Eating dinner.*
5. *Dialing a phone number and then talking to the person on the phone.*
6. *Playing a game that is familiar to the child.*

Leave out a section of the activity that is very familiar to the child. Say, "Tell me what's missing."

Leaving out a section of an event helps the child to develop the ability to put things together, to see things as a whole.

activity 6: creative role-playing

Provide dress-up clothing and other objects in the acting place. Permit children to dress up, play-act, imagine, and create situations.

A FINAL THOUGHT: All children have creative power locked inside them. They have something to say, something that each alone can offer, given the opportunity and encouragement.

the reading place

One of the most important gifts you can give to your child is a love of literature and language. The nurturing of this must begin at a very early age, for the child who is successful with language has had positive contacts with books and reading very early in life.

ARRANGING MATERIALS IN THE READING PLACE: A very special place is needed where books may be kept, read, and relaxed with—either alone or with family members. The reading area should have low open shelves for storing books, a table that is the right size for the child, and a soft carpet and pillows for lying upon.

Comfortable seating for adults should also be included so that adult and child can read together. A bulletin board for hanging pictures about stories encourages interest. The reading place must include objects that children have seen in books. If, for example, you have read Robert McCloskey's *Blueberries for Sal* (Viking Press, 1948), you might put fresh blueberries on the reading table for snacking. Educators suggest that a child's library have at least fifteen well-illustrated picture books. The library should include books with a few words as well as resource books, dictionaries, and magazines.

GUIDELINES FOR SETTING UP THE READING PLACE: Use the following checklist as a guide for placing materials in the place for reading. Responses should be "yes" for the most desirable plan.

	YES	NO
Books are standing so that the cover is shown. Books are not crowded together.		
New books are placed on the shelves weekly. These reflect the child's interests.		
On the shelves are books authored by the child.		
I have read all the books on the shelves.		
I have selected books in which the illustrations and words match.		
I have selected books that interest the child of 3 and 4. These are about the community, the child, and things in the child's environment. There are also books that deal with the child's emotional and social concerns.		

I have selected books that go along with my child's favorite television show.

I have selected books that help my child to classify objects and ideas.

I choose books that deal with the number concepts—few or many, and simple counting.

I have selected books that help my child compare one object or idea to another (examples: large to small, fat to thin, high to low, sad to happy).

I have selected books that help my child to see cause-and-effect relationships.

I have selected books that deal with the time of year, day, or week as well as ones that tell of events in the child's life.

I look at the words in books to see if the vocabulary is interesting and exciting for my child.

SELECTION OF BOOKS: Children's books should be selected by considering (1) the child's physical and motor development, (2) his or her emotional and social growth, and (3) his or her intellectual and language growth. The following booklists include only a few of the many wonderful books available for 3- and 4-year-olds. And Table 4-5 attempts to show the relationship of the child's development and the interest in literature at ages 3 and 4.

physical and motor growth and my body

Arkin, Alan. *Tony's Hard Work Day*. Harper & Row, 1972. A child builds a dream house when he is told that he is too young to help build the family's country house. Suggestions: Child may act out Tony's building activities as the story is read or after reading.

Browne, Anthony. *Through the Magic Mirror*. Greenwillow/ Morrow, 1977. Tony steps through a mirror where dogs walk men, the sky is dark, and other mixed-up things happen. Children will enjoy acting out the silly antics of Tony's imaginative world.

Buckley, Helen. *Josie and the Snow.* Morrow, 1964. Describes family fun in the snow which children can act out.

Clifton, Lucille. *Amifika.* Dutton, 1977. Mother, getting ready for Dad to come home from the Army, has no time for Amifika. Amifika, who is always getting in mother's way, tries to hide under the sink, in the closet, and so on. A warm, tender story with actions to copy.

Table 4–5
child development and literature interests

AREAS OF GROWTH	CHARACTERISTICS	IMPLICATIONS	SUGGESTED BOOKS
Physical and Motor Growth and Becoming Aware of "Me"	Loves movement. Jumps, walks, runs, and climbs a lot. Has great need to use large muscles. Children love to ask, "How am I different; how am I the same as others?"	Has interests in physical activities and needs models to imitate. Needs to experience rhythm through language for the greatest development.	Browne, *Through The Magic Mirror;* Raskin, *James And the Rain;* Ets, *Just Me;* Krauss, *The Growing Story.*
Emotional and Social Growth	Beginning to share. Proud of accomplishments. Is sensitive to people, is curious, and begins to see differences among people.	Has interest in friendship, personal possessions, size, color, and shape differences.	Cole, *The Past Jonathan;* Krasilovshy, *The Very Tall Little Girl;* Krauss, *I'll Be You and You Be Me.*
Intellectual And Language Growth	Can classify objects and ideas. Can learn number concepts— few, many, and ordinal counting. Can compare one object to another (fat/thin or high/low). Can see cause and effect relationships. Has great vocabulary growth potential. Can arrange and rearrange words. Learns that reading is like talking. Can learn left to right page direction. Learns that words are made of letters.	Likes stories that show likenesses and differences and why things happen. Likes an interesting variety of words that feel good when you say them. Likes to retell stories. Likes to follow along the page as adults read.	Barnett, *Animals Should Definitely Not Wear Clothes;* Carle, *1,2,3, To The Zoo;* Oxenbury, *Number of Things;* Rand, *Sparkle And Spin: A Book About Words.*

Cole, Joanna. *Fun on Wheels.* Morrow, 1977. Excitement on wheels that can be acted out and copied by children for large muscle development.

Emberly, Barbara. *Drummer Hoff.* Prentice-Hall, 1971. A lively folk tale in snappy rhyme. A march around the room.

Ets, Marie Hall. *Gilberto and the Wind.* Viking, 1963. Simple childlike responses to different moods of the wind. Easy-to-imitate actions with lots of body movement.

George, Jean Craighead. *All Upon A Sidewalk.* Dutton, 1974. A yellow ant takes a walk on the city sidewalk, running into one natural hazard after another in search of a morsel of special food for the queen. Children will love to imitate the adventures of the little ant in the very big world.

Hargreaves, Roger. *Mr. Topsy-Turvey.* Grosset & Dunlap, 1974. Mr. Topsy-Turvy does everything upside down and inside out. He even speaks backwards. Everyone, by the end of the story, walks backwards. A wonderful book for physical development (ties into visual and physical coordination).

Kraus, Robert. *How Spider Saved Christmas.* Windmill/Dutton, 1973. A spider searches his web for presents to give to friends. The crawling and searching activity will be fun to imitate and copy.

Krauss, Ruth. *The Backward Day.* Harper & Row, 1950. Every-thing happens backwards in this book; from sundown to sunup, funny things are available for imitation and laughter.

Meyer, Renate. *Hide-and-Seek.* Bradbury Press, 1972. A word-less picture story of a boy and girl playing hide-and-seek; includes lots of actions to imitate.

Ruskin, Karla. *James and the Rain.* Harper & Row, 1957. A little boy strolling in the rain is joined by one cow, two ducks, and so on—up to eight cats: All share fun and games in the rain. A wonderful book for imitating the physical movements. A counting book that brings cadence to the language and helps the movement along.

Sendak, Maurice. *Seven Little Monsters.* Harper & Row, 1977. A counting book of monsters who become involved in physical actions. Provides models for acting out, such as drinking the seas, creeping into town, screwing on heads, and sleeping in places other than beds.

Slobodkina, Espher. *Caps for Sale*. Addison-Wesley, 1947. A delightful story where monkeys wear and throw hats. Children will enjoy copying the antics of the monkeys. Lots of physical involvement.

Weigle, Oscar. *The Running, Jumping, Throwing, Sliding, Racing, Climbing Book*. Grosset & Dunlap, 1975. A humorous book in verse where an elephant dives, a giraffe plays tennis, a moose goes skiing, and many other events provide actions for imitation.

Zaffo, George. *The Giant Nursery Book of Things to Do*. Doubleday, 1959. Chasing fires, pulling on coats and boots, climbing imaginery ladders, and other physical activities are provided in this wonderful book of physical things to do.

books that involve the physical awareness of "me"

Aliki. *My Five Senses*. Crowell, 1962. A lovely book with colorful illustrations that help the child to understand how one senses the world.

Cretan, Glasys Yessayan. *Me, Myself and I*. Morrow, 1969. The child will ask, "Who am I?" after reading this book, which provokes thoughtful interactions.

Ets, Marie Hall. *Just Me*. Viking, 1965 (paper). In another of her many books, Ms. Ets portrays for the preschool child the happiness of being oneself.

Klein, Norma. *Girls Can Be Anything*. Dutton, 1973. A new book for today, portraying the physical as well as the mental aspects of girls in today's world.

Krauss, Ruth. *The Growing Story*. Harper & Row, 1947. A story about a boy who watches everything grow but does not realize that he himself has grown until he puts on last year's clothing.

Mayer, Mercer and Mariana. *Mine*. Simon & Schuster, 1970. A book with only two words, "mine" and "yours," which helps the egocentric 3- and 4-year-old to understand property rights.

Slobodkin, Lois. *Magic Michael*. Macmillan, 1973 (paper). Michael, who is not happy with himself, tries to be everything but himself. He is convinced that it is good to be just Michael when he is not permitted to collect a gift intended only for little boys.

books that enhance emotional and social growth

Young children need to know that there are other people in the world who are concerned with the same things they are. Interactions with characters in literature who share their concerns help children to think about their own feelings and behaviors freely.

Bonsall, Crosby. *It's Mine.* Harper & Row, 1964. Problems of sharing are solved when a larger problem occurs.

Cole, William. Illustrated by Tomi Ungerer. *The Pest Jonathan.* Harper & Row, 1970. Problems of a pestiferous child are depicted in themes and pictures.

Deueaux, Alex. *Na-ni.* Harper & Row, 1973. A black ghetto child dreams of a wonderful dream only to suffer a loss. A moving, intense story.

Dunne, Phoebe and Tris. *Friends.* Creative Educational Society, 1971. Photos of friends accompanied by a simple text help to teach the child the value of people who are truly friends.

Flack, Marjorie. *The Story of Ping.* Macmillan, 1971 (paper). A duck learns that he must do as expected or will suffer the consequences.

Keats, Ezra Jack. *Whistle for Willie.* Viking, 1969 (paper). Peter, as hard as he tries, can't whistle for his dog, Willie. He finally does it!

Keats, Ezra Jack. *Peter's Chair.* Harper & Row, 1967. The problems of accepting a new baby sister are handled in a realistically delightful manner.

Krasilovsky, Phyllis. *The Very Tall Little Girl.* Doubleday, 1969. Being taller than everyone can be both a problem and a pleasure.

Krauss, Ruth. Illustrated by Maurice Sendak. *I'll Be You and You Be Me.* Harper & Row, 1954. Love and friendship is the theme of a group of verses that capture a child's feelings for human relationships.

McCloskey, Robert. *Lentil.* Viking, 1940 (Scholastic paperback). A delightful story about good deeds paying off in the end.

Ness, Evaline. *Ameli Mixed the Mustard.* Scribner, 1975. Poems about girls—all sizes and shapes.

Rey, H. A. *Curious George Goes to the Hospital.* Houghton Mifflin, 1966. One in a series of Curious George books that help a child deal with the many new experiences that will occur during a hospital visit.

Ryan, Cheli Duran. *Hildilid's Night.* Macmillan, 1971. Fear of the night causes Hildilid to try to dispose of it.

Sendak, Maurice. *Where the Wild Things Are.* Harper & Row, 1963. A fantasy illustrating the emotions of Max, who is sent to bed for misbehaving. A wonderful story that captures a child's true release of emotions.

Scott, Ann Herbert. *Sam.* McGraw-Hill, 1969. A sensitive story about a black child who always wants to play but whose family is too busy for him.

———. *On Mother's Lap.* McGraw-Hill, 1972. A warm story of sibling rivalry and mother love in an Eskimo setting.

Skorpen, Liesel Moak. *Outside My Window.* Harper & Row, 1968. Loneliness and friendship are dealt with in a delightful manner.

Slobodkin, Lois. *Excuse Me! Certainly.* Vanguard, 1959. A delightful poem whose theme is politeness. Dealt with in a comical and amusing fashion.

Zolotow, Charlotte. *If It Weren't for You.* Harper & Row, 1966. A book to share with brothers and sisters. An older brother speculates on how glamorous it would be not to have to share everything, particularly parents.

———. *William's Doll.* Harper & Row, 1972. When William asks for a doll, the other boys scorn him and his father tries to interest him in conventional boys' playthings. His sympathetic grandmother buys him a doll, explaining that he needs to practice being a father. A very, very special book for boys.

books that encourage intellectual and language growth

Barrett, Jodi. *Animals Should Definitely Not Wear Clothes.* Atheneum, 1971. Absurd and bothersome clothing put on animals evokes laughter. (Classification, comparisons, and imagination.)

Burningham, John. *Mr. Grumpy's Outing.* Holt, Rinehart and

Winston, 1971. Repetition helps to increase the child's memory when Mr. Grumpy's boat is filled with rambunctious animals and children. (Language, cause and effect, few and many.)

————. *Seasons.* Bobbs-Merrill, 1971. An attractive collection of color paintings dramatize the beauty of nature through the year. (Comparisons, time, and vocabulary.)

Busch, Phyllis S. *A Walk In The Snow.* Lippincott, 1971. Photographs provide a study of snow and things that can be done with it. Games to be played in the snow will help to extend the child's knowledge and appreciation for nature. (Classification, vocabulary, and comparisons.)

Carle, Eric. *One, Two, Three to the Zoo.* Collins World, 1968. Beautiful pictures help the child to count. The fold-out last page includes all of the animals. (Ordinal counting and language.)

————. *The Very Hungry Caterpillar.* Collins World, 1972. A counting book and the life cycle of a caterpillar combine to make an exciting and delightful story. (Time, number, and comparisons.)

Dugan, William. *The Sign Book.* Golden Press, 1968. Signs around the child's world will delight the preschooler when the youngster recognizes some. (Comparisons and vocabulary; talking is print written down.)

Freschet, Bernice. *Turtle Pond.* Scribner, 1971. A description of the animal world and survival is the theme. (Cause and effect, classification, and vocabulary.)

Garelick, May. Illustrated by Leonard Weisgard. *Where Does the Butterfly Go When It Rains?* Addison-Wesley, 1961. Simple questions are answered in misty illustrations, but the problem is never solved. (Cause and effect, vocabulary, and comparisons.)

Hoban, Tana. *Shapes and Things.* Macmillan, 1970. A wordless picture book of objects to be identified. (Vocabulary and language into print concept.)

Hutchins, Pat. *Clocks and More Clocks.* Macmillan, 1970. Problems of time differences are presented in a humorous fashion. (Cause and effect and time comparisons.)

Knight, Hilary. *Sylvia the Sloth*. Harper & Row, 1969. The adventures of Sylvia the Sloth as she tries to see life "the other way around." (Space, comparisons, and vocabulary.)

Livermore, Elaine. *One to Ten, Count Again*. Houghton Mifflin, 1973. A counting book where each line is repeated on the next page as a new one is added. (Language, speech into print, and ordinal counting.)

Mari, Iela and Ezo. *The Apple and the Moth*. Pantheon, 1970. A wordless picture book illustrates the life cycle of a moth. (Time, comparison, and cause and effect.)

Memling, Carl. *What's in the Dark?* Parents Magazine Press, 1971. Shows that what is present in the darkness is almost the same as what is present in the daylight. (Comparisons, language, and classifications.)

Merriam, Eve. *What Can You Do With A Pocket?* Knopf, 1964. What can a child do with objects in his or her pockets? (Imagination and vocabulary.)

Miles, Miska. *Apricot ABC*. Little, Brown, 1969. An ABC book with a plot that weaves the alphabet into rhythmical lines and rhymes. (Language and comparisons.)

Munari, Bruno. *ABC*. World, 1960. Colorful illustrations stress language. (An ABC book with an added touch.)

Oxenbury, Helen. *Numbers of Things*. Watts, 1968. Lovely illustrations entertain while they teach number concepts.

————. *ABC of Things*. Watts, 1972. Humorous situations and objects, each representing a letter of the alphabet, interest children in the alphabet. (Letters, vocabulary, comparisons, and classifications.)

Rand, Ann. *Sparkle and Spin; A Book About Words*. Harcourt, Brace Jovanovich, 1957. A captivating adventure with words, their sounds and meanings. (Language, vocabulary, and comparisons.)

ACTIVITIES FOR READING AT AGES 3 AND 4: The following group of activities should be ritualistic. The consistency of action will help to build reading habits.

Table 4–6
guidelines to help adults create positive ideas about reading
for children

CHILD'S BEHAVIOR WITH BOOKS	APPROPRIATE ADULT BEHAVIOR TO FOSTER INDEPENDENT LEARNING
When children select a book . . .	Permit them to choose the book they want.
When children make believe that they are reading, even though they are calling out "words" that are not printed . . .	That's great. This is the very beginning of reading. The child is acting the role of a reader. The child is feeling comfortable with printed language. Leave the youngster alone!
When the child points to words . . .	That's fine. All the child is doing is becoming aware that these are words.
When the child asks to hear the same book over and over again . . .	Great! The youngster is beginning to develop personal tastes in literature and language.
When the child rejects a book that you think is good and selects one that you don't like . . .	Use the child's selection. The youngster is showing asertiveness with books. This will help to build an independent learner.

activity 1: building the reading ritual

There must be a special time each day when the entire family reads together. Set a special time to read for three to eight minutes. No talking, no moving, and no interruptions should be permitted.

activity 2: sharing

Find a special time to share something about everyone's reading. The family dinner table is a natural place for getting together and sharing exciting events. Say, "I read something that was funny in my book yesterday." Share the experience and, if the book is handy, point to it. Do not ask children to share. They will share if you set an example.

activity 3: storyreading

Read to your child at the same times each day. These might be (1) before nap or bedtime, (2) during rest time, (3) after dinner, or (4) after nursery school.

activity 4: setting examples

Be sure that your preschool child sees you reading and enjoying the experience. Make reading materials readily available for your child.

Be sure that you take a trip to the local children's library at least once a week. Use the following guide for appropriate behavior with children in libraries.

1. Permit the child to browse.

2. Pay attention when your child becomes excited about a book or part of a book. Show interest and listen. Show part of your book to the child. Show enthusiasm about your reading.

3. Let your child know that you are selecting books based on a particular interest. Select a group of books for yourself that are all about one subject—for example, tennis, or cooking, or gardening. Show these to your child. Say, "Look, I have lots of books about tennis." You are helping the child to classify materials. This is important for reading and learning later on. The child will begin to imitate your behavior and will begin to select children's books about a particular subject. Do not force this behavior. Just set the example for imitation.

4. Permit your child to take books out of the library. Set a limit as to number. Some libraries already do this. Let the child select the books. If trouble in selection occurs, choose a half-dozen or so books and place them on a child-size reading table. Then go back to your own reading.

5. Many libraries provide story times and activities for children. Find out about these and attend on a regular basis. Build up the experience to be an exciting and important one that just can't be missed.

6. Have a special place at home for the library books—a place that is separate from the one for books that are personally owned. This will help children to learn that library books are very special borrowed property.

7. Be sure that you do not ask your child what the story is about. The preschool child is naturally curious. The youngster will ask questions about the story. Children's questions tell you what they know about stories.

140

activity 6:
guiding
reading with
wordless
books

Wordless books help the preschool child to develop the ability to understand and comprehend the plot of a story. Help the child to "read" one of the books without words suggested in the following list (more titles are listed in Chapter 5 on page 188):

Barton, Byron. *Where's Al?* Seabury Press, 1972.
Goodall, John S. *The Surprise Picnic,* Atheneum, 1977.
Keats, Ezra Jack. *Skates,* Watts, 1973.

As you help the child to "read," follow these steps:

1. *Place the child on your lap.*
2. *Place the book in both your hands and say, "There is a story in this book that is waiting to be told. There are no words. The words for telling come from you. Any story you tell will fit the pictures."*
3. *Direct the child to the left side of the text by placing the child's hand on the left page. Encourage the child to talk about that picture. Accept all of the child's language.*

ACTIVITIES RELATED TO THE DEVELOPMENT OF THE SKILLS NECESSARY TO READ: In order to read, children must be able to understand (1) left to right movement; (2) that words represent pictures and objects, ideas, and feelings; (3) that letters make up words; (4) that certain sounds are like other sounds; (5) that certain shapes are like other shapes; and (6) that oral directions can be translated into physical activity. The following activities will serve as examples for developing each of these skills. Other activities can be developed using these as models.

activity 1:
left-to-right
progression

When you read to your child, use your finger and hand to indicate where you are reading. When you pass a sign in the supermarket, move your hand from left to right as you read it. If the child wants to read it too, place his or her hand at the left side of the poster, and as you read it, move the child's hand along the line of print from left to right.

activity 2: words represent objects, feelings, and ideas	MATERIALS: An apple or an orange, white paper at least 9 × 12 inches, and crayons.
	DIRECTIONS: Put the fruit on a table. Ask the child, "What kind of fruit is here?" When the child responds, write the name of the fruit on the paper. Be sure that the child knows the name of the fruit. Put the fruit on the paper. Ask, "What did I do?" Accept all responses.
activity 3: words represent objects, feelings, and ideas	MATERIALS: Paper, crayons, and objects (toys, fruit, etc.).
	DIRECTIONS: Write the name of an object as the child says it. Ask your child to draw a picture to match the word.
activity 4: letter identification	MATERIALS: A set of letters, either upper or lower case (plastic, magnetic letters that adhere to surfaces are fun), a table, and a book with large print.
	DIRECTIONS: Put a letter on the table and say the letter's name. Ask the child to trace the letter with the pointer finger and say the name of the letter. Ask the child to find that letter in a page of the book. (Letters with magnets can be placed on a refrigerator door.)
activity 5: sounds are like other sounds	MATERIALS: A list of rhyming words: hat, cat, mat, fat, rat, sat. A poem using these words. For example:

I know a cat,
He wears a hat,
He has a fat rat,
He sat on a mat.
The cat and the hat and the fat rat all sat on the mat.

DIRECTIONS: Read the poem to your child. Read the first two lines. Then read the third line and leave out the last word. Encourage the child to insert a rhyming word. It will probably be one that ends with "at." If the child cannot hear the rhyme, stop the activity. Do not use pressure. Go back to rhyming stories and read them daily. The child will rhyme when sufficient development for this skill has occurred.

142

activity 6:
some sounds
are
like other
sounds

DIRECTIONS: Say, "There is a gasoline that rhymes with bell. The gasoline that rhymes with bell is_____(Shell)."
Say, "There is a fruit that rhymes with bear. The fruit that rhymes with bear is_____(pear)."

You can think of lots more. This is fun and can be done anywhere—in the house, in the car, or on the street. It is a difficult game, but it is possible for some 3- and 4-year-olds to enjoy.

activity 7:
letter
identification

MATERIALS: A large piece of drawing paper, a crayon or a marker, and a familiar storybook.
DIRECTIONS: Write the first letter of your child's name on the paper. Say, "Find that letter in your book. Find it as many times as you can." Continue only if the child finds success with the activity.

activity 8:
oral
directions
and reading

DIRECTIONS: Act out setting the table. Ask, "What am I doing?" Say, "Now listen. Go to the drawer. Take out a spoon and a fork." At a later time, increase the directions to three activities. For example: "Go to the drawer. Take out a spoon and a fork and put them on the table. Increase the number of directions at later dates.

WHY THESE ACTIVITIES: The more varied language activities children encounter, the easier it will be to function with words when they read. It is important to observe the child's behavior to see where further growth is indicated. The following list of skills should serve as a general guide for creating more activities and selecting books appropriate for the preschool child.

The desired response for each statement is "yes."

YES   NO

POSITIVE FEELING ABOUT BOOKS
1. The child voluntarily looks at books.
2. Will ask you to read a favorite book over and over again.
3. Will refer to a book as a toy or book toy.

143

4. When asked, "What do you want for a present?", the child will say, "A book."

5. Likes to go to the library.

6. Likes to look at magazines or other printed materials.

PHYSICAL DEVELOPMENT AND READING

1. Can hold a pencil and direct it with ease.

2. Can point to an object across the room and say its name.

3. Favors one hand and foot and uses one eye (right or left) consistently over another.

4. Can hop on one foot.

5. Is beginning to learn to skip.

VISUAL DEVELOPMENT

1. Can see objects with ease—does not squint.

2. Can point to an object and say its name.

3. Moves finger from left to right as if reading when looking at pictures or pages in books.

LISTENING SKILLS

1. Can rhyme words.

2. Likes to hear poetry.

3. Likes to sing songs that rhyme.

Create new activities following the pattern of those included. Do not push or prod children. They will learn as soon as they are ready. Keep reading to them, for this is one of the most effective activities for creating readers.

the playing place:
a place for skill-building

The playing place for the child of 3 and 4 should include games that help to develop the pre-reading skills listed in Table 4–7. Materials that encourage skill development are included.

Table 4–7
developmental pre-reading skills and materials that help them
to develop

PRE-READING SKILLS THAT AID PHYSICAL GROWTH AND ENCOURAGE. . .	APPROPRIATE MATERIALS TO HELP GROWTH
Observing likenesses and differences	Blocks of many sizes with a few in each size Picture dominoes Magnetic alphabet boards Lacing cards (large holes)
Learning that print is language and the eyes move from left to right to follow it. Small muscle development	Toys that stack from left to right Picture books Blocks Food container boxes
Extending oral language vocabulary	Puppets Sewing cards ABC Lotto games Talking toys and records
Comparing, classifying, organizing, and describing materials; for example: Comparing letters and numbers Telling how something looks Putting things with a common element into groups	Toys that encourage children to manipulate, using these skills, include: Dominoes Lincoln Logs Tinker Toys Building Blocks Puzzles Matching games of all kinds

GUIDELINES FOR BEHAVIOR: It is important to remember that play is the child's work. Children must enjoy play, find success in playful endeavors, and be permitted to experiment without fear of adult interference. Following is a guide for adult behavior when children play. All responses should be checked in the "yes" column for the best results.

YES   NO

I observe without interfering.

When the child loses a piece of a toy, I find it and place it within the child's reach.

If the child exhibits frustration with a toy, I do not push it on the child. I understand that the child is not ready for it.

I get letter games for the children when they

begin to show an interest in letters and words.

I look to see if toys are instruction-free—that the child can play with the game without adult help.

I observe the child for signs of interest, so that I can supply books, pictures, and appropriate toys related to those interests.

When directing a child in an activity, the child does the doing, and I serve as a guide.

ACTIVITIES FOR PLAY:

activity 1: observing likenesses and differences (classification and comparing)

MATERIALS: Sandpaper, scissors, a felt-tipped marker, a guide for drawing the letters (see Figure 5–1, page 212), and two strips of plastic 6 inches wide by approximately 78 inches long.

DIRECTIONS: Draw letters on the back side of the sandpaper. Turn the letters face down when tracing, so that they will not be reversed. Be sure that they are at least 3 inches high for lower case letters and 4 inches high for upper case. Cut them out. Put them in a box and label the box "LETTERS." On the plastic strip, first trace all of the lower case letters in alphabetical order. Fill in the letters with a felt-tipped marker. Then on the second strip, trace all the upper case letters—also in alphabetical order—and fill in the letters as before. Roll up each plastic strip and place them in the box with the letters. Put the toy in the playing area. The child, when ready, will roll out the plastic strip and begin to match the sandpaper letters to the drawn ones by placing them on top of the other as shown in Figure 4–2.

activity 2: extending oral language (comparing, describing, and organizing)

MATERIALS: Pictures from magazines, a tagboard, paste, scissors, and a cassette tape recorder.

DIRECTIONS: Paste each picture on a piece of tagboard cut to the size of the picture. Place these in a box. Put these pictures next to the cassette recorder. Show your child how to select a picture, push the correct button to start the tape, and talk about the picture on the tape. Your child will copy this behavior at will.

Fig. 4–2

activity 3:
likenesses
and
differences
with objects
(classifications,
organization,
and decision
making)

MATERIALS: A large plastic bucket, lots of small objects to put in the bucket (buttons, bottle caps, small containers, paper clips, kitchen utensils, rice, macaroni, etc.), four containers that are the same (for example, margarine containers, paper cups), and large paper fasteners.

DIRECTIONS: Collect odds and ends and put them into the bucket. Fasten the paper cups or plastic containers together with paper fasteners as shown in Figure 4–3. Place the fastened containers and the bucket in the playing area. Children will classify objects by placing materials as they see fit into the attached buckets. Say, "Put things in the buckets that go together."

activity 4:
small muscle
development

MATERIALS: A large, sturdy box, big wastebasket, or laundry basket, and small, soft rubber balls or toys.

DIRECTIONS: Place toys in the box and put it on a shelf. The child stands at a distance and tosses the toys into the box. At first, the child may stand next to the box. As time goes on, the

147

Fig. 4–3

youngster will be able to move back and toss and aim. This is a game to play with your child.

activity 5: a sign game

DIRECTIONS: As you ride in the car and pass gas stations, call out the name of a specific station, pointing to the sign that tells its name. For example, if you select Shell, say, "Shell" and point to the sign. Do this for one week with the same sign. The next week, select another gas station and do the same. This time, say the new name as well as pointing out the old name.

activity 6: words are language (comparing and classifying)

MATERIALS: 5 × 8 inch index cards, without lines, 2 large markers in two different colors, and a shoe box

DIRECTIONS: Write the name of one brand of gas on a card. Write it twice, once in one color on one card, and once in the alternate color on a second card. Repeat this with each name. Put all of these cards into a box. You should begin with one name and then increase the number of cards as the child learns to recognize the signs. Say, "This is a matching game. Put two cards together that look the same to you." Children look for only one object characteristic when matching.

activity 7: a game to make (classification and identification)

MATERIALS: Old cereal boxes, scissors, and a shoe or cigar box DIRECTIONS: Cut out the name of the cereal. Put this in the box. Each time you use a box of cereal, cut out that name in the same shape. Put many samples of the same name in the box. Do this with two, three, or four items. Show the child the box of cards. Say, "Put cards that look the same to you in a pile." Accept all responses. If the child does not match as you expected, the youngster is probably not ready to do this activity. Put the game away until success is achievable.

the construction place

The place to construct can be a playroom, a kitchen, the front stoop, or a backyard. Construction can mean crafts—cutting and pasting—or art work as well as building with blocks or sand.

MATERIALS: Certain indoor materials are basic, and a selection should always be available for construction. These include the following:

Glue in a dispenser that can be used easily by a child.

Scissors.

Paper for cutting and tearing—newsprint, wrapping paper, and so on.

Library paste in a jar and an instrument for taking paste out, such as a popsicle stick.

Acorns, beans, peas, and seeds from the out-of-doors.

Boxes, tubes, and egg cartons.

Cellophane and tissue paper.

Confetti.

Corn on the cob—dried.

Cloth, cotton, wool, yarn, and fur.

Cupcake papers and candy cups from boxed candy.

Eggshells.

Meat trays.

Packing materials—excelsior, torn paper, and others.

Feathers.

Grass, twigs, leaves, and flowers.

Gum wrappers, stamps, and holiday stickers.

Macaroni shells, curls, and rings. Large rings may be strung as beads.

Magazines and catalogues.

Wallpaper sample books.

Popsicle sticks and toothpicks.

Paper cups.

Paper scraps—wrapping paper and food wrappers that are not coated in wax.

Wood shavings and sawdust.

Salt or sand.

Spools and wood pieces.

Straws (drinking).

Newspaper cut into strips.

Styrofoam curls and pieces.

Pipe cleaners.

Blocks and building toys.

Materials for cooking and baking (flour; premixes for cakes and cookies).

Sand in a sand box.

Mud.

Large stones to use with the mud.

Outdoor blocks and cut-up tree stumps.

Plastic containers to fill things with.

GUIDELINES FOR ADULT BEHAVIOR: It is extremely important that adults who live and work with children respect their abilities to construct. Materials, space, and time must be provided in an appropriate manner, and adults must observe but not interfere. The checklist that follows should serve as a guide for adult interactions with children when they construct. Positive responses for all statements are desired.

YES   *NO*

Materials are organized and placed for self-selection.

I allow as much as twenty minutes or as few as five minutes for construction, the time depending on the child's interest and desire.

I listen to the child's language as the youngster works, I watch and observe, but I do not interfere with the construction.

When the child says, "It's for you" or "I'm making it for you," I respond by smiling, but I give no verbal response. Your goal for the child is to encourage the youngster to work for self-satisfaction.

I never say, "What is it?" or "I don't like it." I will say, "Oh, how interesting," or "How wonderful to work with those materials," or "Oh, you're enjoying doing that, aren't you?"

If the child is working alongside another child and a disagreement develops, I divert the bothered child by saying, "Oh, look at these beads, John" or "Wow, these strips of paper look exciting."

I do not put values on children's productions.

I encourage the child to talk about the work. I will often say, "Tell me about it," "How do you feel about it?", or "What parts are most interesting to you?"

The child is instructed in cleaning-up activities. Clean-up is as much a part of the construction as the activity in action.

SKILLS DEVELOPED DURING CONSTRUCTION: During construction, children use the small muscles important for writing. They talk about their work, increasing their vocabularies. They learn to organize and compare materials. Construction helps children to develop their understanding of concepts, such as bigger and smaller, before and after, over and under, higher and lower, fat and thin, and others. As children construct, they take pride in themselves and their accomplishments. This is essential for success in reading. Use the following sample activities and develop further ideas that help children to become competent with the physical, emotional, social, and intellectual elements necessary for successful reading.

INDOOR ACTIVITIES FOR CONSTRUCTION:

activity 1: making a collage with out-of-doors materials (organizing and comparing)

MATERIALS: Library paste on a piece of paper or in a shallow cup, leaves, acorns, grass, twigs, flowers, and small pine cones, and paper (approximately 12 × 18 inches)

DIRECTIONS: Place materials, categorized according to item, in boxes on the table. Put all leaves in one small box, all flowers in another, all grass in another, and so forth. Place the paste and a large piece of paper on the table. Children will know what to do.

activity 2: using food for making a collage (organizing and comparing)

MATERIALS: Macaroni, rice, dried beans, library paste, and large paper (18 × 24 inches)— for example, a large piece of brown wrapping paper.

DIRECTIONS: Put the three materials in separate piles on a table. Place the paste and paper near these items. The child will know what to do. After the child has completed the project, say, "Tell me about it" or "Share it with me." Accept all language responses.

activity 3: block building (to help develop size differences— comparing)

MATERIALS: Commercial blocks, homemade blocks made of wood, sponges, or boxes. The blocks should be of many sizes.

DIRECTIONS: Observe the child playing with the blocks. As the child plays, say,

"Find the biggest block you can."

"Find the smallest block."

"Find all of the small blocks and put them over here."

activity 4: blocks (comparing)

DIRECTIONS: As the child plays, suggest the following:

"Build the highest building you can."

"Build the lowest building you can."

Act out these differences with your body to help the child see the comparison.

activity 5: painting with straws (small muscle development)

MATERIALS: One color of paint in a container that has an open top, two straws, a piece of newsprint on a table, and a spoon.
DIRECTIONS: Put the straws in the paint. There should be one for you and one for the child. Show the child how to spoon one spoonful of paint onto the newsprint. Then pick up the straw and gently blow the paint.

activity 6: string and paint (small muscle development)

MATERIALS: One color of paint in a shallow container with a wide mouth, such as a soup bowl, a string about 12 inches long, and a piece of paper at least 18 × 24 inches.
DIRECTIONS: Put the string next to the paint bowl. Place the paper on a table or on the floor. The child is to dip the string into the paint and pull it along the paper. This helps to develop the same ability needed to write with a pencil. The eyes direct the movements of the hands to form a definite pattern on the paper.

activity 7: spools and paint (small muscle development)

MATERIALS: Empty thread spools, one color of paint in a shallow wide-mouth container, and one piece of painting paper 12 × 18 inches.
DIRECTIONS: Show the child how to dip one end of the spool into the paint and stamp it on the paper. As the youngster does this, repeat the following chant to the timing of his printing.

JACK A NORY
I'll tell you a story
About Jack A Nory
And now my story's begun;
I'll tell you another
Of Jack and his brother,
And now my story is done.
NURSERY RHYME

The repetition of the language and the repetition of the printing activity will help the child to build the rhythms of language.

activity 8: pipe cleaners (developing oral language)

MATERIALS: About a dozen pipe cleaners
DIRECTIONS: Place the pipe cleaners on the table. The child needs no instruction. The youngster will begin to twist and turn to create a language through movement. The child will probably talk and twist at the same time. You might sing a song, such as the one that follows, as the child works (for the tune, see Figure 4–4). If you sing this song each time the child plays with these objects, you will help the child to associate the language of the song with the pipe cleaner activity.

THE WHEELS OF THE BUS GO ROUND AND ROUND
The wheels of the bus go round and round
Round and round, round and round.
The wheels of the bus go round and round
All through the town.

TRADITIONAL FOLK SONG[2]

the thinking place

The thinking place for the 3- and 4-year-old is a place to share ideas. This place and time must exist so that the child can be helped to recall experiences. It is a time to think about events, books, toys, ideas, and feelings. It is important to help the 3- and 4-year-old to compare experiences, to organize them, and to make some personal judgments about

Fig. 4–4

[2]From Nancy Larrick, *The Wheels of the Bus Go Round and Round* (Chicago: Golden Gate Junior Books, a division of Children's Press, 1972), p. 6.

154

them. The following activities will help to guide the child to think critically about the activities of daily life.

activity 1: organizing thoughts

Plan a time to share with the child. This can be a time after a nap, after lunch, or after a play period. Say, "Let's think for a moment about all the things you did today where you used your hands." Be quiet for a period of two minutes. Build the habit of quiet silent thought. Then say, "I did the dishes, made the breakfast, and gave the money to the bank teller. When did you use your hands?"

activity 2: classifying ideas

Say, "Think of all the sounds you heard while walking to the food store." Wait for a period of two minutes (or longer, as time progresses). Then say, "What did you hear?" After the child offers sounds, then you offer your sounds.

activity 3: classifying ideas and self-selection

Say, "Of all the books you saw today, which did you want to grab first?" Think for a period of time. Let the child offer contributions. Your purpose here is to help the child to refer to books by name. At another time, say, "Of all the books you looked at (or read) today, which would you like to keep forever?"

activity 4: sharing writing and art

Place all of the books read to a child during a two-day period in a section of a room. During the quiet time, say, "Pick one and sit with it to enjoy it." Put a time limit of two or more minutes on this activity. You and the child should engage in this quiet get-together with a familiar book each day.

activity 5: stimulating ideas

Encourage the child to take a book or toy and go to a quiet place. This helps the child to develop self-confidence when working and thinking alone.

threes and fours and reading: a summary

The fascination with language helps the preschooler learn to use words. Language grows quickly during these years. Impressions of language and books are developed and everlastingly imprinted. These impressions play a major part in the child's later success in reading. Experiences where children are exposed to language and then have an opportunity to create in words and phrases helps to build the skills necessary for reading. It is essential that adults let children grow in these early years as their bodies and minds permit and that they offer as many experiences as possible to help children to love and use the language they will learn to read in books.

5

THE KINDERGARTEN CHILD: JUST BEFORE FORMAL READING BEGINS

How wonderful to be five! This is the age for real school. Kindergartners love feeling grown up and, therefore, want to experience being trusted with responsibility. They adore going on errands, doing household chores, shopping, and even trying to solve family problems. Five-year-olds love to learn new things. Yet their attention span is short. Although they are no longer babies, they need lots of affection and support. Some 5-year-olds will still break down under stress and cry as they did in earlier years.

The first five years of life are an integral part of the reading readiness period. The beginning of schooling at ages 5, 6, or 7 does not contain a magic potion that says, "Read." When the infant dribbles on his or her bed sheet and smells the odor his or her dribble produces, he or she is sharpening the senses, thus developing a skill necessary for reading. When the infant feels a furry pillow, tastes a sour pickle, or sees a giraffe for the first time, language experiences are being built in preparation for reading. When at age 3 or 4, a youngster yells, "Grandma's here," he or she does so because he or she has learned to anticipate a visitor when the doorbell rings. The child has learned to create an anticipatory image, a skill necessary for reading. Readiness to read is happening when the child is involved in experiences. Many kinds of experiences in varying amounts and in different settings are required for the child's intellectual, social, and emotional development. The child will be ready for formal reading when all aspects of growth emerge into "language power"—the power to express, create, and enjoy life through words.

The importance of kindergarten cannot be stressed enough. Kindergarten supplies the time and activities for the development of all aspects of growth. Through field trips, dramatizations, storytelling times, and children's literature and poetry, the kindergarten teacher will build on the child's home experiences in order to create language power and a love of learning.

skill development in kindergarten

Children's physical, intellectual, social, and emotional growth at five years of age permits them to develop the following skills in the kindergarten year.

1. *Left to right movements of hands and eyes when using printed materials.*
2. *The ability to listen and identify likenesses and differences of sounds at the beginning of words and in association with an idea.*
3. *The ability to visually recognize a group of words that are personally meaningful. This is referred to as a "sight vocabulary."*
4. *Knowledge that some letters say their names in words and that others don't.*
5. *The ability to identify colors, shapes, sizes, and numbers of things.*
6. *The ability to describe and interpret pictures.*
7. *The ability to listen to a simple story and to*
   a. *Remember it in the order it was presented.*
   b. *Recall particular sections of the story.*
   c. *Create new endings to the story.*
   d. *Know the difference between a real story and a make believe story.*
   e. *Predict what will happen at the end of the story.*

Skill development happens as children become involved in language activities that develop in conjunction with total growth. Growth patterns of most kindergarten

Table 5-1
growth and implications for preparing environments for maximum development: 5 years old

MOTOR DEVELOPMENT		EMOTIONAL AND SOCIAL DEVELOPMENT		INTELLECTUAL DEVELOPMENT	
ABILITIES	IMPLICATIONS	ABILITIES	IMPLICATIONS	ABILITIES	IMPLICATIONS
Small muscles are developing. Has more eye control.	Is able to sit longer. Can lace shoes, learns left to right, can zipper, hold a pencil, and write with some ease.	Poised. Has inner controls. Can anticipate immediate happenings.	Learns what behaviors are correct and acceptable. Has determined a manner that is used to get his or her own way. Might be a bit dogmatic and offer only one answer to a problem.	Interests widen.	Begins to recognize numbers and letters. Is interested in clocks and time. Is interested in stories about animals that act like people.
Large muscles are well developed.	Can walk a straight line; goes up and down stairs, alternating feet; learns to skip. Can climb on alternating feet; shows an interest in roller skates and pogo sticks.	Cannot change direction in midstream.	Must get off to the right start at the beginning of an event in order to do well.		Can sort. Can place a series of objects in order according to size.
		Very social. Affection is a part of his social behavior.	Will play well with others, including younger or older siblings. Is protective and motherly.	Ability to reason is similar to fours.	Terms like "opposite from" and "across from" begin to take on meaning at the end of the fifth year.
Eyes and hands are becoming well coordinated.	Can play a piano one note at a time. Will use small as well as large blocks. Likes to copy. Likes to watch behavior and copy it. Likes to have outlined pictures to color.	Social with peers. Admires adults. Is concerned with tangible forces.	Plays best with 5-year-olds in pairs. Conforms to adult ideas. Will ask for adult help when it is needed. Is concerned about God and what he looks like. Seems to understand death, but does not relate it to him- or herself.	Space concepts begin to form. Time concepts are vague. Understands a schedule of daily events.	Child knows about "now" and the present, past, or future. Can begin to follow a daily plan and to know own responsibility for learning.

children and their implications for reading readiness are summarized in Table 5–1.

language growth

Observing the development of the child's oral language helps to determine his or her readiness to work with letters and words in a formal manner. Table 5–2 shows the developmental scheme usually found in 5-year-olds.

Table 5–2
language development at 5 years: implications
for reading and writing

BEHAVIOR	IMPLICATIONS
Easily uses sentences such as "Shut the door," "The boy was hit by the girl," "I gave it to him so he won't cry," and others. These are complex sentence constructions.	When using these constructions, he or she will begin to understand them more easily when hearing them. Will begin to dictate complex sentence structures when creating a story.
Asks where a letter is in a word: "Where is a word that starts like jelly with a 'J?' "	Is ready to play games related to letter matching. Can hear initial consonant sounds and will begin to distinguish words by noting letters and their sound relationships.
Wants to write a description on pictures he or she creates.	Begins to understand the difference between oral and written language.
When dictating, will begin to say letter names in each word.	Can begin to write his or her own words on paper.
When looking at an ABC book, will say, "Oh, an ABC book." Will point to the letters "A," "B," and "C."	Is ready to look at detail in the letters in words.
Asks for a notebook to write in.	Is probably ready to begin to write his or her own first book.
Will begin to write his or her name and the names of street signs and gas stations.	Likes to write language and should be encouraged to build a group of words to write (see the section in chapter 5 on writing, pages 166-74).
Will point to words when seeing them in books, on posters, and on food boxes.	Is interested in words and should be encouraged to play games that involve words and phrases.
Is aware of sound similarities in words. Will make up words that rhyme with other words. Can hear letter sounds at the beginning of words.	Is probably ready to play simple decoding games that teach word spelling patterns. Will have fun writing and hearing rhymes and words with word family patterns.

Based on the works of Buhler, N. & C. Chomsky, Dale, Elkind, Menyuk, F. Smith & Miller, Weir, and others. All references are cited in the Bibliography.

the listening place

A 5-year-old switches on the television set or a radio as soon as he or she wakens in the morning. In a neighboring room, the child's sister turns on another television station. Mother is in the kitchen listening to the weather report in order to know how to dress the children for the day. Dad's electric razor hums over the running water in the bathroom sink. The school bus arrives with its horn honking, drowning out the sounds of a family getting ready for the day. Words and sounds are all around us. This means listening to different things at different times for different purposes. Where does one listen first?

Children in school are expected to spend more time in listening than in any other activity, so we must prepare them to develop the ability by:

1. *Following simple directions.*
2. *Hearing the likenesses and differences of:*
   a. *Sounds around the environment.*
   b. *Words (rhyming).*
   c. *Letters and syllables.*
3. *Hearing details.*

materials for listening

Materials for listening should be simple. Children need to listen to a radio, a television set, recordings, and voices placed on cassette tapes. The most important material, however, is an adult who truly cares about listening. This means that the child has an adult's full attention. Following is a guide for adult behavior during listening.

Have a special listening place where you and the child can go to chat and listen to each other.

When the child talks, listen with your eyes as well as your ears. Look at the child and smile to show your interest.

Make sure that listening times are short and direct.

Create instant listening activities in the car, in the bath, on the bed, or at the park. Say, "Listen, remember, and tell what you heard." Then say, "Make the sounds."

When the child responds, notice his or her span of attention to the different sounds; this will help you to plan further activities.

When you ask children to listen, direct them by providing a purpose for listening. Say, for example, "Sh-h-h-h, listen to hear the birds," or "Listen to the running water."

Provide a private time to listen to the child. When the child asks to tell you something, do not say, "Wait."

Let the youngster tell it now. Young children cannot wait.

LISTENING ACTIVITIES: The suggested activities will help the child at age 5 to grow to become a creative listener who enjoys the sounds of language.

activity 1: hearing language that rhymes; increasing the ability to recall

Put the following poem on a cassette tape.

IF ALL THE WORLD WAS APPLE PIE
If all the world was apple-pie,
And all the sea was ink,
And all the trees were bread and cheese,
What should we have to drink?

MOTHER GOOSE[1]

Set the recording in the listening place.
DIRECTIONS FOR USE: When you and the child have a moment together, listen to the tape. Then, ask one of the following questions:
1. What did you hear? (Seeks general information)
2. What did you like about it? (Seeks impressions)
3. Tell about the things that you remember the most. (Seeks imagery)
Accept all responses.

activity 2: listening for likenesses and differences— sounds at the beginning of words

TEACHING: Say a word that begins like the child's name. Say the word over and over and over. Point to a toy that begins with the same letter and sound as the child's name. Say, for example, "Look at the toy, Tracy. It is a truck." Continue the

[1]From *Mother Goose Nursery Rhymes*, illustrated by Arthur Rackman. Reprinted by permission of Viking Penguin Inc.

activity by developing a simple language activity, such as the following:

Tracy and truck,
Tracy and truck,
Truck and Tracy,
Truck and Tracy,
Tracy is a girl,
Truck is a toy,
Tracy and truck,
Truck and Tracy.

Say this movingly, swinging a part of your body so that the child will imitate the movement and say the ditty.

activity 3: beginning sounds— likenesses and differences

DIRECTIONS: Select a group of words that begin with the same sound as your child's name. If his name is Darren, for example, say, "I have a new game. Listen. David, dog, doodle, Darren, Dot. How are these the same?" The expected response is, "They have the same sounds at the beginning." If the child does not say this, this indicates that the child is probably not ready to hear the likeness. Play similar games. Say a string of words that begin with the same sound. Ask the child to say a word that goes with the group. Say, "Straight, string, strap, stripe, stride."

activity 4: likenesses and differences teaching beginning sounds.

This activity will help children to hear sounds at the beginning of words.
DIRECTIONS: Say, "Listen to me. A-a-a-a-a-a-a-a-a-a-a-a-a-ap-ple." Hold onto the sound of the "a" as long as you can. Say, "O.K., get ready to say the word 'apple,' but hold onto the beginning of the word as long as your breath will go. Get ready, go! A-a-a-a-a-a-a-a-a-apple." After the child has completed the sounding, say, "Let's do another. I will say animal and hold onto the beginning of the word. Ready, listen: A-a-a-a-a-a-a-a-animal." This activity can be done with all letters that can be held without changing the sound. These include consonants and long and short vowels; for example, the long vowels that appear in the beginning of the words "*a*pe," "*e*at," "*i*ce," "*o*pen," and "*u*se"; and the short vowels that appear in the beginning of the words "*a*pple," "*e*gg," "*i*ndian," "*o*n," and

"*u*nder." Some consonant sounds can be held without change. These include the "c" in "*c*ircus," the "f" in "*f*ish," "h" in "*h*igh," "l" in "*l*olly," "m" in "*m*an," "n" in "*n*ice," "r" in "*r*un," "s" in "*s*un," "z" in "*z*ebra." Ask the child to find pictures of things that begin like "a-a-apple." This can be done with all of the above-mentioned letters.

activity 5: television and listening— testing the child's ability to match letters with their sounds

MATERIALS: 10 cards—3 × 10 inches, a dark Magic Marker, a shoe box, and pictures that represent children's television programs.

DIRECTIONS: Write the name of one of the child's favorite television programs on each card. All should begin with sounds that can be sustained without being distorted. These might include "Sesame Street," "Zoom," and "Flintstones."

Put these cards in the box. Paste the picture representing each program onto the cards. Say, "I am thinking of the name of a television show that has the same sound at the beginning as the sound in the beginning of the word 's-s-s-s-smile.' See if you can find it." Hold onto the "s-s-s-s-s" as the child looks for the picture. Encourage the child to hold the sound with his or her own voice as well.

activity 6: listening for story detail— encouraging a love for language and literature

PURPOSE: To encourage an awareness of story detail.

MATERIALS: A storybook with a simple plot, such as

Carle, Eric. *The Very Hungry Caterpillar.* Collins-World, 1969.

deRegniers, Beatrice Schenk. *May I Bring A Friend?* Atheneum, 1964.

Lionni, Leo. *In The Rabbit Garden.* Pantheon, 1975.

DIRECTIONS: Read the story to the child. At a later time, talk about the story. Say, "Gee, I loved that hungry little caterpillar." The child will begin to discuss the story details with you. Encourage the conversation, laughing and chatting about the wonderful adventures of the "eating insect."

activity 7: following directions and increasing memory power

PURPOSE: To increase the memory for listening.

DIRECTIONS: Give the child some simple directions. Increase the directions to two things, then to three. For example:

Directions—Activity 1: Walk to the window.

Directions—Activity 2: Walk to the window and turn around.

Directions—Activity 3: Walk to the window. Turn around and sit down.

Directions—Activity 4: Walk to the window. Turn around. Sit down and tap your knee.

Directions—Activity 5: Walk to the window. Turn around. Sit down. Tap your knee and look at me.

activity 8: records and responding— developing the listening habit

MATERIALS: Types of recordings to use are: songs, rhythmic music, and popular tunes.

DIRECTIONS: Play records during the time the child is in the listening place. Make listening to records a daily activity. Children respond to sounds based on their experiences and development. Observe ways in which the child responds to sounds. Ask yourself:

1. *Does the child listen and imitate exactly? If so, the child is able to remember well.*

2. *Does the child listen and point out likenesses or differences in sounds? If so, the child is able to hear sound differences, which is important for "sounding out words" when reading.*

3. *Does the child listen for details? If so, the child will tell you lots and lots about one or two things he or she has heard.*

Provide listening experiences that teach. Such experiences provide the child with a model to copy and with answers to problems. Provide listening experiences that test. These ask your child for specific responses. DO NOT *TEST* UNTIL YOU TEACH. You may frustrate the child and turn him or her away from the sounds of language.

the writing place

Children are aware of written forms of language long before their fifth birthday. Adults create this awareness when they point to the name of a cereal on a cereal box or to gas station signs, street signs, and simple directions on toy containers. The year in kindergarten helps the child to solidify the ideas that oral language, especially his or her own, can be written for others to enjoy.

Adults must capitalize on the many opportunities that help children to understand the importance of writing to reading.

Let us look at a situation where the meaning of print is taught naturally as part of a daily routine:

Mom and the 5-year-old are in the kitchen preparing for a birthday dinner. She scurries all around looking for ingredients to make the main dish as well as the birthday cake. She finds everything but the things needed to frost the cake. She suggests that her kindergartner get a pencil and paper so that she can make a list of the things she needs to buy. When she receives the paper, she sits down and says, "Now, what am I missing?" Both she and the child add words representing ingredients to the shopping list.

This meaningful explanation that "speech is print" evolved intuitively, stressing some very important facts about written language. Many situations like the one above occur frequently at home. These provide the opportunity for parents to stress the function of written language and its relationship to reading.

The writing place is the place where the 5-year-old begins to record ideas and feelings by using symbols to represent ideas. It is the place where the child *must* feel free to experiment with written language in order to become a written communicator of ideas.

materials in the writing place

At 5, children's small muscles have developed so that they can control writing tools. Paper can be unlined for writing and as small as 9 × 12 inches in size. Pencils, pens, and crayons should be thick and round. It is important that the table at which children are expected to write be not too big, and not too small. An easel and paint is appropriate for the 5- and 6-year-old. Because they have grown, they are able to better control paint drippings. However, paints should be thick. Materials need to be kept where the child can get them when he or she desires. A set of upper and lower case letters in manuscript form should be posted in the writing place. The letters should be written as shown in Figure 5–1:

Fig. 5–1

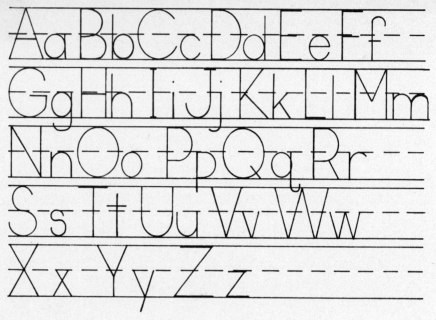

These letters should be placed at the child's eye level when he or she is standing, so that the letters can be traced with the finger.

The first book that the child reads should be a story dictated by the child to the adult. This helps the child see that written language represents spoken words. After the adult writes the child's talk down, he or she can copy it. The child will request more words, and the book writing process begins. It is in the writing place that youngsters become authors and readers.

guidelines for
adult behavior

It is important that adults become astute observers of children's behavior when they write and draw. Writing behaviors are good indicators of the children's readiness to read. Table 5–3 will help you to become aware of signs of readiness behaviors and their implications for reading. Eighty percent of these behaviors should be observed for each child. This indicates a readiness for successful writing experiences.

Table 5–3
growth of written expression and implications
for writing at age 5

AGE 5	BEHAVIOR	IMPLICATIONS
(in kindergarten)	Drawing is much more than a pleasant experience.	It is a means by which the child develops relationships and shares thoughts that are personally important.
	The child enjoys, with intense vigor, drawing the picture.	The final product is not as important for the child as the creating process.
	The child's drawing changes in mood and shows great flexibility.	The child's thinking at 5 is very concerned with a mixture of fantasy and reality and with the scientific aspects of the environment.
	Some drawings by 5-year-olds are detailed; others are not.	The more detail, the more aware children are of things around them.
	The child often shows emotional sensitivity to events through his or her art work.	The child will draw exaggerated body parts, those with which there is emotional involvement (i.e., an oversized mouth and tooth if there was a dentist visit, etc.).
	Children draw themselves and parts of their body larger than their surroundings. They are usually the center of all art.	The child is the center of the world, and drawings about self are important representations of the child's attempt to identify with the environment.
	When they begin to paint or draw, they usually begin with an idea.	The child's productions are usually recognizable.
	At the beginning of the fifth year, the details are few.	Indicates less awareness of environment than is needed for formal instruction in written expression.
	Small muscles are beginning to develop rapidly.	Child can cut on a line, fold paper, and copy figures—triangles, circles, and so on.
	Will stretch or bend to see the end of a zipper on a coat when closing it.	Small muscles and eyes and hands are not coordinated as fully as is needed for writing letters and numbers easily.
	Will reverse letters and numbers from the top to the bottom of the page from right to left.	Needs large, unlined paper and little or no direct instruction for writing formally. Indicates that the child is not ready for formal reading.
	Likes to copy; will make an outline and color it in.	Needs models and outlines pictures for coloring.
	Shows a preference for one hand over another.	Will paint, cut, fold, or fill in spaces with crayons. (Will sometimes use the other hand for throwing, eating, etc.)

skills developed when children write

There is a strong relationship between the skills important to reading and those necessary for writing. The skills usually mastered in the fifth and sixth year include the following:

Painting or drawing with deliberate intention.
Drawing and copying figures.
Talking about creative drawing and writing experiences.
Left to right movements of hands and eyes.

ACTIVITIES FOR WRITING

activity 1: skill, color awareness, and visual recognition

MATERIALS: Red paint, an easel or flat surface, 1 large bristle brush, and large paper (18 × 24).

DIRECTIONS: Take a walk with your child. Notice all of the things that are red. After walking, paint something you both saw that was red. Learn the following poem and say it as you walk and after the painting experience.

RED
I love red
Warm red
Bright red
Red streaming across the sky like a blazing flame
Red flaming lights.

Happy red—
Red party balloons
Red cake frosting
Red ribbons on packages.

Red is hot blistering red peppers
Red is wildly moving flames
Nights and days are red—
humid, red hot days in summer.

Red brightens your life—makes faces shine and rosy
Cold is red—
Cheeks are rosy red in cold

and rosy red in heat
Red is happy, hot, shimmering
I love red.

S.M. GLAZER

Say the poem many times on different occasions. At another time, suggest that the child paint as you read.

activity 2: copying figures— left-to-right movement: visual identification

MATERIALS: Five or more pieces of tagboard cut into rectangles, 4 by 5 inches, a box to hold the cards, dark felt-tipped marker or crayon, and unlined paper.

DIRECTIONS FOR CONSTRUCTION: Draw the figures shown in Figure 5–2, one on each card.
Place the cards in a box.

DIRECTIONS FOR USE: Put the box of cards on a table. Next to the box, put as many pieces of drawing paper as there are figures to copy. Put the crayon or marker on top of the paper and leave these materials in the place to write. The child will go to the activities. As the child reproduces the pictures, observe the copying skills. Ask yourself:

1. *Does the child copy all of the figures?*
2. *Are they like the originals?*
3. *Does the child do the activity easily, quickly, and over and over again?*

If the answer to all of these is yes, the youngster has acquired one of the skills necessary for beginning reading activities.

Fig. 5–2

Fig. 5–3

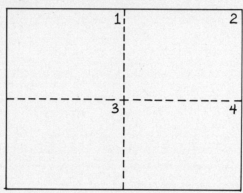

activity 3:
left-to-right
progressions

MATERIALS: A large piece of painting paper (18 × 24 inches) folded into four parts and numbered, from left to right, 1, 2, 3, and 4, and crayons.

DIRECTIONS: Say to the child, "Make four pictures." Point to each box. Hold the child's hand and put it in each box, saying, "First do 1, then 2, then 3, and then 4." If your child is unable to do this easily, save it for a month or two and try it again.

activity 4:
noting color
(visual
distinction)

MATERIALS: Four cards, each with a different shape and color, as shown in Figure 5–4, a large piece of painting paper, and four markers, one in each of the colors of the figures.

DIRECTIONS: Place the cards in a box in the writing area. Put the painting paper on the flat surface and place the markers next to the paper. When a child approaches the game, say, "This is a copying game. Copy the shapes and color them."

Fig. 5–4

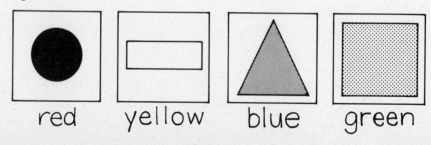

red   yellow   blue   green

172

activity 5:
copying your
name (visual
discrimination:
left-to-
right)

MATERIALS: A 3 × 10 inch card with the child's name printed on it.

DIRECTIONS: This should be available for the child to copy at all times. Use as many opportunities as you can to help your child to write his or her name: on greeting cards, drawings, thank you notes, and so on.

activity 6:
"go-together"
pictures
(sequencing,
left-to-right,
associating
pictures with
verbal
expressions)

MATERIALS: Paint and two pieces of paper.

DIRECTIONS: Write the numbers "1" and "2" on the paper. Ask the child to draw a story. Encourage the child to tell about something that happened. Say, "Draw the first things that happened on the paper marked with a '1.' Draw the last thing that happened on the paper marked number '2.'" After the youngster completes the drawings, tape them together, as in a book. Give the child time to tell about the pictures.

activity 7:
telling about
a painting
(describing/
interpreting
pictures)

MATERIALS: One painting by a child.

DIRECTIONS: When the child shows you the painting, say, "Tell me one thing about your painting." As the child talks, write what he or she says on the back of the creation. Say, "I am putting the words you are saying on paper so that they can be saved forever."

activity 8:
retelling an
art story
(remembering
sequencing,
and reading
comprehension)

MATERIALS: One book with a simple story plot, paper, and crayons or markers.

DIRECTIONS: Read a story to the child. Say, "Draw pictures to tell the story to a friend." Ask your child to retell the story after drawing the pictures to test the child's ability to recall facts.

activity 9:
my writing
book
(left-to-right
and
describing)

MATERIALS: A notebook for the child, a notebook for the adult, and a writing tool (pencil, pen, crayon, or marker).

DIRECTIONS: At a special time each day, for a period of not more than three minutes, you and the child write in your books. There is to be silence and no interruptions.

Writing in kindergarten means receiving personal gratification and pleasure from the productive artistic experiences. Adults must facilitate the growth of written expression by encouraging children to experiment with writing. Experimentation builds confidence. Confidence brings a willingness to try to succeed in order to learn to read.

When children scribble, they are involved with the same types of motor activities they need in order to learn about color, design, lines, and space on paper. When children see differences in lines, spaces, designs, and colors, they are, in a sense, beginning to see differences within themselves.

the acting place

Imagination is important, not only to children, but to businessmen, scientists, and educators. All of these professionals see their imaginations as the magic force that directs them beyond the mastery of facts and techniques in the search for new ideas. The ability to imagine and create by acting is present in all humans. It is not merely a talent possessed by a gifted few. Acting provides the 5-year-old with an opportunity to use new ideas, language, and symbols.

materials for acting

At 5, children need space to move and experiment with their bodies, translating experiences into body language. Children at 5 like to act out roles and need props. Collect as many of the following as possible and put them where acting occurs.

Cereal boxes
Baby food jars
Empty cans of fruit, vegetables, fish, and meats
Plastic containers
A small carton or two
Hats
Badges (policeman, fireman, metermaid, etc.)
Dresses
Shoes

Pocketbooks

Doctor's bag, filled with old or play equipment

Gardening materials (rake, gloves)

Insects, ants

Pets, fish, gerbils, hamsters, guinea pigs, hermit crabs

Large cartoons

Puppets

Pictures of popular T.V. charcters

Props that represent T.V. or film personalities

adult behaviors when children act

It is important that children feel that their acts are acceptable expressions of experiences. The following checklist will guide adults to encourage maximum growth through acting. "Yes" is the desired response to all behaviors.

YES   NO

Time is provided for independent dramatic play to act out feelings, ideas, and adult roles.

There are times when the adult works with the child. During these times, children are directed to act out a particular behavior.

There are times that children tell about experiences by acting with and without words.

Props in the acting place are periodically changed.

There are books in the acting place.

Children are often encouraged to act out the main idea of a story.

When children dramatize in front of two or more persons, they do this voluntarily.

There is a place where a child can act alone in privacy (example: a large carton—one that a refrigerator has been packed in).

reading and language skills developed through acting

1. *Acting helps to make words come alive.* Dramatization permits the child to discuss experiences and act upon them. The child is able to translate listening and seeing experience into physical behavior.

2. *Acting permits children to test their ability to hear sounds and letters and to build an initial sight vocabulary.* Children, at 5, will continue to role-play as they did in nursery years. They will, however, become more aware of details. If, for example, children have simulated a supermarket, a child will "buy" a particular cereal and find the box. On the box he or she will note letters and words. The child will begin to compare one cereal box to another, noticing the name of the cereal, the number of letters, and even the similarities in words and phrases. Acting permits this spontaneous reading behavior to occur.

3. *Acting helps youngsters to increase their oral vocabulary.* Acting out ideas brings multiple meanings to words. One child may know that the word "honey" refers to a sticky sweet substance. Another child, who has heard the word "honey" in another context, "Hello honey," might use it and act the greeting, thus gaining the meaning that "honey," in this context, might be a person.

4. *Acting helps build the child's imaginary powers.* Imagination is the foundation for building the ability to live vicariously through reading.

activity 1: first time activity (following directions/ recalling information)

ACTIVITIES FOR ACTING:

MATERIALS: The music and a piano or a recording of the following:

HERE WE GO LOOBY-LOO
Here we go looby-loo
Here we go looby-light

176

Here we go looby-loo
All on a Saturday night.

DIRECTIONS: Say, "Find a place in the room. I am going to play the music. Walk to the music." Repeat this, telling the children to jump, hop, skip, and run to the music.

activity 2: translating speech to body language (building imaginary powers)

MATERIALS: A drum.

DIRECTIONS: Beat the drum and say, "Walk to the music." Change the drum beat and say, "There is grass under your feet. Walk on the grass." As the child walks, say, "The grass is very soft. It is very cool. Make believe you are taking off your shoes. Walk in the grass without your shoes." Or you might use the following alternative activities. Say, "There is ice under your feet. It is v-e-r-r-r-ry slippery. It is very difficult to walk on the ice. It is very dangerous." Or say, "You are a dancer, dancing to the music. The music is soft and flo-o-o-o-owing. Your costume is fluffy. It moves with your body."

activity 3: poetry and movement (one or more children)

THE MISCHIEVOUS RAVEN
A farmer went trotting upon his gray mare,
Bumpety, bumpety, bump!
With his daughter behind him so rosy and fair,
Lumpety, lumpety, lump!

A raven cried, "Croak!" and they all tumbled down,
Bumpety, bumpety, bump!
The mare broke her knees and the farmer his crown,
Lumpety, lumpety, lump!

The mischievous raven flew laughing away,
Bumpety, bumpety, bump!
And vowed he would serve them the same the next day,
Lumpety, lumpety, lump!

NURSERY RHYME

[2]See Nancy Larrick, *The Wheels of the Bus Go Round and Round* (Chicago: Golden Gate Junior Books, 1972), p. 18.

DIRECTIONS: Read the poem to your child. After a second reading, say, "Make your body move when you hear the moving words." Read slowly, following the child's actions.

activity 4: the joys of nature through poetry (building vocabulary)

MATERIALS: An apple or two. The following poem:

IF I WERE AN APPLE
If I were an apple and grew on a tree,
I think I'd drop down on a nice boy like me;
I wouldn't stay there, giving nobody joy;
I'd fall down at once and say, "Eat me, my boy!"

ANONYMOUS

DIRECTIONS: Place a few apples around the kitchen. Find a picture of an apple tree full of apples. Post it on the refrigerator door or the family bulletin board. Say the poem as you work around the kitchen or other places in the home. The child will learn it and say it by rote. When you are in the kitchen, near the picture and the apples, say the poem. At a later time, ask one of the following questions:

1. *How would you feel if you were an apple that fell from a tree?*
2. *Why would you want to fall down, anyway?*
3. *What would you do if you were a lima bean (a carrot, a head of lettuce, an egg, etc.)?*

activity 5: choral speaking (building oral language)

MATERIALS: The following poem written on a large piece of tagboard:

If all the seas were one sea
What a great sea that would be!
If all the trees were one tree
What a great tree that would be!
If all the axes were one axe
What a great axe that would be!
And if the great man took the great axe
And cut down the great tree
And let it fall in the great sea . . .
What a great SPLASH that would be!

AN OLD FOLK POEM

DIRECTIONS: Read the poem. Post the poem in a place where it can be easily seen. At another time, re-read the poem and ask the child to say it along with you. The repeated language pattern permits children to learn the poem quickly. After many readings, say the first line and encourage your child to say the second line.

activity 6:
listening and
acting with
body parts
(following
directions;
sequencing)

THE BEEHIVE
Here is the beehive. Where are the bees?
Hiding away where nobody sees.
They are coming out now,
They are alive.
One! Two! Three! Four! Five!

A FOLK POEM

DIRECTIONS: Chant the counting rhyme and show the children the finger actions illustrated in Figures 5–5 through 5–8.[3]

This old finger play helps the child to translate words into physical actions.[4]

activity 7:
the church
and
the steeple

MATERIALS: Use same as Activity 6.

Here is the church,
And here is the steeple;
Open the door,
And see all the people.

activity 8:
acting stories

For the kindergarten child, acting out stories is a form of reading. The child listens to a story and sees a prop to act out all or part of the story action. The activities following can be adapted for many stories. These are wonderful entertainment for children's parties.

[3]Reprinted with permission of Macmillan Publishing Co., Inc., from *The Rooster Crows: A Book of American Rhymes and Jingles* by Maud and Miska Petersham. © 1945 by Macmillan Publishing Co., Inc., renewed 1973 by Miska F. Petersham.
[4]Ibid, Maud and Miska Petersham.

Fig. 5–5, 5–6, 5–7, and 5–8

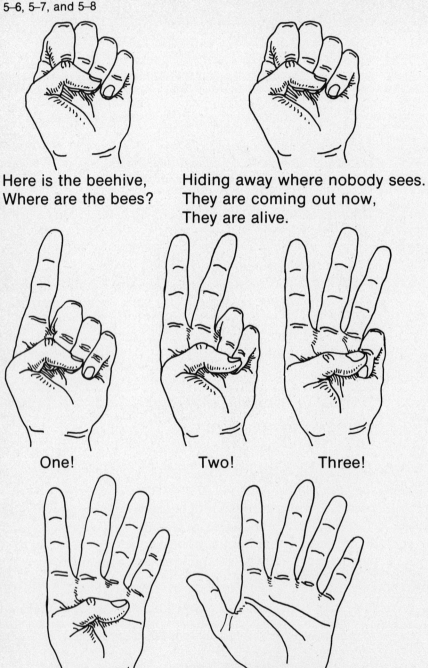

Here is the beehive,
Where are the bees?

Hiding away where nobody sees.
They are coming out now,
They are alive.

One!   Two!   Three!

Four!   Five!

Fig. 5–9, and 5–10, 5–11, and 5–12

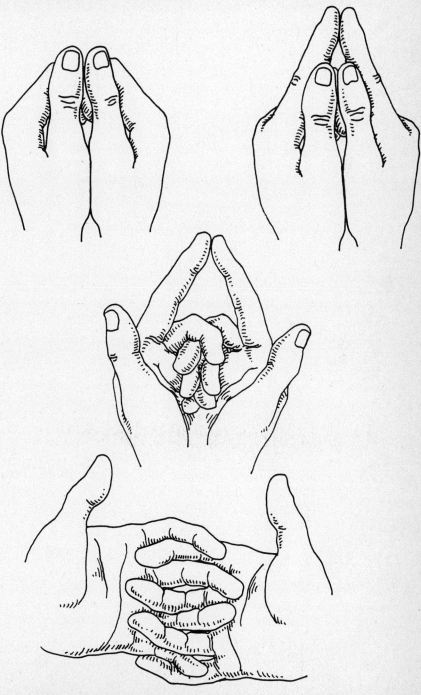

this is the
house
that jack
built—
a nursery
rhyme

MATERIALS: Sticks or tagboard rolled like sticks, masking tape, colored felt-tipped markers, and clear Contact paper.

THE HOUSE THAT JACK BUILT

This is the house that Jack built.

This is the malt
That lay in the house that Jack built.

This is the rat,
That ate the malt
That lay in the house that Jack built.

This is the cat,
That killed the rat,
That ate the malt
That lay in the house that Jack built.

This is the dog,
That worried the cat,
That killed the rat,
That ate the malt
That lay in the house that Jack built.

This is the cow with the crumpled horn,
That tossed the dog,
That worried the cat,
That killed the rat,
That ate the malt
That lay in the house that Jack built.

This is the maiden all forlorn,
That milked the cow with the crumpled horn,
That tossed the dog,
That worried the cat,
That killed the rat,
That ate the malt
That lay in the house that Jack built.

This is the man all tattered and torn,
That kissed the maiden all forlorn,
That milked the cow with the crumpled horn,
That tossed the dog,
That worried the cat,

182

That killed the rat,
That ate the malt
That lay in the house that Jack built.

A NURSERY RHYME

DIRECTIONS FOR CONSTRUCTION: Create the characters from this wonderful tale, as shown in Figures 5–13 through 5–20. First make the stick puppets by drawing each on the tagboard. Then cut out each character and color them with the felt-tipped markers. Cover each stick character with clear contact paper in order to insure durability and long-term use. Cut around the dotted lines. This will permit a child to put his or her face into each of the puppets and become that character.

DIRECTIONS FOR USE: As you read the story to the children hand each one a puppet. Say, "I am going to tell the story. When

Fig. 5–13 through 5–20

I point to you, say, 'This is the house that Jack built,' if you are the house. If you are the rat, say, 'This is the rat.' " Proceed to tell the story and encourage the child to recall and repeat as much language from the story as possible. This is wonderful for increasing the child's memory for the sequence of the story. It is also helpful for the child who will not voluntarily act to recall, reinforce, or just enjoy literature.

the carrot seed (prop drama)

MATERIALS: Ruth Krauss's *The Carrot Seed* (Harper & Row, 1945), a package of carrot seeds, and a brown paper bag.

DIRECTIONS: Read the story to the child. Put the seeds and the book in a brown paper bag with a representative picture and the words *The Carrot Seed* written on the front of the bag. Put this in the acting place. Children will read the book and will find ways to act out the story, using the props provided. A list of stories adaptable to prop and face puppet drama follows:

Arkin, Alan. *Tony's Hard Work Day* (Harper & Row, 1972) (prop story).

Burningham, John. *Mr. Gumpy's Outing* (Holt, 1970) (face puppets).

Crockett, Johnson. *Harold and the Purple Crayon* (Harper & Row, 1958) (prop story).

Eastman, Philip D. *Are You My Mother?* (Random House, 1960) (face puppets).

Ets, Marie Hall. *Play With Me* (Viking Press, 1955) (face puppets).

Martin, Bill. Illustrated by Eric Carle. *Brown Bear, Brown Bear, What Do You See?* (Holt, 1971) (face puppets).

Sendak, Maurice. *Where the Wild Things Are* (Harper & Row, 1963) (face puppets).

Slobodkina, Espher. *Caps for Sale* (Young Scott, 1947) (prop story).

Stobbs, William. *Henny-Penny* (Follett, 1970) (face puppets).

Zolotow, Charlotte. *The Quarrelling Book* (Harper & Row, 1963) (face puppets).

Wonderful story telling tips can be found in Lesley Mandel Morrow's *Super Tips For Storytelling*, (Instructor Publications, 1979).

**activity 9:
role playing**

Arrange materials for the following role-playing experiences:

A firehouse and firemen
A classroom teacher
A physician in a hospital or office
A dentist and a technician
A veterinarian in an animal hospital
A homemaker
A clerk in a supermarket

Place appropriate chairs, tables, and props in the acting place. Alternate materials weekly or when the children request changes.

Materials for role-playing are suggested on page 174 of this chapter. A suggested arrangement follows for the supermarket: empty food boxes, cans, paperbags, aprons for clerks, and a sign that says "Supermarket."

the reading place

How nice it is to relax with a book. The place to read should be a relaxing place filled with things that invite children to read. The reading place should have soft chairs, small throw rugs, and good lighting. Posters, pictures, and toys related to books and stories should be included. The library for the child of 5 should include personally owned books as well as borrowed books from the school and public libraries. Books should be arranged and placed by topic—animal books, fairy tales, and so on. Books should be placed on low shelves that display the covers.

materials for the
reading place

Five-year-olds love to read books about life and living, about animals, and about funny things, and they like books with poems and interesting language. Four kinds of books are needed for the 5-year-old: (1) books that your child can listen to you read, (2) books without words, (3) books with only a few words, and (4) books that match recordings and television programs.

LISTENING BOOKS: Books for listening are books to be read to children. They help the child to develop the attention skills needed in school. Books for listening should have the following characteristics:

1. *Vivid pictures that match the language on each page of print.*
2. *Simple plots with one main character.*
3. *Repetitive language.*
4. *Topics related to the interests of the child of 5 include the immediate environment: animals, taking the parts of various people; stories with happy endings; stories that help them to deal with daily experiences: fear, danger, growing, fights, privacy, illness, responsibility, death, birth, and holidays.*

Following is a list of a very few of the many books to ready to 5-year-olds.

Adoff, Arnold. Illustrated by R. Himler. *Make A Circle to Keep Us In* (Delacorte, 1975). This poetry book, which deals with fears and feelings, is printed so that the language flows along the page.

Brown, Margaret Wise. Illustrated by R. Charlip. *The Dead Bird* (William R. Scott, Inc., 1958). This book deals with death in a charming manner.

Davis, Alice. Illustrated by G. B. Wiser. *Timothy Turtle* (Harcourt Brace Jovanovich, 1970). Timothy is an overweight turtle who will help the overweight child handle the social problems encountered with obesity.

Emberly, Barbara. Illustrated by E. Emberley. *Drummer Hoff* (Prentice-Hall, 1967). Repetitive language and rhyme help the child to see a sequence of delightful events unfold.

Ets, Marie Hall. *In the Forest* (Viking, 1967). A walk in the forest results in a parade with animals dreamed from a child's wonderful imagination. Repetition and lovely language add much to this listening book.

Leaf, Munro. *The Story of Ferdinand* (Viking, 1936). This classic story will help the "different" child realize that others are also different.

Preston, Edna Mitchel. *Pop Corn and Ma Goodness* (Viking, 1969). Love, marriage, birth, and death are dealt with in delightful language that repeats.

Raskin, Ellen. *Who Said Sue, Said Who?* (Atheneum, 1974). Repeated language patterns help this story bound through the nonsense adventures of animals.

Serraillier, Ian. Illustrated by E. Emberley. *Suppose You Met A Witch* (Little, Brown, 1973). This delightful book helps the child to deal with fears of the imagination.

Thomas, Marlo, Steinman, Gloria, and Pogrebin, Letty C. *Free to Be . . . You and Me* (McGraw-Hill, 1974). The world of feelings is shared through stories, poems, and pictures. This is a "yes" book that says, "Hey, I'm O.K."

Urdy, Janice. Illustrated by Maurice Sendak. *Let's Be Enemies* (Scholastic Book Service, 1971). Fighting and sharing is the theme.

Viorst, Judith. *My Mama Says There Aren't Any Zombies, Ghosts, Vampires, Creatures, Demons, Monsters, Fiends, Goblins or Things* (Atheneum, 1973). Handling the concept that Mamas are not always right all the time is difficult. This book will share these difficult feelings in a fanciful way.

Warburg, Sandol. Illustrated by L. Weisgard. *Growing Time* (Houghton-Mifflin, 1974). Death and facing death are the themes.

Williams, Garth. *The Rabbit Wedding* (Harper & Row, 1958). Companionship and friendship are the underlying concepts that result in the marriage of two rabbits.

Zolotow, Charlotte. *The Night When Mother Was Away* (Lothrop, Lee and Shepard, 1959). Loneliness and a motherless family are the themes of this well-written book.

————. *My Grandson Lew* (Harper & Row, 1974). Lew and his mother share the memories of Grandpa. A wonderful book for understanding the concept of death.

WORDLESS PICTURE BOOKS: Why wordless picture books? Wordless books need children to give them language. The pictures encourage the child to tell stories. The child's language becomes the language of the book. This provokes the development of vocabulary. The pictures are the child's visual clues for selecting language. Wordless books help children to realize that authors are people who talk and then write that talk down to share with others.

Wordless books are as personal as the child who reads them. Each story creation is acceptable, for it comes from the child.

The following characteristics are important when choosing a book without words for young children.

1. *The book should have vivid illustrations.*
2. *If the book has a plot, it should be simple, with repetitive actions.*
3. *All wordless books do not need plots. They may include objects. These object picture books should be clear, colorful, and simple in design.*

Following is a list of wordless books:

Anno, Mitsumasa. *Topsy-Turvies* (Weatherhill, 1970). A wordless book with delightful pictures.

Barton, Byron. *Where's Al?* (Seabury Press, 1972). Tells the story of a boy who loses his dog.

Goodall, John S. *Jacko* (Harcourt Brace Jovanovich, 1971). Adventures of an organ grinder's monkey and his friend end happily when the monkey finds a natural home in the forest.

———. *The Surprise Picnic* (Atheneum, 1977). Surprises at a simple picnic turn it into an adventure.

Hoban, Tana. *Look Again* (Macmillan, 1971). Black and white photographs of familiar objects will lead to wonderful language production.

Keats, Ezra Jack. *Skates* (Watts, 1973). Dogs and skates twirl and slide and bump and flip their way along an adventure in pictures that ends with the dogs realizing that skating is not their sport. A wonderful book.

Krahn, Fernando. *How Santa Claus Had A Long and Difficult Journey Delivering His Presents* (Delacorte Press, 1970). A picture story that is wonderful at holiday time.

Mayer, Mercer. *A Boy, A Dog, And A Frog* (Dial Press, 1967). A boy and a dog fail to catch a frog.

Stoddard, Darrell. *The Hero* (Aro Publishing Company, 1974). Part of a series of indestructable waterproof books.

Turkle, Britan. *Deep In The Forest* (Dutton, 1976).

BOOKS WITH A FEW WORDS: Part of the early excitement attached to learning to read is recognizing words. Books with a few words are important for building sight vocabulary and for building good feelings about printed materials. The following books have only a few words. These words enhance the pictures that tell the story.

Berkley, Ethel. Illustrated by Kathleen Elgin. *Big and Little, Up and Down* (Addison-Wesley, 1951). The words "little," "narrow," and "short" are described so that children will learn the relationships of these adjectives.

Brown, Marcia. *All Butterflies: An ABC* (Scribner, 1974). An ABC book.

Skaar, Grace. *What Do Animals Say?* (Addison-Wesley, 1968). Limited vocabulary helps children to guess the noises that familiar barnyard animals make.

Ungerer, Toni. *Snail, Where Are You?* (Harper & Row, 1962). This 11-word "tell it yourself story" is beautifully illustrated.

Winter, Paula. *The Bear and the Fly* (Crown, 1976).

BOOKS, RECORDINGS, AND TELEVISION: There is something magical about making a book come alive through language and song. Records help to make story books everlasting experiences for the child. Still another exciting experience is to see a favorite television character in a story book. That familiar character makes the book experience a personal one that connects written language to language heard on television. Following is a listing of books that are also available on records. Included, too, are television programs that have grown from classical literature for children.

190

nursery rhymes and poetry in books and records	Biggs, Raymond. Illustrator. *Mother Goose Treasury* (Coward-McCann, 1966). Recording: Weston Woods. Randolph. Illustrator. *Hey Diddle Diddle and Baby Bunting* (Warne Publishing Co., 1882). Recording: Weston Woods.
books that have influenced television programming	Baum, L. Frank. *The Wizard of Oz.* Illustrated by Evelyn Copelman. Bobbs-Merrill. Originally published in 1900 by George M. Hill Company with title: *The Wonderful Wizard of Oz.* Full-Length film shown on T.V. at least once a year. Chase, Alice. Walt Disney's *Mary Poppins.* Edited by Annie N. Bedford. Illustrated by Grace Clark. Western, 1964. Lofting, Hugh. *The Story of Doctor Doolittle.* Illustrated by author (Lippincott, 1920). Dell (Paperback) Walt Disney's full-length film, *Doctor Doolittle,* is shown at least once a year during a holiday season. Wilder, Laura Ingalls. *Little House on the Prairie.* Illustrated by Garth Williams (Harper & Row, 1935). This book is the basis for a weekly television program that is delightful listening and viewing for the entire family.

guidelines for selecting books for 5-year-olds

Many books are available to meet the social, emotional, and physical needs of the child. Even more good books can be found that help children to begin the formal reading process. Use the following checklist as a guide for selecting books for 5-year-olds. Desired responses should appear in the "yes" column.

	YES	NO
The book has a single plot.		
The book has one main character.		
Words and phrases are repeated throughout the book.		
Sentences are simple.		
Only a few adjectives and adverbs are used.		
Few pronouns are used throughout the text.		
Illustrations help to tell the story.		

191

YES   *NO*

Some books are small and some are large.
Books are different shapes (rectangular,
square, etc.).
Books are selected so that a child can relate
to the story character because that character
has something in common with the child (a
concern, a physical problem, a feeling, a
similar mood, etc.).

reading activities for 5-year-olds
The following activities center around the development of the skills necessary for beginning reading. Each activity includes a list of the reading and thinking skills that are being taught.

READING TO CHILDREN:

activity 1: listening to matching sounds of language

MATERIALS: Edna M. Preston's *Pop Corn and Ma Goodness* (Viking, 1969), or another book that rhymes, a large easel and a piece of paper, and a marking pen or crayon.

DIRECTIONS: Read the story to the child. Prepare the child for this book by repeating the rhyming words a day or so before the story is read. As you approach the familiar words, saying them clearly and keeping time with your head or foot, encourage the child to chime in with familiar words. At the end of the story, casually write a pair of rhyming words on the easel, saying the words as you write. As you write, focus should be on the visual and sound similarities of these words.

EVALUATIONS: You are encouraging children to (1) organize their thoughts, (2) compare sounds and word patterns, (3) make judgments about their discoveries, and (4) come to some decisions about their observations.

activity 2: listening (vocabulary development)

MATERIALS: Judith Viorst's *My Mama Says There Aren't Any Zombies, Ghosts, Vampires, Creatures, Demons, Monsters, Fiends, Goblins or Things* (Atheneum, 1973), or other books with interesting language, colored chalk and a chalkboard or a large piece of paper, and crayons.

DIRECTIONS: After reading the story, say, "What other words can you think of that go with zombies, ghosts, vampires, and monsters?" Write the words suggested by the child on the chalkboard or large paper.

EVALUATION: You are encouraging the child to (1) use vocabulary, (2) classify ideas, (3) compare ideas, and (4) use his imagination.

activity 3: listening to increase attention skills

MATERIALS: A cassette recorder and tape, and a story book selected by the child.

DIRECTIONS: As you read, tape the story. At the completion of the story, rewind the tape and say, "Listen." Hand the book to the child and encourage him or her to look at the book and listen to your voice.

EVALUATION: You are encouraging the child (1) to move from left to right, (2) to pay attention, and (3) to compare words to visual images.

USING WORDLESS BOOKS TO ENCOURAGE READING SKILLS:

activity 1: reading wordless books— a beginning approach

Hold the child on your lap and the book in front of him or her. Look at the cover and ask, "What do you suppose this is about?" Open the book and show the title page. Turn to the first page and say, "Tell about the picture." Go on to the next page and say, "What's this?" or "Now what's happening?" Continue in this way until the end of the story. Encourage the child to go through the book independently. Suggest, for example, that the child put this special book where it is easy to get.

activity 2: a story with objects

MATERIALS: A large piece of drawing paper, a dark marker or crayon, some green leaves, a branch of a tree, a small pile of dirt, a watering can with a bit of water, and a tin can.

DIRECTIONS: As you tell the following story, make the homemade tree. Tell the story slowly, so that your words match the activity.

Once upon a time there was a can, a very empty can.
He thought "Gee, I'd love to be useful."
So he found some dirt and filled himself up.
Then he found a branch and put it in the dirt.

He got some water and watered the branch. And guess what!
Some green leaves grew on the tree.

After telling the story, say, "Now you try it." Provide materials for the child. Encourage the child to make the tree and tell the story at the same time.

EVALUATION: You are helping the child learn to (1) collect information, (2) organize it, (3) summarize the main idea, and (4) think sequentially.

activity 3: drawing a story

MATERIALS: A large piece of drawing paper, a dark marker or crayon, some green leaves, a branch of a tree, a small pile of dirt, a watering can with a bit of water, and a tin can.

DIRECTIONS: Tell the story, drawing as you talk. At the conclusion of the story, say, "Now you tell the story."

EVALUATION: You are helping your child to (1) translate written language (pictures) into spoken words, (2) sequence ideas, and (3) recall facts.

activity 4: reading pictures

MATERIALS: Some wordless books, such as the following—
Hutchins, Pat. *Changes, Changes* (MacMillan, 1973).

Keats, Ezra Jack. *Skates* (Watts, 1973).

Mayer, Mercer. *A Boy, A Dog, and A Frog* (Dial, 1967).

DIRECTIONS: Make a display of books without words. Photograph or draw pictures like those shown in Figure 5–21 and place the books near them.

Fig. 5–21

Tell A Story

Snail, Where Are You?

My Story

These displays will encourage the children to read the books.

WORD RECOGNITION—BOOKS WITH VERY FEW WORDS:

activity 1:
matching
words
to pictures

MATERIALS: A book with a few words (see the list on page 189)

DIRECTIONS: Read the book to the child. As you approach a word, point to it. Read the book a second time. Show the pictures. Point to the word, saying it slowly. Children will imitate and join in the reading.

EVALUATION: Children are learning to (1) associate words with ideas in pictures and (2) recognize words.

activity 2:
matching
words

MATERIALS: A book with few words and some cards with one word from the book written on each.

DIRECTIONS: Write the word or words, one on each card. Be sure that the word is written as it appears in the text. Place these cards in the back cover of the book. Put the book with the cards in the child's library. Children who are ready to do so will find the words in the book and will discover that the words on the cards match the text.

EVALUATION: You are testing your child's ability to discriminate visually between words in print.

activity 3:
recognizing
words

MATERIALS: A familiar book with few words, a large sheet of paper, and a marker.

DIRECTIONS: Make a list of the words in the book. Be sure that there are only a few (not more than five). Hang the list of words in the reading place. Place the book that contains these words near the posted lists.

EVALUATION: You are helping your child to discover that words have meaning in and out of books.

ACTIVITIES THAT HELP CHILDREN WITH SEEING, LISTENING, AND SPEAKING:

activity 1:
using a book
and a record
together

MATERIALS: A recording of a folk song, a book that matches it—for example, Ezra Jack Keats's *Over in the Meadow* (Four Winds, 1972; Record and Filmstrip: Weston Woods), or *Hush Little Baby* (Illustrated by Aliki; Dutton, 1975, record and

196

filmstrip: Weston Woods)—and a record player that the child can use without help.

DIRECTIONS: Place the recording on the record player and the book next to it. Children will play the record and look through the book on their own.

EVALUATION: This helps the child to understand that print is talk that is written down. It also helps the child to develop the left to right movements necessary for reading.

activity 2:
television
and books

MATERIALS: A large carton from a washing machine, dishwasher, or refrigerator, paint, and a poster-size picture of a favorite television character.

DIRECTIONS: Cut a section of the box so that it looks like a television set. Place the poster in the opening. Paint the carton so that it resembles a television set. Put books around the set that match television broadcasts. Children will go to the books and will begin to match television characters and events to those in the texts.

EVALUATION: Children are learning to (1) see a relationship between pictures in books and visual images on television, and (2) they are discovering that there is a connection between seeing pictures and seeing words.

activity 3:
sharing story
plots

MATERIALS: A worksheet that looks something like that shown in Figure 5–22:

DIRECTIONS: Encourage the child to draw a picture or to write something that tells the plot of the book. Hang it up to share with other family members.

EVALUATION: You are helping your child to (1) summarize the story and (2) remember information.

activity 4:
storytelling

Storytellers must be energetic, enthusiastic, and in love with books and literature. It is the storyteller who brings oral language and printed words together for children.

When you tell a story to your child, hold the child in your lap or sit next to him or her. Learn the story and tell it by rote. Use repeated language patterns and interesting words and phrases. Retell the story often, until the child can tell it to you.

activity 5: puppets and storytelling

Puppets make stories come alive. There are many stories that adapt easily for puppet plays for the 5-year-old. Old folktales and stories with repetitive language, simple plots, and rhythmic sentence patterns are the kinds most often selected by children. The following stories and books lend themselves to dramatization with puppets.

Carle, Eric. *The Very Hungry Caterpillar.* Collins-World, 1969.

Cook, Bernadine. *The Little Fish That Got Away.* Young Scott, 1965.

deRiginers, Beatrice Schenk. *May I Bring A Friend?* Atheneum, 1964.

Duvoisin, Roger. *William's Doll.* Harper & Row, 1972.

Emberly, Barbara. *Drummer Hoff.* Prentice-Hall, 1972.

Ets, Marie Hall. *Play With Me.* Viking Press, 1955.

TYPES OF PUPPETS FOR 5-YEAR-OLDS: Puppets appropriate for 5-year-olds are those that are easy for children to control. Most are also easily made.

hand puppets

PAPER BAG PUPPET: This is made by painting the face of a person or animal on the fold of a closed paper bag. You can also paint on

Fig. 5–22 and 5–23

Book:_____

Eyes Open   Mouth Opens   A Look Inside

eyes, as is shown in Figure 5–23. Hair, clothing, and a costume may be added.

MILK CARTON PUPPET: Secure an empty quart size milk carton. Cut through three sides of the carton in the middle. Close the opening at the top of the carton by folding it down as shown in Figure 5–24. This will create a flat surface at the top of the milk carton. Fold the carton back, bending at the uncut section.

Fig. 5–24

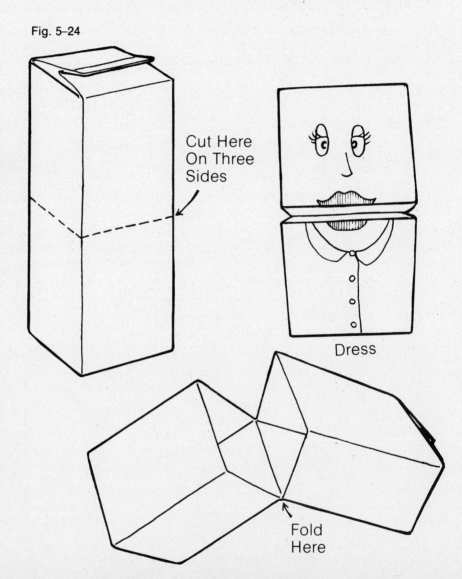

Cut Here
On Three
Sides

Dress

Fold
Here

A face can be painted on the one side that is not cut, as shown. When using the puppet, the child places his or her fingers in the upper section of the carton and the thumb in the lower section. The puppet's mouth will open and close as the thumb and fingers are brought together.

STICK PUPPETS: Pictures of a story character can be drawn, cut out, and pasted on tagboard. The stiffened shape is taped to a stick or a plastic drinking straw (see Figure 5–25). The storyteller grasps the stick and moves the puppet back and forth behind a screen. The audience will see the body of the puppet above the screened area.

assessing the environment that's best for my child when learning to read

All individuals have developed unique behavior styles for many things early in life. This includes not only activities such as running, swimming, walking, and talking but also reading and learning. All humans develop in accordance with his or her physical, social, and emotional growth. All develop, too, the ability to work in certain environments under certain conditions. Many of us work best when given special directions; others need only a few; and some need none. Some work best in quiet places, and others like a clutter of noise. The "how" of learning the conditions under which one learns information needs to be observed for each child. We must ask

Fig. 5–25

ourselves, "Does the child learn best when sitting still?" " Does the child need to move about from one area to another, or are there a few different learning styles for my child?" Use the checklist following to discover the atmosphere that helps your child learn. Then create the learning/reading place that best suits his or her learning style.[5]

	YES	NO

The child seems to work best:

In a small area.

In a room with lots of materials displayed and available.

In a room where there are few materials displayed and where things are available when the adult provides them.

Near an adult.

Away from an adult.

DIRECTIONS TO ACTIVITY
The child seems to need:

An adult to direct him to materials. ("Look, John, here are two books about a boy named John. Find out if there are boys in there who are about your size.")

Little direction to accomplish goals.

Limitations of alternatives in the selection of materials and activities. (The child needs an adult to say, "John, you may use one of these two toys—books, records,—during this time.")

Short time periods for working.

Long time periods to complete projects.

[5]The descriptions of learning modalities and the practical experiences needed for each learning style were developed with the help of the following texts: Louis Raths, Arthur Jonas, Arnold Rothstein and Selma Wassermann, *Teaching for Thinking: Theory and Application,* Columbus, Ohio: Merrill, 1967; Marshall B. Rosenberg, *Diagnostic Teaching* (Seattle, Wash.: Special Child Publications), 1968.

The same materials over and over again.

Different materials day after day.

Directions to go to projects in order to complete them. ("John, you need three more pieces of paper in order to finish your tower.")

INTERACTIONS WITH CHILDREN
The child seems:

To work best alone.

To work best when around other children, yet he or she works alone rather than with others.

To work best with a small group:

1. As the leader/director.

2. When directed by another child who acts as leader.

To like to work with the same child(ren) over and over again.

MATERIALS The child needs to:

Touch things when seeing them.

Listen in order to enjoy a story.

Look at pictures while hearing a story.

the playing place: skill building

The place to play is the place to sharpen pre-reading skills. Five-year-olds need two kinds of games: those that teach reading skills and others that test these skills. It is important to remember the distinct difference between teaching games and testing games. The game that teaches permits the child to offer many responses. The error-free game makes success inevitable. Teaching games can require specific responses if the mechanical aspects of the materials allow for this error-free concept. If, for example, the child were to learn that the little word "at" following many consonants makes many rhyming words, the materials for teaching this concept would be prepared so that each letter would fit "into" the little word. This concept is illustrated in Figure 5–26.

Testing games, on the other hand, have only one correct response. The child plays the game by giving that response. Board games, card games, and lotto games all permit children to test their abilities to handle reading skills.

The place to play should have flat surfaces and room to move. Games should be stored on low, easy-to-reach shelves. Games that teach and test the same skill should be stored together. This helps the child to categorize ideas.

materials for playing

Testing and teaching games comprise the playing materials needed for the development of reading skills. When selecting and preparing materials, the following must be considered. It is important to develop the child's ability to:

1. *Use small muscles easily and proficiently.*
2. *Move his eyes from left to right when using printed matter.*
3. *Match objects, pictures, letters, and words.*
4. *Recognize letters and words.*
5. *Match sounds with objects that represent initial letters.*
6. *Remember information sequentially and develop sequential order in things.*

Fig. 5–26

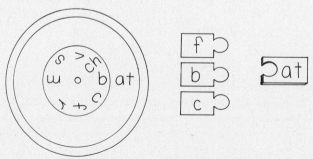

7. *Remember details and use words to describe these details.*

8. *Make inferences about literature and language based on stories.*

9. *Organize information so that it can be summarized.*

10. *Make an educated guess about ideas based on given information.*

guidelines for play:
selecting materials

Materials purchased should be selected for the pre-reading skill that they help to develop. The following chart (Table 5–4) should serve as a guide for play materials that develop these skills.

Table 5–4

SKILLS	TOYS THAT ENCOURAGE THEIR DEVELOPMENT
Small muscle development (fingers, eyes)	Colored pencils, pens, and markers Tool boxes, Lincoln Logs, small wood building blocks Toys with small pieces that build and stack (Lego, etc.)
Left to right hand and eye movement	Magnetic alphabet and arithmetic boards Printing sets Sewing cards Follow-the-dot activities
Matching activities Objects, pictures, letters	Shape and number pictures, dominoes Blocks Toys with matching pieces Puzzles Lotto games
Recognizing letters and words	Magnetic alphabet boards Printing sets ABC Lotto games
Matching sounds with beginning consonants	Talking toys with books to match. These often require the child to pull a string or push a button for the sounds of language.
Comparing ideas	Puzzles and lotto games develop these skills.
Remembering details and using words to describe them Making inferences Organizing information and summarizing it Taking educated guesses	Toy barns, farms, hospitals, stores, fire engines, tents, doll houses, and colorful posters encourage children to use all of these thinking skills. Toys with many parts that fit "in and out," and require the arranging and rearranging of materials help children to develop these skills.

adult behavior in
the playing place

Children need time to play by themselves. Adults should step in only when asked. The following checklist is a guide for adult behavior during playing. Responses should be checked in the "yes" column for the best adult behavior.

	YES	NO

*I direct children to materials that are
appropriate to their level. I might say, "John,
there is a game that seems just right for you,"
or "There is a game that will help you learn
to hear the letters we spoke about."*

*I encourage my child to select a teaching
game over and over again.*

*I watch children for signs of frustration (loss
of interest, leaving the game, crying, eye
rubbing) and redirect them to games where
they can find success.*

*After children have used a teaching game a
number of times, I direct each to the game
that tests the same skill (see pages 204 to 213
for examples).*

*I am sure that all games are safe, durable,
and attractive.*

ACTIVITIES FOR PLAY:

activity 1: using small muscles.

MATERIALS: Sewing cards made from tagboard, a picture from a magazine, a hole puncher, glue or paste, wool or rug yarn, clear Contact paper, and a box.

DIRECTIONS FOR CONSTRUCTION: Cut tagboard into 8 × 8 inch square. Paste a picture onto the card, punch holes in the picture, and cover the card with clear contact paper. Cut pieces of yarn 30 inches long. Finish the ends with masking tape. Put all the materials in a box. For illustrations of these materials, see Figure 5–27 through 5–29.

DIRECTIONS FOR USE: When the child selects this game, demonstrate sewing the yarn through the holes. Permit the child to

Fig. 5–27, 5–28, and 5–29

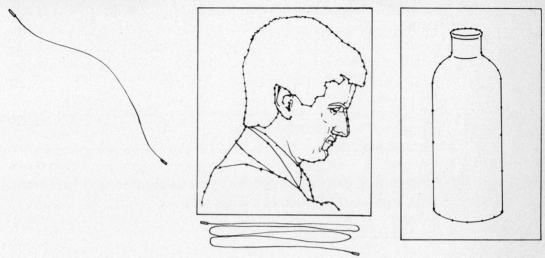

sew in any manner. There is no one way to sew the cards. The purpose of the game is to help the child use the fingers and aim the yarn into a hole.

activity 2: small muscle development

MATERIALS: Scissors, a box for storing all the materials, and the shapes shown in Figure 5–30, drawn on individual pieces of paper 9 × 12 inches.

DIRECTIONS: Draw one figure on each piece of paper. Place the pictures and the scissors in a box. Write the word "cut" on the box. Place the materials in the playing place. When the child chooses the activity, he or she will be able to cut easily on the lines.

Fig. 5–30

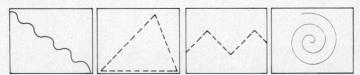

| activity 3: teaching left-to-right movement | MATERIALS: A story book |
| | DIRECTIONS: As you read to the child, point to the page, moving your fingers from left to right along the line of print. Continue to do this each time you read until the child automatically moves his or her head first to the left and then to the right when you turn the pages. |

activity 3: teaching left-to-right movement

MATERIALS: A story book

DIRECTIONS: As you read to the child, point to the page, moving your fingers from left to right along the line of print. Continue to do this each time you read until the child automatically moves his or her head first to the left and then to the right when you turn the pages.

activity 4: left-to-right progression

MATERIALS: Oak tag, scissors, Magic Markers, a children's story, and a small box.

CONSTRUCTION: Cut the oak tag into strips 4 inches by 15 inches, divide each strip by cutting it into puzzle pieces, as shown in Figure 5–31, and then draw a story in sequence from left to right—one on each puzzle piece.

This teaching game allows the child to put a story into sequence and organize the story plot.

SUGGESTED EXTENSIONS OF THE GAME: After putting the puzzle together, ask the child to (1) act out the story or (2) tell about the story on tape. To make this a testing game, cut the puzzle pieces in squares.

activity 5: making a book

MATERIALS: Five pieces of tagboard, 10 × 10 inches each, a hole puncher, and some pipe cleaners.

DIRECTIONS: Punch holes on the left side of each piece of tagboard. Cut pipe cleaners into small pieces, putting these through the holes and twisting them together. Write "My Book," as shown in Figure 5–32. Say to the child, "Make your own book. First, number each page." If the child understands left to right progression, numbering the pages from left to right will be an easy task.

Fig. 5–31

Fig. 5–32 and 5–33

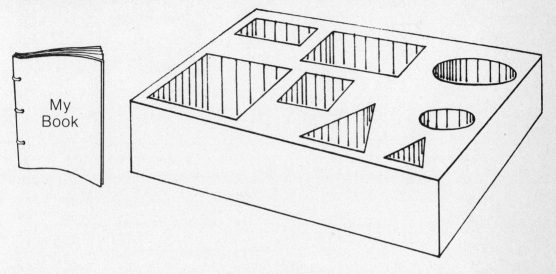

activity 6:
matching
objects—
a game to test
the child's
ability
to distinguish
between
shapes

MATERIALS: Different shaped blocks—a large and small triangle, a large and small square, a large and small rectangle, a large and small cylinder, and a box with shapes cut out (as shown in Figure 5–33).

DIRECTIONS: Use commercial blocks from a block-building set. Trace the outline of each block onto the top of a cardboard box. Cut out on the outline. Replace the box top and seal it with tape.

OBJECT: To match the block to the shape by placing it into the hole.

activity 7:
matching
pictures—
a teaching
game

MATERIALS: Oak tag cut into 8- × 4-inch pieces, a Magic Marker, and scissors.

DIRECTIONS: Select two objects that go together. Objects could include pairs, such as those shown in Figures 5–34 and 5–35. Draw one of the pair on top of the oak tag card and the second from the pair on the bottom of the card. Divide the card by making a puzzle-like division at the center portion of each card. Put the pieces in a box labeled "Puzzle Matching Game."

OBJECT: The child is to put the pieces of the puzzles together, matching objects.

207

Fig. 5–34

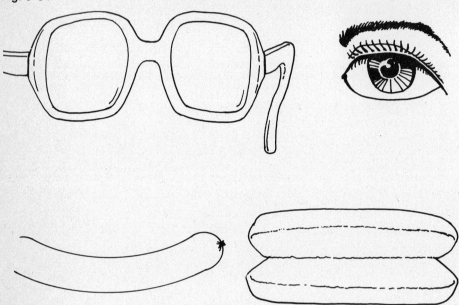

Fig. 5–35

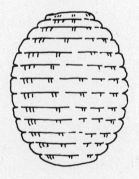

activity 8:
recognizing
words and
letters—
teaching
word
recognition

MATERIALS: Tagboard, cut into 3- × 10-inch pieces, a felt-tipped marker, and some photographs—one of the child, one of mother or father, one of his favorite toy.

DIRECTIONS: Write the child's name on one card, the name of a favorite toy on another, and "Mommy" or "Daddy" on a third. Paste the photo onto the word card that matches the photo.

DIRECTIONS FOR TEACHING: Show the child the card with the picture. Say, "What do you suppose this word says?" Encourage the child to guess until the child comes upon the correct word. Say, "You've got it" or "That's right." Then say, "What does this word say?"

activity 9:
word
recognition

MATERIALS: A marker, a 3 × 10 inch piece of paper, a shoe box, and a large piece of paper or chalkboard.

DIRECTIONS: Ask the child one of the following questions.

What is your favorite toy?
What do you like to do most?
What is your favorite food?
What do you really hate?

Write a single word on the card. Review the words with the child in a playful, nonpressured, happy manner, telling him or her the words he or she does not recall. Speak as soon as you discover hesitation in the child's voice. This helps to teach words that children may not remember.

activity 10:
testing word
recognition

MATERIALS: An envelope, tagboard, cut into 3 × 10 inch pieces, and a felt-tipped marker.

DIRECTIONS: Write the child's words, one on each card. Place them in the envelope. Label the envelope "Darren's Words."

DIRECTIONS FOR USE: Place all of the cards face up on a flat surface. Say, "I will call a word. You find it."

An Important Note: It takes at least nine and up to fifty-five viewings of a word in order for the word to become part of the child's sight vocabulary. Be patient.

**activity 11:
letter
recognition—
a teaching
activity**

DIRECTIONS: Hold up a letter. Say, "This is an E-e-e-e-e-e.
Say it with me: E-e-e-e-e-e-e-e-e-e."
Then say:

E is for eagle
E is for even
E is for eat
E is for eleven
E is for elephant
E is for eraser
E is for egg
E is for Evelyn.

Then say, "Say this with me." Encour-
age children to repeat with you by saying this slowly, with a
chant. They will say the first part of the rhyme easily and will
catch the rest of the words as the poem is repeated.

Follow-up: Make charts like those
shown in Figure 5–36. Hang them on a wall, and as you pass,
with the child, read the chart and point to the words.

**activity 12:
matching
letters to
sounds in the
beginning
of words**

MATERIALS: Scissors, oak tag, glue, and pictures of objects that
begin with the long sounds of the letter "i" (as in "ice").
DIRECTIONS FOR CONSTRUCTION:

1. *Cut out pictures of objects that begin with the letter "i." Objects
   might include: ice cream, ice, iron, iris, island, and icicle.*
2. *Paste each picture onto a piece of oak tag cut to fit the picture.*
3. *Make a series of cards, 3 × 5 inches in size, as shown in Figure
   5–37.*
4. *Place all the materials in an envelope and label it "A Matching
   Game."*

DIRECTIONS FOR USE: This game may be constructed using all
of the vowel sounds. Select one letter, and reconstruct the game
for that letter. The child is to match the letter card to each
picture, saying the name of the picture each time there is a
match.

210

Fig. 5–36

Ee Elephant

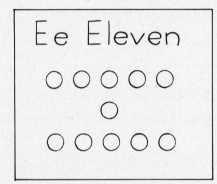

Ee Eleven

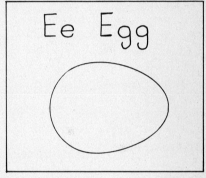

Ee Egg

activity 13:
a game testing
the child's
ability to hear
sounds in the
beginnings
of words (long
or short vowel)

MATERIALS: Scissors, felt-tipped markers, pictures cut from a magazine or photographs, and oak tag cut into 3- × 10-inch pieces.

DIRECTIONS FOR CONSTRUCTION: Collect pictures of objects that begin with all of the vowel sounds. These might include ice cream, ocean, umbrella, eraser, apricot, and ape. Place each of these pictures on a card. Cover the picture with clear Contact paper. On a second set of cards, write each of the vowels, as shown in Figure 5–38.

Fig. 5–37

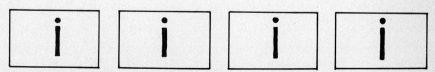

Fig. 5–38

DIRECTIONS FOR USE: Direct the child to match the vowel to the picture of the object that begins with that vowel's sound.

**activity 14:
a teaching
game
—sequencing**

MATERIALS:

*I see a bee
I see a bee and a bug
I see a bee, a bug, and a bear
I see a bee, bug, bear, and baboon.
I see a bee, bug, bear, baboon, and buffalo
The bee, bug, bear, baboon, and buffalo see me.*

S. M. GLAZER

DIRECTIONS: Say the first line. Ask the child to repeat it. Continue saying a line and asking the child to repeat that line. Each time you do this type of activity, the child will probably hold more items in his memory. Do this same activity with numbers.

**activity 15:
a teaching
game—
comparing
and
sequencing**

MATERIALS: 5 × 7 index cards, pictures cut from a magazine or newspaper, glue, and a cigar or shoe box.
DIRECTIONS: Cut pictures from newsprint or magazines and paste them on the cards. Place the cards in the box.
Ask the child to select a picture and tell a story about it.

**activity 16:
comprehension
game
testing—
recalling
facts
sequentially**

MATERIALS: A story book, such as Marie Hall Ets's *Play With Me* (Viking, 1955) or Espher Slobodkina's *Caps For Sale* (Young Scott, 1947), pictures of a few pages throughout the story (these can be drawn or copied), glue, and tagboard.
DIRECTIONS: Paste each picture onto a piece of tag board. There should be as many pieces of board as there are pictures. Place them in a large envelope with the name of the story

written on the front. Ask the child to retell the story, using the pictures. Accept all responses in order to tell what the child remembers.

the constructing place

For 5-year-olds, the place to construct is a place that stimulates verbal learning. The child needs concrete materials, small group projects, rules and standards, and role-playing activities as aids for handling ideas in the environment. At this age, the environment must be touched, tasted, and smelled as well as heard and seen in order for ideas to take on meaning. So very much is learned by "doing" that construction is an essential part of language learning and reading. The child creates an idea or an object and compares it to one made previously. When a child constructs, just as when he reads, thinking occurs. Construction involves the same thinking skills necessary for successful reading.

Construction activities for 5-year-olds are handled differently than in earlier years. Rules may be followed, and some decisions should be made with children. Making the decision is now part of the activity. The self-made rules permit children to discover how they can move from one activity to another.

materials for construction

Materials for construction must help children to translate abstract ideas into concrete objects. This concept is difficult for young children. They must, therefore, reconstruct the ideas for themselves by creating. Letters must be three dimensional. Words need to be accompanied by the objects that they represent. Materials for construction include the following:

Letter-making materials
String
Straws
Yarn
Cotton

Play-acting materials
Construction paper in many colors
Tagboard that can be easily cut
Patterns for tracing
Yarn

Rope
Pipe cleaners

Buttons
Fabric
Large blunt needles and thread
Popsicle sticks
Toothpicks

Natural materials for art work

Leaves
Stones
Twigs
Natural animal homes—cocoons,
  hives, bird's nests
Sand or dirt

Printing materials

Sponges, erasers
Styrofoam pieces

Papier-mâché materials

Balloons
Newsprint
Wallpaper paste

Construction materials

Tempera paints
Large paint paper

Woodworking

Wood pieces
Rulers
Hammers
Screw driver
Simple clamp vise
Bucksaw

General purpose materials

Masking tape
Hammer
Nails
Workbench with vise
Saw
Wood pieces for construction
  with hammer and nails
Clay
Play dough
Plasticine (clay with an oil
  base that does not harden)
Wood pieces
Tagboard
Yardstick
Markers (different colors)
Scissors

material storage in the constructing place

Materials should be easily available to children. All materials should be labeled. Straws should be kept in one box, fabric in another, and so on. Categorizing materials helps the child to categorize ideas. Tools, because they are dangerous, need to be stored at a workbench or in a homemade tool storage box. Nails should be kept in individual containers and should be separated according to size.

guidelines for construction

A decision concerning the use of tools is necessary. Some safety rules must be made by the adult and the child together. The following rules are suggested:

1. *Always keep hands away from a sharp-edged tool while using it.*
2. *Always be sure that the handles, blades, and other parts of tools are securely fastened.*
3. *Always carry only one tool at a time.*
4. *Always watch out for others when carrying tools.*
5. *Always use tools at the woodworking area.*
6. *Always report an accident as soon as it happens.*

adult behaviors when children construct

The child must be freed to express individual ideas by developing a personal creation. To free a child's imagination to construct means stepping back and becoming an active observer of his or her behavior. The following guide (Table 5–5) will help adults to become active observers of children's behaviors when they construct. This should be used only as a guide, for all children are individuals and each works in his or her own manner.

construction activities for the 5-year-old

The following activities will help children to use language to accompany the products resulting from their constructions.

activity 1: letter making

MATERIALS: Homemade or commercial blocks with the letters in the child's name on them, a large piece of white paper, placed on a flat surface, white paste or glue, and cotton.

DIRECTIONS: Place all the materials on a table or flat surface. Direct the child by saying, "Make your name with the letters. Then make your name with the cotton. Paste your cotton name on the paper." When the child has completed the name picture, say, "What have you done?"

Table 5–5

CHILD'S BEHAVIOR	ADULT BEHAVIOR
If the child cannot stick to an activity until it is completed . . .	The child must be directed to shorter projects or to those that are less intricate.
If the child talks about the construction during working time . . .	Great! This is the kind of language behavior that should begin to grow during construction.
If the child does not talk about construction . . .	Encourage language by asking the following: 1. "How do you feel about your project?" 2. "What does it make you think of?" 3. "What else is like that?" 4. "Where have you seen something like that before?"
If the child always works alone . . .	That's fine. Lots of people enjoy working by themselves.
If the child never chooses to construct . . .	Encourage the child to do so by saying, "Take two pieces of paper and some sticks and paste, or take two round things, two soft things, and two hard things and paste them together." Any language that directs children to specific materials will encourage construction.
If the child does not complete a project and says, "I want to do it another time". . .	This is fine. The child should be directed to put the object away and go back to it at another construction period.
If the child wants to display objects . . .	That's great; but those who do not should not be forced or directed to.
If the child comes to an adult and tells about constructions . . .	Permit the child time to talk to an adult or to use a tape cassette if preferred.
If the child talks lots about objects . . .	Find the time to write the talk down as the child describes the products.
If the child's product looks awkward, misshapen, or unattractive . . .	That's fine—as long as the object is made by the child. Never put your hands on the child's work to help make it "better." THE BEST PRODUCT IS THAT WHICH IS PRODUCED BY THE CHILD!

EVALUATION: By copying, the child is developing eye–hand coordination.

EXTENSION: This activity can be done using string, yarn, or rope.

activity 2: collage with natural materials

MATERIALS: Feathers, leaves, stones, twigs, paper, scissors, glue or white paste, and pieces of plants.

DIRECTIONS: Place the materials in piles on a table top. Put the paper on the table and place the scissors and an open jar of paste next to the paper. Say, "Take some materials from each pile and create something by pasting them on the paper." As your child works, say, "Tell me how that feels" or "What do you like about the feathers?"

activity 3: papier-mâché with balloons

MATERIALS: A balloon, blown and fastened, wallpaper paste, a large shallow dish, water, and newsprint in strips about 1 inch wide.

DIRECTIONS TO ADULTS: Tear or cut newspaper into strips; mix the paste according to the directions on the package and place it next to the balloon along with the pile of newsprint strips.

DIRECTIONS TO CHILDREN: Cover the balloon with the strips of paper. Dip one strip of paper into the paste. Get it all wet. Then wrap the strip around the balloon. Wrap the balloon three times. (This does not have to be done in one day.) While the child is working, say, "Tell me what you are doing." Record the child's language by writing it down on a piece of paper. Place the language on a large piece of oak tag and read it to the child. You are helping the child to see that reading is talk written down.

activity 4: play-acting and construction— a cutting activity

MATERIALS: Scissors, paste or white glue, tagboard and unlined paper.

DIRECTIONS: Say to child: "Draw a large face and cut it out. Give the face a name." When the faces are completed, say, (1) "Tell about your face." (2) "How does that person feel?" (3) "What do you suppose made him look that way?"

EVALUATION: You are encouraging children to use language to describe feelings.

activity 5: woodworking

MATERIALS: A work table, a saw, a hammer, wood, and nails.

DIRECTIONS: Supply materials in the appropriate place and permit children to construct with wood at will.

EVALUATION: Woodworking helps the child to develop the large and small muscles that are necessary for writing. Children will relieve their frustrations by banging. They will also create objects, when ready, that translate ideas into reality for them. They may talk about their products. This can be encouraged in the following way. Say, "Tell me about your wood work," "Tell me how you made that," or "Where would you use that?"

the thinking place

The thinking place must be quiet. It might be the corner of a room, a large refrigerator box, a private study carrel, or just a pillow on the floor. What is needed most is time set aside for thinking activities. Adults and children must engage in these thinking times together. Adults must not send children off alone to think. To set an example, you should perform the activity with your children.

adult behavior when children think
To help children think means to:

1. *Engage in thinking activities with children.*
2. *Work alongside of the child. Do not look at the child's work unless you are asked to do so by the child.*
3. *Concentrate on your own work, setting a model of behavior.*

ACTIVITIES THAT DEVELOP
THINKING READERS:

activity 1: sustained silent reading to build the "reading habit"

MATERIALS: A book or two or three.

DIRECTIONS: Begin the sustained reading as follows: Say the following:

1. *You select a book and I am going to do the same.*
2. *Come over here (to the reading place) and get comfortable.*
3. *I am going to set this timer for three minutes. (You might use a three-minute hourglass or a timer with a bell.)*
4. *There are some rules for this quiet reading time. First, everyone will read. Second, we will not answer the telephone, door knocks, or bells, nor will we permit anyone who is not in the room to enter. That's why we have written "Do Not Disturb" on the front of the door. When the timer bell rings, we will stop.*
5. *O.K. Take your book, get comfortable, and let's read.*

Continue the activity at the same time each day. Increase the time over a period of weeks from three to five or seven minutes. Do not ask children to tell about reading. You may set an example by saying, "Oh, I read the funniest thing." Your child will eventually copy your example and share what he or she has read.

activity 2: sustained silent writing— building the "language habit"

MATERIALS: Writing tools and paper, a surface on which to write, and a timer.

DIRECTIONS: Sustained writing should begin as soon as the child can write anything. Writing means letter making and picture making as well as writing words. Sustained writing fosters the writing habit. It provides a daily period of uninterrupted writing time. Children will choose their own topics, tools, and places to write. Sustained writing gives children an opportunity to (1) practice penmanship, (2) practice writing words that they can spell, (3) learn to spell and write new words, (4) discover patterns of language, and (5) allow ideas to come without interruption or interference.

SUSTAINED SILENT WRITING (SSW)
1. *Each child and adult must have his or her own notebook or pad, writing tools, and his or her own place to write.*
2. *Words must be available for children to copy. This means that there should be a box of words available or a listing posted near the writing place.*
3. *Time must be provided for sharing writing, if children desire. This helps children to see language and to share vocabulary with others.*
4. *Sharing and adult direction will often lead to further writing.*

DIRECTIONS TO CHILDREN: Say, "I am getting my notebook for sustained writing. Get yours, too. Find a spot to write. I will set the timer. Remember, no getting up to answer the phone or the doorbell—or for anything else. We will just write until the time is up. Ready? Begin."

At the completion of the writing time, say, "Oh, boy, listen to what I have written" or "Look at my writing." If the child wants to share, your offer to share will encourage the child to show, read, or display his or her productions.

a final thought

Growing up and going to school means "thinking." However, the thinking habit begins at birth and must be nurtured through childhood. A kindergartener needs freedom to think about the new world of school. It is the adult who must help the youngster to build the confidence and respect necessary to share ideas and to bring the school and home together to unify the thinking, learning, and reading experiences in order to create children who will read for a lifetime.

THE BEGINNING OF FORMAL READING INSTRUCTION IN SCHOOL

First grade, 6 years of age, and learning to read are generally thought of as happening at the same time. The instant children enter the first year of formal instruction, they are expected to learn to read. But age is only a small part of being ready to read. Like cutting teeth and toilet training, most children will read, but each will learn in his or her own time.

what makes 6 the readiness year?

Six-year-olds are hectic, inconsistent in behavior, and clumsy; they dawdle and work in spurts. Their work habits vary. One day they will work well and the next, not at all. This typical behavior often frustrates adults. Six-year-olds are able, however, to learn a great many things, particularly those related to reading.

The 6-year-old has a marvelous self-concept. This big ego helps the child to handle the strains of formal instruction. It also helps the youngster get into dilemmas by opposing his or her teacher, mother, and dad. The new values and expectations of school and the great pressures placed on the child to learn to read will sometimes cause the youngster to act younger and to engage in activities more typical of a 3-, 4-, or 5-year-old. Six-year-olds do have positive attitudes about school and, therefore, have a certain magical readiness for reading. Although many do not share school events with adults, it is important for them to share their paperwork and reading with those they love. Praise from mother and father is of high value to six-year-olds. These usual 6-year-old experiences prepare the child for formal reading instruction. Skills related directly to reading must be present for the child to succeed. Table 6–1 is a summary of these skills. Next to each category is a simple device for discovering if your child has competence in the skills needed in order to engage in formal reading instruction.

Along with these abilities, youngsters must have a happy, healthy attitude toward books.

In order to make reading a part of the child's life, you must first make it a part of your life. Children will join you in sharing their joys from reading. They will treasure the feelings received from the wonderful language in good books for young readers.

how children are taught to read in school

Most beginning reading programs include two parts: The first is the recognition of words. Some instructional procedures require that children recognize words as whole units, and others use a phonics method. In this approach, the child is expected to learn the sounds of letters and basic letter groups, such as "th," and then be able to analyze (sound out) the words. The second part is comprehension. In order to comprehend, the child must understand or make sense of the information printed on a page. Only things to which the

Fig. 6–1

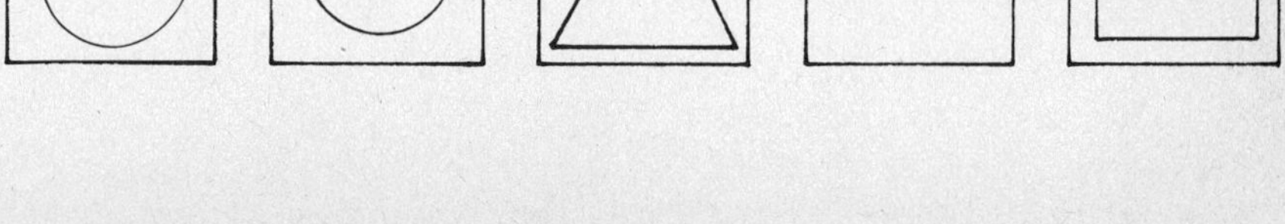

Table 6–1
discovering skill abilities

READING READINESS SKILL	DISCOVERING YOUR CHILD'S SKILL DEVELOPMENT
Can recognize the letters of the alphabet in print.	(1) Write each letter on a card and flash it before the child. The child is expected to say its name. (2) Show an alphabet book, and have the child select and name the letters (suggested books include the following: Bruno Munari's *ABC* (Collins-World, 1960). Helen Oxenburg's *ABC Of Things*, (Watts, 1972)
Can print his or her name.	Send a birthday card to a relative or friend and ask children to sign their names.
Can copy figures or words.	(1) Write the child's favorite words on individual cards 3 × 9 inches in size. Ask the child to copy them on a piece of paper. (2) Ask the child to copy the series of figures shown in Figure 6–1.
Knows each of the following: Over and under	Ask the child to climb *over* a box. Ask the child to get *under* a chair.
Left to right	Ask the child to show you the left hand. Ask the child to show you the right foot (hand, eye, etc.).
Beginning and ending	Ask the child to tell you the beginning of a story. Ask the child to tell you the ending of an event.
Before and after	Ask the child to stand before "you." Ask the child to tell you what happens after dinner or after he or she goes to school, and so on.
Front and back	Ask the child to stand in front of you (in back of you).
Can name the colors when looking at them.	Show an object and ask its color.
Can rhyme words.	Say, "I know a man. He lived in a *van* (accept man, tan ran, or any other rhyming word). I know a cat. He lived in a _____ (child should offer a word that rhymes with cat—hat, mat, rat, flat, etc.). These can be nonsense words.
Can identify some words by sight.	Make cards with one word on each. Place them face up on a table and ask the child to pick one and tell what it says.
Has a keen interest in learning to read.	Will say, "Tell me that word," when you read him a story or, "Where does it say that?"

224

READING READINESS SKILL (cont.)	DISCOVERING YOUR CHILD'S SKILL DEVELOPMENT (cont.)
Can solve simple problems.	Ask your child to put many things into a container that is just big enough to hold the quantity. The problem to solve is the "tight squeeze." Does the child stick to the task until the pieces fit into the container?
Is able to remember simple directions.	Give the child a simple chore that has one direction (i.e., "Put your coat away"). Add a second direction to the first ("Put your coat away, and get your milk").
Can speak clearly, without speech problems.	If there is a concern, speak to the child's teacher.
Has normal hearing, sight, and good general health.	If there is concern, see a physician or consult the school nurse.

child can relate will be meaningful to him. Therefore, parents and teachers must be sure that instructional materials, books, magazines, and workbooks for beginning readers have information or situations familiar to the child. The child must have some information about the new data in order to make contact with it. Here is where comprehension instruction begins. Let's imagine that your child is familiar with boats and sailing. The youngster knows about the front and back of boats but is unfamiliar with the words "bow" (the front) and "stern" (the hind part of the boat). In order to teach the child the meaning, you casually refer to the "bow," pointing it out to the child when referring to the boat's front end. When this occurs, you are asking your child to compare what is known—the word "front"—to the new word, "bow." The child compares the terms and begins to organize the ideas about the new word "bow," gathering all the information in order to describe the elements that represent "bow." By pointing to the bow, you are telling the child that it means "front." The child is able to take an educated guess to make sense of the new word and to comprehend its meaning. Our task, then, is to know the child very well. We must understand how and where the child learns best so that we can provide learning activities that help each youngster to make sense of the information and remember it.

discovering how children learn words
(sounds of language)

It is important for parents and teachers to work together to discover how children learn best. Adults must be astute observers of children's behavior in learning situations. After watching a child, the adult should be able to tell how the child retains information. The observer might say of one child, "Brian learns best when he listens. I know, because he remembers more facts and gets more excited about reading when he hears than when he sees the materials." The following guide will help you to determine how your child remembers information. Use it with caution, for as children grow, their learning styles may change and grow as well.

ACTIVITIES FOR OBSERVING CHILDREN'S
ABILITY TO REMEMBER WORDS—DEVELOPING VOCABULARY

activity 1: learning a whole word by looking (sight words)

Ask the child for the name of his favorite food, toy, or game. Write it on a piece of paper 3 × 10 inches in size. Use manuscript writing, as illustrated in Chapter 5, page 168). Say the word. Have the child repeat the word. Say, "Tell me what you are thinking when you read that word."

activity 2: learning a whole word by sight and touch

Say to the child, "Tell me in one word what you love most" (hate most, one child's favorite foods, toys, and so on). Write that word on a 3 × 10 inch piece of paper. Say the word. As you say it, take the child's finger and slowly trace over the word, holding onto the vowel sounds as long as the breath will last. For example, if the word is "ice," say, "i-i-i-i-i-ice." Repeat the tracing and have the child say the word as it is traced. After three or four tracings, direct the child to say the word and write it at the same time, without looking at the word on the card. Say, "If you think you are wrong, stop, come back, and trace again."

activity 3: learning a whole word by recognizing patterns

Present the following string of words to the child: cat, hat, mat, fat, pat, sat, bat. Write the word "cat" on a 3 × 10 inch card. Ask the child to read it. Ask, "What do you notice about it?" Then present the child with the other words, each on a separate card. Lay all the cards on the table and ask, "What do you notice?" Take the cards away. Say, "Write as many of the words as you can remember."

**activity 4:
learning
words
by sight
and sound**

Ask the child to tell you one word that describes a favorite toy, meal, or activity. Write the word on a 3 × 10 inch card. Say that word as the child looks at it. Put your voice on tape and repeat that word. Say the word in a sentence. Ask the child to say the word that is heard on the tape and encourage the child to use it in a sentence after listening to yours. As the child sees the word, run the cassette and ask the youngster to tape the word each time it is heard. Try this once every two days.

Wait twenty-four hours after each type of activity and test to see if the child remembers the word. Ask yourself the following questions:

1. *Does the child remember it best when looking at the whole word?*
2. *Does the child remember it best when looking, saying, and tracing it?*
3. *Does the child remember it best when looking at other words with the same spelling pattern? (cat, fat, sat, etc.).*
4. *Does the child remember it best when seeing it and hearing it on tape?*

Look to see which learning style is best for your child. You can begin to teach words in the style in which the child remembers words most easily. If two styles work, alternate one and then the other for word learning. Be relaxed, unpressured, and reassuring to your new reader. Tell the child what you are doing. Say, "Let's find out how you remember words best." Informing children about themselves and their activities is one of the most important ways to build self-confident readers.

**making sense of ideas
in print—comprehension
style activities**

For years, children have been expected to answer questions after reading a passage. This questioning procedure is used to check the child's comprehension in order to find out how much is remembered after reading. Questioning is only one of the many ways children can let us know that they have retained information. As a matter of fact, children who ask questions about things they have read are telling us that they have made sense of the squiggles in print. Many children, however, cannot tell us what they know about reading by responding to questions. Some can tell us by writing, others by acting out parts of the information, and still others by drawing pictures or rewriting the information. The following activities will help you to learn how the child reports and retains information from print. Remember that these are only a guide and should be used carefully.

comprehension model 1: retelling after reading Ask the child to read a passage silently. The passage should not be more than ten sentences in length. Then ask the child to tell you everything he or she remembers about his or her reading. The child may tell you by talking, by acting, or by drawing a picture about it.

comprehension model 2: retelling after listening You read a passage to the child. After you have completed the passage, say, "Tell me all you can remember about the reading." The passage should not be more than ten sentences in length. The child may share the memories about the listening experience by acting, drawing, telling, or writing.

comprehension model 3: listening and reading together Read a passage on tape. Give the passage of print to the child. Ask the child to read it and listen to the tape at the same time. Encourage the child to listen to the tape without reading. Ask the child to read without listening to the tape. Then say, "Share all that you remember from the listening and reading."

comprehension model 4: reading words and pictures together Ask the child to read a passage that has pictures to help tell the story. Be sure that there are no more than ten sentences in all. Have the child read the story. Say, "Tell me as much as you can remember about the story."

Children will begin to report information from reading in the style they are most comfortable with. They will listen and read, or look and read, or read aloud, or read silently. They are, in a sense, finding out for themselves how they best remember information.

the relationship between learning modes and habits and learning to read

"Darren never completes his homework. Honestly, I'm so disgusted. I got him this model airplane. He began the project, got halfway through it, and never finished." These often heard adult complaints about children's learning habits are indications that understanding behavior is important for guiding children to become readers. Each child has certain needs that express themselves through behaviors in their work and play. Adults must begin to look at children's habits in order to find out how these needs and habits are expressed. Telling a child to think for him- or herself or to pay attention is not direction. Each child needs adult guidance in order to be directed in the development of the productive work habits necessary for creating readers. Table 6–2 illustrates some behavior often observed by adults. The behavior is described, and the usual adult reaction and response is given. An interpretation of the behavior and the implications for changes in the child's environment are suggested.

learning places and self-direction: self-scheduling for the beginning reader

Self-direction means independent behavior. Children need guides for learning independence. First, they must know what is expected and how to carry out expectations. Schedules can serve as reminders for the completion of tasks. The suggested reminder sheets shown in Figure 6–2 will help children as well as adults to remember language activities.

As the children grow and acquire more language ability, they should be encouraged to take on more responsibilities. They can be assigned some specific activities, and they can select others for themselves. The activity schedule shown in Figure 6–3 is appropriate for children who can recognize at least fifty words. The activity sheet corresponds with the learning places.

Some children will need verbal guidance along with self-scheduling guides. The following statements will help children to direct themselves into language activities.

Be careful not to use punitive statements, such as "You're not doing what I asked," "Your work can be better than that," or "I'm surprised that you picked such a baby book." This only helps children to move backwards. Think about how you would feel if someone said these things to you. If they make you feel good, continue. If they make you feel self-conscious, humiliated, depressed, and inferior, then children will feel the same.

Table 6–2
observing behaviors indicative of independent learning

BEHAVIOR	USUAL ADULT REACTIONS	IMPLICATIONS FOR ENVIRONMENT
When asked a question, will answer haughtily. (I know that's correct. You're wrong.)	Child is referred to as bratty, fresh, and lacking respect for authority. The child is impulsive about most things.	Child needs to be helped to slow down. Needs to be given alternatives—for example, a few answers at a time to choose from.
Will constantly ask for adult approval. ("Do you like it?") Will ask for help each step of the way, fearful of making an error.	Is referred to as a "brown-nose" by peers, as a pest by adults, and is often called a "baby" by other children.	The child is overdependent on adults. Planning with this sort of child ahead of time, giving a self-made step-by-step plan, and then reviewing after the completion of task will help to create self reliance.
Will pester others involved in projects. Will get up and down and move about when activities call for sitting times.	Adults say, "He can't concentrate." "He is a nuisance." "He likes to annoy others."	Has little ability to concentrate. Has missed the connection between the "means" and the "ends" of situations. Needs an environment that forces back-tracking of activities, recalling that which has been done and where to go from there.
Will say, "I don't know" in response to questions. Will ask, "What is it all about?" or "Tell me again."	Adults will say, "He can't think," "He doesn't listen," or "He never understands what I'm trying to do."	Child misses the meaning of language. Needs to have experiences getting meaning in different ways—ask questions, listen to ideas, see ideas, draw ideas. Needs pinpointing of experiences in order to identify meanings.
Uses phrases like, "I always go faster than you" or "I do all my work better than you." Words like "all," "never," "always," and "nobody," are always part of his or her language behavior.	"He thinks he's the greatest," "He's a spoiled brat," and "He thinks he's always right" are comments made by adults who interact with children who show this kind of behavior. Children pick books that are too hard and insist that they can read them.	The dogmatism gets them into trouble. The assertiveness needs to be questioned. Must be asked to compare, contrast, and use words like "pretty certain" and then justify that opinion. Needs to be given guides and instructions in self-selection procedures.
Always selects books on the same topic. Sits the same way in the same place and shares materials in one fashion.	Will say, "At least he does it, but it's so boring, it's always the same. He won't do it any other way." Child gets upset if	The rigidity of this child needs to be loosened. The child needs to be offered alternatives for planning independently, for ways to

BEHAVIOR (cont.)	USUAL ADULT REACTIONS (cont)	IMPLICATIONS FOR ENVIRONMENT (cont.)
	routine or procedures are changed.	share books to select, for seeing things in different ways.
Never volunteers to share work. Will throw work away. Will talk self down—"I'm terrible; my work is awful." Fears ridicule, so withdraws.	Adult will say that the child is insecure, is afraid of being criticized. Other children will ridicule and make fun of behavior because the insecure child invites this. Others see the child as one who is afraid of making a mistake.	Needs open-ended experiences—those where there are many correct responses, so that the child can't make an error. Needs to know where success is possible. Never use words like "good" or "bad" to describe work. Say, "How you have improved!" or "What else might work?"

The learning styles and how to adjust the environment to meet developmental needs is derived from Marshall B. Rosenberg, *Diagnostic Teaching*, Special Child Publications, Seattle, Washington; 1968.

Parents must supplement school programs and engage children in additional activities. The more and varied experiences beginning readers have with printed materials, the better their success in reading will be. Consideration for each child's mode of learning, interests, and abilities to become independent should be part of the activities for enhancing the development of reading.

Fig. 6–2

Fig. 6–3

My Reminder Sheet		Check Here
I read a book. It is _____		
I wrote something.		
I acted something.	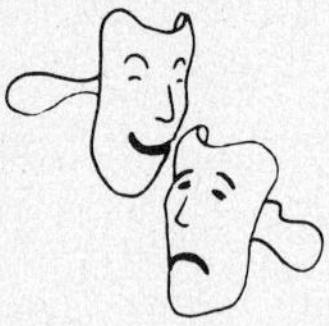	
I constructed something.		
I also did —		

the listening place for beginning readers

Developing attention skills is important for beginning readers. The atmosphere for listening in the beginning reading years should provide the child with a place to listen and look at language. This special place should include pictures, recordings, mobiles, and special posters. An area for private listening should be available for the child. This might be a large refrigerator carton or a table covered with a sheet. All learning requires listening. Children must learn to sift out the sounds that they need to remember and reject the sounds that

232

Table 6–3

SITUATION	ADULT STATEMENTS
When a child has some problems selecting an activity . . .	Say one of the following: "Here are two; pick one" or "Which do you think you might like?" "Which one of these books (games) do you suppose you might like best?" (Using tentative language gives children freedom to respond without worry or error—they do not have to predict the responses that they think adults want to hear.)
When the child looks but cannot find something to do . . .	Say one of the following and place your hand on his or her shoulder or head: (1) "I believe I saw two books that remind me of things I saw in your rock collection (doll, game, etc.)." Relate materials to the child. (2) "Which of these do you think is best for you?"
When a child is not completing an activity . . .	Say one of the following: (1) "Leave it there, but come back and complete it before going on to the next activity." (2) Point to the activity, smile, and say, "It really must be finished. Watch the clock to judge your time" (give a time allotment). (3) "Check your list of things to do."
When the child seems unhappy with a selected activity and says something like, "But I like Brian's better." . . .	If materials are self-selected, there is a built-in response—"It's your selection, and it is expected that you complete the activity." Often, children do not complete something they have started. That's O.K.—with justification. Think to yourself, "How would you feel in the same situation?" Then judge the restrictions you place on your child.
When the child doesn't know where to work . . .	Ask, "Where do you suppose you should work with the clay (or writing, or cooking, etc.)?" or "Where should that kind of work be happening?"

they do not need. The listening place will help children to respond to language and to develop the selection–rejection ability that will help them to become critical listeners.

materials for listening
The listening place should include a record player, a cassette tape recorder, rhythm instruments, recordings (cassettes and records), and listening books for children to hear.

233

Rhythm instruments are wonderful for developing listening skills. Instruments include (1) beat sticks, (2) sandpaper blocks, (3) wrist and angle bells, (4) tambourines, and (5) jingle bats.

HOMEMADE RHYTHM INSTRUMENTS: 1. Beat Sticks. A broom handle sawed into two sticks, each a foot long, will make sticks for beating. These should be sanded and painted for decorative purposes.

2. Sandpaper Blocks. Wrap a piece of sandpaper around a piece of wood approximately 5 × 3 inches. Fasten on the side with tacks or staples.

3. Bells. Ankle or wrist bells can be made from a 6 × 8 inch circle of elastic (constructed from a discarded pair of panty hose). Fasten two or three large bells together (loosely, so that they will jingle) with electrical wire that has been coated with plastic. The plastic-coated wire keeps the metal bells from cutting the thread. Sew the wire with the bells onto wristlets or ankle bands, as shown in Figure 6–4.

4. Tambourine. Encircle an embroidery hoop with a plastic-covered wire threaded with at least four sleigh bells. Cover the hoop with rug yarn (see Figure 6–5).

5. Jingle Bar. Drill holes in a discarded wooden paddle. With heavy wire, lace sleigh bells through the holes (see Figure 6–6). Paddles can be found in toy stores. They usually have a ball attached to a rubber band and are used for paddle ball.

BOOKS AND RECORDINGS: Listening to recordings and looking at books at the same time is a wonderful experience. These

Fig. 6–4

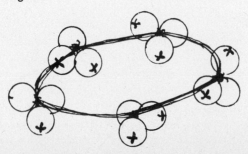

Fig. 6–5 and 6–6

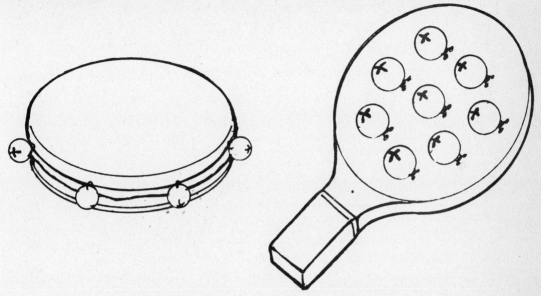

activities help children to see and hear the sounds of language together. Using the eyes and ears together is an important reading skill. Records help to develop this skill. Encouraging children to listen to recordings while looking at the accompanying book helps children to develop the integrated use of their ears and eyes. Weston Woods has produced many favorite stories for children to hear. Some of these include:

Brown, Marcia. *Stone Soup.* Scribner, 1947.

Brown, Margaret. *Wheel on the Chimney.* Lippincott, 1954.

Daugherty, James. *Andy and the Lion.* Viking, 1938.

Galdone, Paul. Illustrator. *Old Mother Hubbard and Her Dog.* McGraw-Hill, 1960.

————. Illustrator. *The House That Jack Built.* McGraw-Hill, 1961.

Hoff, Syd. *Danny and the Dinosaur.* Harper Row, 1969.

Johnson, Crockett. *Harold and the Purple Canyon.* Harper Row, 1955.

Keats Ezra Jack. *Whistle for Willie.* Viking Press, 1964.

Krasilovsky, Phillis. *The Man Who Didn't Wash Dishes.* Doubleday, 1950.

Langstaff, John and Rojankovsky, Feodor. *Over In The Meadow.* Harcourt Brace Jovanovich, 1955.

McCloskey, Robert. *Lentil.* Viking, 1940.

Potter, Beatrix. *Tale of Peter Rabbit.* Golden Press, 1970.

Yashima, Taro. *Crow Boy.* Viking, 1955.

There are many chilren's books that rhyme that are fun to read out loud. These books have similar spelling and sentence patterns. Reading these to children helps them to become familiar with the sounds of these spelling and sentence patterns. This will help them to read these patterns when they see them in books. Adults can tape these and produce a recording for children to hear. Children will read along as the adult's voice plays. Hearing the language and seeing the words is a marvelous way to develop readers; they will be able to integrate the sights and sounds of language.

The books in Table 6-4 rhyme. They will help children to hear and see patterns of language. The patterns that are used in each book are listed in the chart.

ADDITIONAL HOMEMADE RECORDINGS: Hearing the sounds of their own words brings a new dimension to children's language experiences. Recording sounds is like writing. The sounds become permanent—to enjoy forever. Record sounds for listening. Some suggestions follow.

1. *Sounds around the house—water, the telephone, the vacuum cleaner, dogs, children, and so on.*
2. *Sounds in the neighborhood—a car starting, a lawn mower, a motorcyle, and so on.*
3. *Sounds from community helpers—firemen, policemen, medical services, and so on.*
4. *Sounds that remind us of characters in literature, such as*
   A whistle like the whistle in Whistle for Willie, *Ezra Jack Keats (Viking Press, 1964).*
   A "kerkerboom" like the cannon shooting in Drummer Hoff, *Barbara Emberley (Prentice-Hall, 1967).*
5. *Famous language phrases from literature—"'Not I,' said the pig,"* from The Little Red Hen.
6. *Scary sounds—creaky doors, wind blowing, a loud bang.*

Table 6–4

books and language development

AUTHOR	TITLE	PUBLISHER	LANGUAGE ACTIVITY DEVELOPMENT
Brewton, Sarah and John	*I Know An Old Lady/The Magic Fish*	Crowell, 1969 (Recording available: Weston Woods)	Repeated language in consistent language patterns makes this an easy early reading experience.
Eastman, Philip	*Are You My Mother?*	Beginner Books, 1960	Limited vocabulary delightfully handled in a story with a simple plot, repeated language patterns, and a happy ending.
Galdone, Paul	*The Little Red Hen*	Scholastic Book Service, 1975	Repeated sentence patterns and a simple plot aid in making familiar language from earlier years a part of reading.
Graboff, Abner	*Old MacDonald Had A Farm*	Scholastic Book Service, 1970	Repeated language and language patterns help children to learn by rote and then realize the likenesses and differences of language in print.
LeSieg, Theo	*The Eye Book*	Random House, 1968	Few words are repeated in simple language patterns.
LeSieg, Theo	*Ten Apples Up On Top*	Random House, 1961	Sentence and word patterns are simple; "up" and "op" patterns and numbers in word form are dealt with.
Lionni, Leo	*Frederick*	Pantheon, 1966	Simple plot in which the pictures follow the language.
McGovern, Ann	*Too Much Noise*	Houghton Mifflin, 1967	Sounds of the world are used and spelling patterns are aided in the development of the plot about a man who learns to live with everyday noise.
Perkins, Al	*The Ear Book*	Random House, 1968	Few words, easy to read. Simple, repeated language patterns.

Table 6–4
books and language development (continued)

AUTHOR (cont.)	TITLE (cont.)	PUBLISHER (cont.)	LANGUAGE ACTIVITY DEVELOPMENT (cont.)
Prokofiev, Serge & Chappell, Warren	*Peter and the Wolf*	Knopf, 1940 (Available from many recording companies)	Music helps the child to appreciate the simple plot that deals with one main character. The music helps to develop the character's personality and actions.
Dr. Seuss	*Fox In Socks*	Beginner, 1965	Spelling patterns "ox," "ick," "ock," "ack," "oom," "iddle," "oodle," and so on.
Dr. Seuss	*Hop On Pop*	Beginner, 1963	Deals with spelling patterns "all," "ay," "ent," "other," "ed," "ack," "up," "ing," "it," "ight," and so on.
Dr. Seuss	*Green Eggs and Ham*	Beginner, 1960	Patterns "am," "an"; simple plot; good illustrations.
Dr. Seuss	*One Fish, Two Fish, Red Fish, Blue Fish*	Beginner, 1960	"ish" pattern and word numbers; the pictures go wonderfully with the words.
Dr. Seuss	*The Cat in the Hat*	Beginner, 1957	Simple plot; rhyme; repeated language patterns; spelling pattern "at" stressed.

7. *Happy sounds—laughter, circus music, clapping hands.*
8. *Holiday sounds—jingle bells, gobbling turkeys.*
9. *Quiet sounds—snoring, a light switch.*
10. *Noisy sounds—honking horns, a loud crash.*

guidelines for listening

Guiding children's listening means directing them into listening experiences so that they pay attention to the sounds of language. Some children must be told what to listen for, and others can tell themselves. The following checklist will help to guide adults in directing children into listening. The desired response for all adult behavior is "yes."

YES   NO

I provide direction to the child before listening. I find simple directions, not more than two sentences, that are no more than ten words long.

I repeat simple directions at least three times.

After giving spoken directions, I ask the child to repeat them.

I do **not** *interfere while the child is listening. Interfering means stopping the experience and talking to the child. This causes distraction.*

I schedule listening experiences based on the child's attention. If, for example, the child moves about after three minutes of listening, then I schedule only three minutes and increase the time only a fraction of a moment the next time.

reading skills in the listening place

Children are developing (1) the ability to recall the plots, places, people, and times of events in literature. They are also developing (2) the ability to hear sounds of language, such as rhyming words and sentence patterns.

activities for listening

activity 1: responding to listening

MATERIALS: Props that reflect some of the characters in recorded stories—A piece of red fabric, for example, might trigger thoughts of Little Red Riding Hood—and pictures that represent characters or scenes from stories on recordings.

DIRECTIONS: Place props or pictures near the listening area. Be sure that the recording represented by these props is available for listening. The presence of the pictures, posters, and props will help children to select the recording and will bring their attention to the particular details pointed out by these materials.

EVALUATION: This helps children to organize ideas and to describe the story in order to build vocabulary.

activity 2:
personal,
silent
listening

MATERIALS: A large painted carton or a table covered with a sheet, a record player

DIRECTIONS: Put the recording and the record player into the carton or under the table. Tell your child, "I put the record player in a private place, just for you."

EVALUATION: Privacy is important for relaxing while listening.

activity 3:
developing
reading
skills—
the rhythm of
language
(sentence
patterns)

MATERIALS: A cooking pan, and a set of beat sticks, one for the adult and one for the child.

DIRECTIONS: Beat the stick once, saying "Do my beat." Beat the stick two times; say, "Do my beat." Then make a combination, beating two small taps and one large, hard one. Say, "Do my beat." Then tell the child to make a beat so that you can imitate it.

EVALUATION: This helps to develop the ability to hear sound differences. This skill is used in sounding out words.

activity 4:
listening
to bells—
developing
reading skills

MATERIALS: A tambourine or other rhythm instrument.

DIRECTIONS: Clap once. Ask your child to shake the bells once. Clap twice. Ask your child to imitate that sound with the instrument. Create other beats with your hands and feet and ask your child to imitate the rhythm with the instrument.

EVALUATION: The child is being asked to listen for sound differences and to build the ability to remember information. This skill is the same as listening for sound differences in words and building sight vocabulary.

activity 5:
listening
to stories (a
comprehension
activity)

MATERIALS: A story record with one main character—for instance, Virginia Lee Burton's *Mike Mulligan and the Steam Shovel* (Houghton Mifflin, 1939) or Ezra Jack Keats's *Whistle For Willie* (Viking 1964).

DIRECTIONS: Say, "Listen for the most important person in the story." After listening, ask the child to tell why that person is the most important.

EVALUATION: This questioning technique helps the child see the main idea of the story.

activity 6: listening for story details (a comprehension activity)

MATERIALS: Use Robert Kraus's *Whose Mouse Are You?* (Macmillan, 1970) or Janice May Urdan's *Let's Be Enemies* (Harper & Row, 1961).

DIRECTIONS: Say to the child, "Listen to see if you can remember all of the things that happened." Have children relate the information by drawing it, telling it, or saying it onto a tape cassette.

EVALUATION: The child is recalling details.

activity 7: listening for story place (a comprehension activity)

MATERIALS: Story books that designate a place in which the story occurs—for instance, John Langstaff & Feodor Rojankovsky's *Over in the Meadow* (Harcourt Brace Jovanich, 1955) or Taro Yashima's *Crow Boy* (Viking, 1955).

DIRECTIONS: Direct the child to listen to see if he or she can decide where the story happens. After the story is read, ask the child to recall the place by telling or drawing it. Ask why he or she thinks the story happened in that place.

EVALUATION: Children are being guided to listen for story setting.

activity 8: listening for time (a comprehension activity)

MATERIALS: Stories that occur at a particular time of day, year, hour, or season—for example, Philip D. Eastman's *Sam and the Firefly* (Beginner Books, 1958) or Peter Spier illustrated *The Fox Went Out On a Chilly Night* (Doubleday, 1961).

DIRECTIONS: Ask the child to listen to find out when the story takes place. Suggest times: "Does it take place during the day, in winter, at night?"

EVALUATION: Children are being guided to listen for time.

activity 9: listening with feeling (a comprehension activity)

MATERIALS: Books about people in situations—for example, Serge Prokofiev & Warren Chappell's *Peter and the Wolf* (Knopf, 1940) or Esphyr Slobodkina's *Caps For Sale* (Addison-Wesley, 1947).

DIRECTIONS: Ask the child to listen to the story. As the child listens, say, "Listen for things that you would be happy about or things that would make you sad."

Before reading the story to the child ask, "What kind of problem do you have?" After the child tells the problem, say, "Someone in this story has a problem. Listen to see who has the problem."

EVALUATION: You are helping the child to deal with personal concerns, and at the same time, you are listening to find out if the youngster hears the story details.

activity 10: listening for rhymes of language (sounding words)

MATERIALS: Books that rhyme—for example—Al Perkins's *Hand, Hand, Fingers, Thumb* (Random House, 1969) or Dr. Seuss's *There's A Wocket In My Pocket* (Random House, 1974).

DIRECTIONS: Record the story on a cassette or read it directly to the child, stressing the rhyming word. Continue one fourth of the way through the story and begin to leave out the rhyming words that come at the end of the line. Look at the child and signal in your own way for your child to fill in the missing word.

EVALUATION: The filling-in process helps the child to listen not only to the story but also to the sounds of the language. The child is learning spelling patterns.

activity 11: listening to sentence patterns

MATERIALS: Children's books with the same sentence pattern used over and over again—for example, Philip D. Eastman's *Are You My Mother?* (Beginner Books, 1960), Al Perkins's *The Ear Book* (Random House, 1968), or Julian Scheer's *Rain Makes Apple Sauce* (Holiday, 1964). Many poems, too, will help the child to play with sentence patterns.

DIRECTIONS: Ask the child to listen to the story as you read. After reading the poem or story once, write one of the language patterns on a piece of paper. When you re-read the poem, leave a word or phrase out of a sentence and ask the child to replace it. Do not ask him or her to do it. Just leave out the word, look at him or her as you hesitate, and he or she will offer the word.

EVALUATION: The child is becoming aware of the sentence pattern—*subject, verb, direct object.*

activity 12: listening to spelling patterns (sound words)

A list of spelling patterns is included on page 269, of this chapter.

MATERIALS: A children's poem or story with consistent spelling patterns—for example, the "at" pattern:

I have a cat
Who has a hat
And in the hat
There lives a rat.
And with the rat
There lives a bat,
Who is very, very, very fat.

The rat and bat
Sleep on a mat,
Inside the hat
That's on the cat.
They play and eat and sleep
and chat,
Inside the hat of that cat.

S. M. GLAZER

DIRECTIONS: After reading the poem, ask, "What words sound the same?" As the child says the words with the rhyming pattern, write them on a piece of paper. Point to the words and ask, "What do you notice?"

EVALUATION: By stressing one spelling pattern, you are helping the child to learn that pattern. The game will further help to teach spelling patterns.

activity 13:
listening to
letter sounds
(decoding)

MATERIALS: The following, recorded on cassette tape:

G is for giant
gigantic, Oh gee,
He has a gem from the bottom of the sea.

J is for jolly, jovial and Jean
joke and Joan and jelly bean.

S. M. GLAZER

DIRECTIONS: Ask the child to listen to the tape. Say, "Listen for all of the words that begin with the same sound as 'jack.'" At the completion of the listening, say, "Tell me the words you remember." You can use this as an independent activity for testing the child's learning. Ask the child to find pictures of things that begin with the same sound as "jolly," "giant," "jack," "joke," and so on.

EVALUATION: You are teaching the child to hear consonant sounds at the beginnings of words. This can be done with all consonants.

**checking children's
ability to use
reading/listening skills**

The following group of activities can be used to test the child's ability with reading skills that involve listening.

**activity 1:
testing the
ability to
hear vowel
sounds at the
beginning
of words**

MATERIALS: A cassette tape with the following recorded by the adult.

A says A A A-a-a—a-a-a-a-a-a for a-a-a-ape.
Now say it with me—a-a-a-a-a-a-a-a-ape.
Can you think of other a's like ape?

S. M. GLAZER

DIRECTIONS: Play this for the child. The youngster can be directed to play it independently. This activity can be used for all vowel sounds. Use the following list of words for testing the ability to hear other vowel sounds.

Long Vowels	Short Vowels
a———ape	a———apple
e———eat	e———egg
i———ice	i———indian
o———open	o———octopus
u———use	u———up

**activity 2:
testing
beginning
consonant
sounds**

MATERIALS: Record the following:

Freddy fish
fries funny french fries
five full times in five days.

S. M. GLAZER

DIRECTIONS: Ask the child to listen to the silly ditty. Say, "Listen for one sound that you will hear over and over again."

When the tape stops, say, "Tell me *a* word that begins with the letter you heard over and over again."

the writing place

The writing place for beginning readers has two purposes: (1) to develop the mechanical writing skills, including punctuation, spelling, and handwriting and (2) to develop the writing skills that help children to transcribe their emotions and ideas into written form. There must be space for mechanical writing on tables and at desks, and there must be space for writing for relaxation. When children write to relax, they need not share or worry about the mechanical writing skills, if they choose. The writing place must be relaxed, well lit, and comfortable. The more children write, the more comfortable they will be with words in print. The first books children read by themselves should be self-written. In this way, children will understand the process of creating language for reading. This is extremely important for creating readers.

materials for writing

Materials for writing should be available to the child at all times. These include pencils, felt-tip pens, crayons, and chalk. Unlined and lined paper should be available. A guide for copying the correct letter shapes (see chapter 5, page 168) should be visible, displayed at eye level when the child is standing.

guidelines for writing

Adults and their behaviors concerning writing have great effects on children's writing growth. Two kinds of adult behaviors when children write must be considered: behavior when children write mechanically and behavior when children create ideas and express their feelings in writing. The following checklist should help adults to interact with children in ways that will encourage them to write. The desired response for each is "yes."

YES   NO

Children have available to them letters made of plastic, sandpaper, or wood, which they may use to trace.

Chairs and tables are child-sized.

There are erasers available for the child who can't stand a mess.

There are fat pencils and crayons and thin ones so that the child can select the one that seems easiest to use.

There is a pencil or crayon sharpener available.

There is plenty of paper available so that the child can take a clean piece at any time.

When children ask for help in drawing a letter or word, a model is provided so that he or she may copy the correct form.

When children ask to spell a word, it is written on a card. It is not spelled out.

guilding children's creative writing abilities

Children learn to write by writing and by seeing others write. As they have had freedom to speak in the very early years of life, so they must also have freedom when they learn to express ideas by writing. It is easy to accept children's immature speech, but we have a more difficult time accepting immature writing. Children must move through stages of writing as they have moved through stages of learning to speak. They must first scribble, then make lines deliberately on paper, then draw immature representations of the word, and then move into writing letters and words and, later, sentences and stories. They need time to share and evaluate their own writing growth.

The following guide will help adults encourage children to become creative writers. The response for all statements should be checked "yes" for children's maximum growth in written language.

YES   NO

I have provided materials to copy.

When children write, I encourage the behavior by acknowledging it with a smile, a positive gesture of my own, or a nod of the head.

When the child shows me the writing, I respond with one of the following remarks:

"Oh, I'm so glad you are writing."

"Tell about it."

"Read it to me."

"Oh, that's so good, Stephanie."

"Wow—You are writing lots. That's great!"

I instigate situations where children must use mechanical writing skills. Such situations might include the following:

An invitation.

A letter to a friend who is sick.

A letter to Santa Claus.

A thank you note.

A publication for the home library or a local library (the classroom, the school, the local children's branch of the library).

I do not use a red, blue, or green marking pencil to correct errors. I tell the child verbally and point with my finger only.

If the child wants to display a piece of creative writing—fine. Children can hang writing at any place they choose (refrigerator doors, bulletin boards, on the walls, on a door).

skills developed by writing

When children have the opportunity to practice mechanical writing skills, they will (1) develop the ability to form letters correctly; (2) use proper punctuation; (3) develop spelling skills; and (4) present original stories in a neat, well-constructed format suitable for sharing. Children will develop the ability to express themselves, their ideas and emotions, when writing for themselves. Without pressure to produce for sharing, they will compare ideas, describe feelings, and organize and summarize information. As they become adept with writing skills, they will prepare their creative writing excerpts to share with others.

activities for writing

Following are a series of activities for developing the mechanical or formal writing skills and for helping children to become creative writers.

activity 1: mechanical writing (letter formation)

MATERIALS: A chalkboard or pad

DIRECTIONS: Make letters to copy (see Chapter 5, Figure 5–1) and have a chalkboard or pad available for the child. He or she will use it to write, copy, and create letters and words.

EVALUATION: Children are teaching themselves to write.

activity 2: creative writing with oilcloth

MATERIALS: A piece of oilcloth or a piece of large, firm plastic sheeting, a broad felt-tipped marker, and a rag.

DIRECTIONS: Cut and then tape the oilcloth or plastic to the table top. Put the writing tool in a can or box and place it on the table. Leave the rag on the table so that the child can erase and clean the table covering after completing the writing experience. The child will go to the table and write.

EVALUATION: This provides an opportunity to write freely, to make shapes, and to use the muscles that are necessary for writing.

activity 3: posting words— creative writing

MATERIALS: A piece of tagboard and a magic marker.

DIRECTIONS: Write a list of words on the tagboard. These words should have meaning for the child. They should be posted in the places where children write. Suggested word lists include the following:

1. *Characters from favorite stories or T.V. shows.*
2. *Names of family members.*
3. *Names of favorite foods.*
4. *Special interest words—names of insects, pets, plants, or toys.*

Children will copy words to write stories. Give children new words upon request, writing them on cards 3 × 10 inches in size. Do not spell them. Write them on a card, say them to the child, and point to the word, running your finger under the letters as you pronounce it.

EVALUATION: Children are teaching themselves to read by writing.

activity 4:
spelling
patterns
for writing

MATERIALS: The movable charts shown in Figure 6–7, posted in a writing place. The strips of letters can be removed, and replaced with blends (sl, pl, tr, st). Pull the strips up and down, and make many words. The double circle is also movable. The smaller, inner circle turns if both are fastened with a paper fastener.

DIRECTIONS: Post the charts in a place where the child writes. Post the rotating charts so that a child can play with them. Make paper and writing tools available. Children will learn the words by copying them. If ready, children will say one of the following: "They all end in "at." "The charts have words that all end with "ate." Ask the child to notice the difference in the two words.

EVALUATION: Children are learning the spelling patterns.

activity 5:
creative
writing

MATERIALS: Cards (5 × 8 inches or larger) with the following phrases on them:

I like to eat————————————————————————————

——

I like to play with my——————————————————————

——

DIRECTIONS: Put these in a place to write. Encourage the child to complete the sentences. Do not correct any writing. Remember that this is creative writing.

EVALUATION: Children are organizing, comparing, and describing, using oral writing expressions.

Fig. 6–7

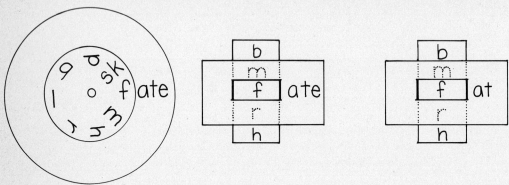

activity 6: more enticement into writing

MATERIALS: The following phrases, each written on a 5 × 8 inch card:

I like _____

I hate _____

I wish _____

I eat _____

I drink _____

If I could go anywhere in the world _____

If I could throw one thing away _____

I wish I had _____

My favorite person is _____

If I were an old pair of shoes _____

If my dog could talk _____

I'm very sad when _____

What is your favorite animal? _____

What is your favorite color? _____

What is your favorite food? _____

What is your favorite holiday? _____

I get upset when _____

_____

_____

EVALUATION: The child is organizing, comparing, and learning new words.

activity 7:
an apple tree

MATERIALS: A strong tree branch painted a bright color plastic bags, apples, small, strong pieces of string, labels, and a container filled with stones.

DIRECTIONS: Put one apple in each plastic bag. Tie the bags with pieces of string. Hang each bag on a branch and place the branch in the container filled with stones. This will secure the branch. Place a label around the tie of each bag (see Figure 6–8). Directions on each label should read as follows:

Label #1: Complete the following and then take an apple for eating.

When I eat an apple, I feel like _____

I feel that way because _____

Label #2: Complete the following, and take an apple. How many things can you do with an apple?

Label #3: Complete the following, and take an apple. What would a squirrel do with an apple? What do you do with an apple?

EVALUATION: Writing helps the child release ideas. It helps the child organize, compare, and classify ideas.

Fig. 6–8

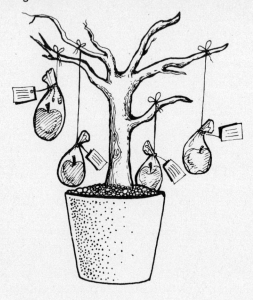

activity 8: conducting an interview

MATERIALS: The following Interview Sheet:

What is your name? _____

What do you like to do best? _____

What is the thing you hate most? _____

If you could pick one thing in the whole world, what would it be? _____

PROPS: *Reporters Visor*—Use an old baseball cap or construct as follows: Cut a strip of hard tagboard so that it fits around a child's head. The band should be about two inches in width. Fasten it with a staple. Cut a half-circle and tape it to the band to serve as a visor.

Microphone—Staple a styrofoam hamburger container from a fast-food restaurant together. Leave a small opening at the bottom. Place a tongue depressor in the opening. Paint the entire microphone with black paint. Use a white or yellow paint to dot the top part of the mike.

DIRECTIONS: Put the materials and props in a box labeled "Reporter for Local News." Your child will take a questionnaire, put the props on, and get to work. Help with spelling if asked. Do not correct.

EVALUATION: The child is learning to translate speech to print.

activity 9: writing letters

MATERIALS: The following slips of paper, each in an individual envelope labeled "Write a letter":

Write to get an autograph from your favorite television character.

Write to find out if you can visit the president.

Write to find out how ice cream is made.

Place a letter form like the following one with the envelopes:

Dear —————————

I would like to know ————————————————————

————————————————————————————————

————————————————————————————————

Thank you,

—————————————

DIRECTIONS: Place all of the materials in a box labeled "Write a letter." Invite your child to do one. You do your own.

EVALUATION: Creative writing and individual writing skills are practiced in this activity.

activity 10: punctuation— "a period means stop"

Write the following on a card or a large piece of tagboard:

Red means stop.
A sign means stop.
Watch when you come to the end of a sentence.
The dot says stop.

S. M. GLAZER

Make the following worksheets:

I like ice cream.	*I like ice cream*
I like tea.	*I like tea*
I like children.	*I like children*
Children like me.	*Children like me*

DIRECTIONS: Place the two worksheets together. When children select them, ask, "How are they different?"

EVALUATION: You are helping your child to see likenesses and differences and to learn how a period is used.

activity 11: poetry extension

MATERIALS: Each one of the following, written on a card:

I wish ————————————————

I promise ————————————————

I remember ————————————————

I imagine ————————————————

DIRECTIONS: Read one card to the child. Ask the child to complete the sentence. At a later time, say, "Use a color when you write the sentence." (Example: I wish I had a super *yellow* car.) Parent and/or child collect and compile these to make a poem.

EVALUATION: You are guiding your child in sentence construction.

activity 12: writing poetry

MATERIALS: Put each of the following on a card:

Love is a feeling that lasts a while.	*Ideas come sometimes And fade easily.*	*Friends Are rare and precious.*
The wind flys by In a storm.	*A butterfly flits up and down, up and down Until away.*	*A puppy grows to be a dog; How lovely!*

DIRECTIONS: Place writing paper and writing tools in a box with these cards. Say, "Clap the little poem. Be sure that you use as many claps as the poem on the card. Then write your own poem."

activity 13: the balloon surprise

MATERIALS: Write messages on small slips of paper. Roll one up and slip it inside a balloon. Inflate the balloon and tie.

DIRECTIONS TO CHILDREN: Take a balloon, pop it, and write an answer to the message.

SUGGESTED MESSAGES:

1. *You are an icicle and the temperature has just risen to 100 degrees. What will you do to save your life?*

2. *You have just returned from a trip where you have discovered the treasures of an ancient kingdom. What would you tell the world about it?*

EVALUATION: These are writing incentives that guide children in written expression.

activity 14: sustained writing time

MATERIALS: An egg timer, writing tools, a table or desk to write on, and a notebook for each person.

DIRECTIONS: Each person should have his or her own note pad and find a place to write. Say, "I am going to set the timer. When it begins, you write. Do not look up or get up. We will not answer phones or talk. Ready? Write." Rules must be followed, and writing must be practiced daily. If sharing takes place, it should be voluntary. Adults may encourage children to share by saying, "Oh, listen to what I have written" or "Look at my writing." Accept all writing, pictures, scribbles, and copied language. These are beginnings for developing creative writers.

EVALUATION: You are helping to build the writing habit. The child is practicing mechanical and creative writing skills.

the acting place

Acting for the beginning readers is a way to respond to stories, language, and pictures in literature. Some children will act out their own stories, using the details from a story they have read or heard. Others will borrow plots from authors and add their own details. Children will take their own points of view about ideas in literature and act them to confirm their opinions. Since these acting experiences are personal, they make the literature an intimate experience.

The acting place should be roomy—for movement. Fabric, stuffed animals, toys, telephones, dress-up clothing, and books should be included. These props will help children to remember characters, times, places, and incidents in literature.

guidelines for adult behavior
when children act

Observing children at play provides us with information about their comprehension ability. We watch how and what they make sense of. The following checklist offers suggestions for adult behavior when children act. Checking "yes" for each category says that you are an astute observer who is guiding children to releasing their ideas by acting.

YES   NO

When a child is acting alone, I do not interfere.

I do not question a child about acting. I encourage the child to talk about it by saying one of the following:

"You enjoyed acting, didn't you?"
"Tell me about your acting."
"What toys do you like to act with?"
"What do you think about when you act with these toys?"

I encourage acting by providing props for children (clothing, dolls, household items, etc.). I schedule adult acting activities on a regular basis for children who prefer acting in small groups and who respond to total group direction.

I provide hand puppets, dolls, marionettes, and other "hide-behind" actors for children who cannot act for themselves.

I provide activities that direct children to move from physical, nonverbal drama to drama with oral language.

When the chlld acts, I do not interfere. I understand that acting is a form of expression controlled by social, emotional, and physical development.

reading skills developed in the acting place

When children act, they manipulate ideas with their bodies. This helps them to interpret, to make sense of—for themselves, in their own ways—the characters' times, places, and ideas in literature. When children act, they are developing their abilities to compare characters and story themes, one to another. They are making decisions about their literature choices, developing their own sense of taste. They are increasing their abilities to use adjectives to describe incidents in books.

acting activities that help beginning readers

activity 1: acting to interpret story theme

MATERIALS: Two pieces of children's literature—for example, Marcia Brown's *Once A Mouse* (Scribner, 1961) or Ruth Krauss's *Happy Day* (Harper & Row, 1949).

DIRECTIONS: Place the two stories or books next to one another. Be sure that the children know these stories. Ask the children to act how they feel about these books. Offer one of the following directions:

1. *Act out how you feel about the story titles.*
2. *Act out how you feel about the places in which the stories occur.*
3. *Act out how you would feel if you lived in either of the places the story occurred.*
4. *Act out how you would feel if you were in the same situation as one of the main characters (be specific). How would you change one of the characters to make him happier (sad, unique, excited, enlightened)? Act it out.*

EVALUATION: The child is comparing his own experiences with those he or she has heard about in literature.

activity 2: making decisions about literature

MATERIALS: Props related to several characters in stories that each child has read.

DIRECTIONS: Ask children to select two props that remind them of two characters in the story. Ask them to act out all of the things they remember about each.

EVALUATION: You are asking children to recall and to classify information. This also involves getting story details.

activity 3: describing literature

MATERIALS: A few pieces of cloth, each a different color.

DIRECTIONS: Ask children to select a piece of fabric that reminds them of a special book. Then say, "Find the book." Read the book as each child acts out part or all of the story, using the fabric as a prop.

EVALUATION: Children are interpreting the story in their own way. This is the same as rewriting a story or retelling it.

activity 4: classifying ideas from literature

MATERIALS: Use Syd Hoff's *Albert The Albatross* (Harper & Row, 1961) or Joseph Low's *A Mad Wet Hen and Other Riddles* (Greenwillow Books, 1977).

DIRECTIONS: Ask your child to do *one* of the following at a time:

1. *Act out all of the funny things you remember about the story.*
2. *Act out all of the sad things you remember about the story.*
3. *Move your body into the shape you would be in if you were in the same situation as the major character (name the character).*

EVALUATION: Your child is classifying and describing story content.

activity 5: becoming sensitive to writing styles

MATERIALS: A poem with a consistent sentence pattern—for example:

DRUM BEAT
Hear the story of the drum,

Hear its BEAT BEAT BEAT,
While you read or you listen
Feel the pulse—tap your feet.

Up in front or in back
Calling, "DUM DUM DUM,
Keep in time, follow me
Heed the rhythm of the drum."

Yes, in pre-historic times
I was FIRST BEAT BEAT
And by now I've been marched
In parades on ev'ry street,

In parades with a band
I am STRAPPED THIGH HIGH
There I bobble up and down
People wave as I go by.

But on stage in a band
On a SLANT I STAND
Hear the drummer sound the beat
With the drumstick in his hand.

All this tickles, tickles me
so I GRIN GRIN GRIN
For the snares underneath
Shake and wiggle near my skin.

In Peru or Iraq
I go DUM DITTY DUM
Hear the drummer sound the beat
With his fingers and his thumb.

In Sudan, for example,
I can TALK TALK TALK
For my beats are like words
Flying faster than a hawk.

North or South, East or West
I call "DUM DUM DUM
Keep in time, follow me
Heed the rhythm of the drum."

Flutes and tubas and the strings
Also PLAY WITH ME
And the drummer tunes my kettle
So it fits the music's key.

Big or small, loud or soft
I'm a CHUM CHUM CHUM
That is why people dance
To the rhythm of the drum.

From the stage or the street
When you HEAR BEAT BEAT,
Keep in time, follow me
Feel the pulse—tap your feet!

RONALD HYMAN[1]

DIRECTIONS: Say, "I am going to read this poem. Listen to it. I will read it a second time. As I read, you move to the beat of the language."

EVALUATION: You are asking children to become sensitive to the language of literature by translating it into physical activity.

activity 6: literature and drama for the child alone

MATERIALS: A full-length mirror, free-standing, a paper bag with the name of a story or poem written on it, the book that contains that story or poem, and props that fit the characters in that story or poem.

DIRECTIONS: Place the bag next to the book on a table. Post the following sign next to the bag:

ATTENTION!
There are things inside this bag
that go with this book.
Open the bag.
Take out the things and act.

EVALUATION: You are asking the child to recall the story.

[1] Ronald Hyman's poem is reprinted with permission of the author.

**activity 7:
acting
special
words**

MATERIALS: A group of 3 × 5 inch cards, each with one of the following written on it.

happy   miserable   tired   exhausted
starved   battered   worn   furious
as loud as thunder   as hungry as a bear
as old as a dinosaur   as cold as ice
as dirty as garbage   as quiet as a mouse
as shiny as a diamond

DIRECTIONS: Put all the cards in a box. Label the box as follows: "Pick a card. Act it out."

EVALUATION: Children are reading language and illustrating it by acting out their abilities to make sense of the information.

**activity 8:
puppets and
drama**

MATERIALS: Puppets that represent story characters, books that accompany the puppets, and a puppet stage or a table to use for a stage.

DIRECTIONS: Place the books and puppets together in the acting place. Children will go there to act out the stories.

EVALUATION: Children are responding to literature, developing their ability to recall details and make summaries.

the reading place

The reading place for the young reader is a study at home, in school, or in a public library. It must have a variety of books and magazines based on children's interests and reading abilities. It should invite children into reading. Colorful shelves for storing books and comfortable cushions, chairs, and rugs for lying upon and reading should be all around. There must be books that have limited numbers of words and books that are written by children themselves. There should be books for reading to children so that they can listen. The reading place is everywhere, but book storage should be in one central location.

materials for reading

A place to store books and organize them is important in order to stimulate enthusiasm about books. Shelving can be purchased, but it is easily made and inexpensive to construct. Shelving can be easily constructed from bricks and boards. For building such book shelves, the design shown in Figure 6–9 is suggested.

MATERIALS: 24 bricks and 3 pieces of wood 1 × 12 × 36 inches.

arranging materials

Books ought to be classified according to content. Animal books should be with other books about animals. Dictionaries should go together. Folktales and fantasy books should be shelved together. It is important to remember to classify books according to content, not reading level. Designating a grade level to books says, "Stay away, I'm not for you" to some children. Children will learn for themselves which books they can read.

books for beginning readers

Books included in the beginning reader's library should be based on children's interests as well as their reading ability. Take your child to the public library. Notice the books that the child selects. Observing which books are selected will give you a fairly good indication of the child's interests.

Fig. 6–9

If your child has a difficult time select-ing books, place a few of the children's books on a table. Say, "Select one." Observe the child's choices. The following check-list will serve as a guide for determining your child's reading interests.

YES   NO

CATEGORY 1
My child selects books about:
  Family members, daily home activities,
  daily problems.
  Sharing, responsibility.
  Gaining self-confidence.
  Learning in school, accomplishments,
  tasks, or chores.
  Adult occupations.

CATEGORY 2
Stories will usually have an animal as the main character.
My child selects:
  Tall tales and humorous stories.
  Plays with dialogue.
  Stories with animals that do the talking.
  Stories that have a moral (often a fable).
  Stories that deal with emotions.
  Stories that teach a lesson on life.
  Informational books about plants, animals,
  weather, and so on.

CATEGORY 3
My child selects books:
  With many pictures.
  With single words on a page.
  With words repeated over and over again.
  With large print.
  With short sentences.
  With repeated sentence patterns, such as
  "I like apples," "I like peas,"
  "I like cake."

Only a few of the many books available for the new reader are listed here. Use this list as a guide for selecting others as needed.

EASY-TO-READ BOOKS:

Charlys, Remy and Supree, Burton. *Mother, Mother, I Feel Sick* (Parents Magazine Press, 1966).

Emberly, Barbara and Emberly, Ed. *One Wide River to Cross* (Scholastic Book Service, 1970).

Gackenbach, Dick. *Mother Rabbit's Son Tom* (Harper & Row, 1977).

Harlan, Glen. *Petey the Pup* (Scholastic Book Service, 1972).

Hoff, Syd. *Albert the Albatross* (Harper & Row, 1961).

———. *The Horse in Harry's Room* (Harper & Row, 1970).

Merriam, Eve. *Mommies at Work* (Scholastic Book Service, 1973).

Minarik, Else H. *Father Bear Comes Home* (Harper & Row, 1959).

———. *Little Bear* (Harper & Row, 1957).

———. *Little Bear's Visit* (Harper & Row, 1961).

Thompson, Vivian. *Sad Day, Glad Day* (Scholastic Book Service, 1970).

Van Gelder, Rosalind. *Tricky Questions to Fool Your Friends* (Scholastic Book Service, 1971).

Weil, Lisl. *Monkey Trouble* (Scholastic Book Service, 1972).

Wells, Rosemary. *Noisy Nora* (Scholastic Book Service, 1976).

OLD FAVORITES: Some favorites and "musts" for all young people's libraries are suggested below. These should be read and re-read again and again, for they are the ageless wonders of talented authors who know about children's interests.

Low. Joseph. *A Mad Wet Hen and Other Riddles* (Greenwillow/ Morrow, 1977).

McCloskey, Robert. *Homer Price* (Viking, 1943).

Parish, Peggy. *Thank You, Amelia Bedila* (Harper & Row, 1964).

FAVORITE FOLKTALES, FAIRYTALES, FABLES, AND LEGENDS:
Annett, Cora. *How The Witch Got Alf* (Watts, 1975).

Brown, Marcia. *Dick Whittington and His Cat* (Scribner, 1960).

———. *Once A Mouse* (Scribner, 1961).

Brown, Margaret Wise. *Goodnight Moon* (Harper & Row, 1957).

Brown, Margaret Wise. *Brer Rabbit: Stories From Uncle Remus* (Harper & Row, 1941).

Burton, Virginia Lee. *The Little House* (Houghton Mifflin, 1942).

Courlander, Harold. *Terrapin's Pot of Sense* (Holt, Rinehart and Winston, 1957).

Fatio, Louise. *Happy Lion* (McGraw-Hill, 1954).

Galdone, Paul. *The Old Woman and Her Pig* (McGraw-Hill, 1960).

Milne, A. A. *The World of Pooh* (Dutton, 1957).

Mosel, Arlene. *Tikki Tikki Tembo* (Holt, Rinehart and Winston, 1968).

Potter, Beatrix. *The Tale of Peter Rabbit* (Warne and Scholastic Book Service, 1972).

Sendak, Maurice. *In The Night Kitchen* (Harper & Row, 1970).

———. *Nutshell Library* (Harper & Row, 1962).

———. *Where the Wild Things Are* (Harper & Row, 1963).

Steig, William. *Sylvester and the Magic Pebble* (Simon & Schuster Inc., 1969).

guidelines for adult behavior

The following checklist will help adults to guide children when they read. The desired response is "yes" to all statements.

YES   NO

The place to read is comforable and child-like with small chairs, tables, some cushions or carpet squares, and good lighting.

I read to the child daily. I schedule a daily time when children read for themselves.

Sustained Silent Reading (see chapter 5, page 218) is a routine event.

When children select books, I observe and collect information about their selections in order to discover their interests and habits.

*When the child asks, "Is this book O.K.?",
responses might be one of the following:
"If you like, it is fine." "How do you feel
about it? Of course." "Did you check with
the fist full of words rule?" (described on
page bottom).*

*When children select, I respond by saying one
of the following: "I'm glad to see that you
have chosen a book yourself" or "Oh, how
nice that you chose it on your own!"*

*If the child chooses to read aloud and misses
a word, I tell it to the child immediately. I
do not say, "Sound it out." That breaks the
story comprehension.*

*I do not stop the child in the middle of
reading to ask questions. This, too, interrupts
comprehension.*

*I do not discourage a child from selecting the
same book over and over and over again. I
understand that the selection of the same
book builds confidence with printed
language.*

helping children to select books

It is important that children learn to select books that they like, ones they are able to read independently. Adults must provide children with a tool for self-selection so that they will be able to choose books on their own. The "fist full of words" check is one that has served as a guide for many youngsters. Present the following rules to the child.

1. *You may select any book you like.*
2. *When you pick the book, you must be sure that you are able to read it. This is how you check yourself: Begin to read the book and hold up one hand with your fingers closed to make a fist. Each time you do not know a word, lift one finger. If you lift five fingers before you reach the end of the page, the book is too hard.*
3. *Try another book, and begin again.*

activities in the reading place

It is important to remember that the place to read can be anywhere. The following activities will guide in the development of places for developing independent readers.

activity 1: reading inside and outside

MATERIALS: Easy to read books

DIRECTIONS: Place two or three books next to your child's bed, in the pantry, in the play yard, in the car, in the garage—anywhere there is room. This will help the child to realize that reading is an activity that happens everywhere.

activity 2: reading together as a chorus

MATERIALS: Books with repeated language—for example, Bernadine Cook's *The Little Fish That Got Away* (Addison-Wesley, 1956) or Barbara Emberly's *One Wide River To Cross* (Scholastic Press, 1970)—and poems, including "1-2 Buckle My Shoe" (nursery rhyme) and Paul Galdone's illustrated "The House That Jack Built," (McGraw-Hill, 1961).

DIRECTIONS: Read the story or poem to the child. As you read, have the child say as much of it as possible with you. Make the book available for the child at leisure. At a later time, re-read the story to the child. Encourage the youngster to read it with you. This is chorus-like reading. You have read as a choir reads.

activity 3: sustained silent reading

MATERIALS: A timer, a book for each family member, and a place to relax with the book.

DIRECTIONS: SSR activities (as described in Chapter 5) can become longer as the child reads more fluently. A maximum of fifteen minutes is suggested. Certain days may be set aside for sharing reading experiences. Encourage sharing by saying one of the following: "I read the most exciting thing in my book!" "I liked a part of my book and want to tell you about it."

activity 4: oral reading

MATERIALS: A book and a listener.

DIRECTIONS: An important note—The child must see a purpose to oral reading. The child should never be asked to read aloud without reading the material silently first. Reading aloud is performing and therefore requires rehearsal. Oral reading is then becoming re-reading with purpose. Valid purposes for children to re-read aloud include the following:

1. *Sharing some part of a book or poem that they found exciting, interesting, or fun.*
2. *Reading a dialogue where other people are involved.*
3. *Proving something by going to the book and finding the facts.*
4. *Reading just because the child wants to.*

Oral reading without a purpose is a senseless and unnatural behavior.

activity 5: reading children's writing

MATERIALS: Books and poems written by children that have been saved over the years.

DIRECTIONS: Set aside a special place where books authored by all family members are kept. A special time should be set aside, at least once a week, for reading and looking at literature, poetry, captions, phrases, and pictures created by members of the family. Be sure to collect enough to form a home family library.

the playing place: building skills

Games that teach and test decoding (sounds of language) and comprehension (sense of language) comprise the materials for play. All materials should be classified according to the skill each tests and teaches.

adult behavior when children play

Keenly observing children's behavior is the most important way to find out which skills they are able to use for reading. The following checklist will help you to observe each child's readiness for formal reading.

skill development for play

The following list of skills are generally mastered during the first two years of formal reading instruction. Use this table as a guide for developing and selecting games for play.

Table 6–5

CHILD'S BEHAVIOR	ANALYSIS OF BEHAVIOR
The child selects the same game over and over again.	That's usually good. It is built-in drill. That's how children teach themselves and learn.
When the child selects games that involve two or more people, the youngster always wins.	That's probably why that game is selected. Success breeds success.
The child never selects a game without my help.	Then the child must be directed to the materials. Label a game with the child's name or offer a choice of two games.
The child wants to play reading games instead of other recreational activities.	That's great. The child is self-teaching. That's a goal for all children.
The child prefers homemade games to those I buy.	The child is telling you that personal attention is needed from the adult. The child needs the warmth and security of the adult in order to confirm his or her success.

                                                          YES   NO

DECODING SKILLS FOR FIRST-, SECOND- AND THIRD- YEAR READERS:
Can hear consonant sounds at the ends of words.
Can identify the following consonant blends:

bl, cl, fl, gl, pl, sl,
br, cr, dr, fr, gr, pr, tr,
sc, sk, sm, sn, sp, st, sw, tw
dw, qu, ke

Can identify three-letter blends (consonant clusters): str, spl, thr, sch, spr, scr, shr
Knows long vowel and short vowel sounds.
Knows inflectional endings: 's, ed, ing.
Understands the concept of compound words—that a compound word is two separate words that form a new one with a new meaning.
Recognizes basic spelling patterns:

		Yes	No
ad	*ape*		
ed	*epe*		
id	*ipe*		
od	*ope*		
ud	*upe*		
ag	*ar*		
eg	*er*		
ig	*ir*		
og	*or*		
ug	*ur*		
am	*at*		
em	*et*		
im	*it*		
om	*ot*		
um	*ut*		
an	*ade*		
en	*ede*		
in	*ide*		
on	*ode*		
un	*ude*		
ap	*ake*		
ep	*eke*		
ip	*ike*		
op	*oke*		
up	*uke*		

Knows how to pronounce au, aw, and al with l, or the following:

au, as in haul
aw, as in hawk
al with l following, as in all
al with k following, as in walk
al with t following, as in salt
ow, as in cow
oi, as in oil
ai, as in tail
ue, as in true

Knows the two vowel rule ("Two vowels go
walking, the first one does the talking" or "Say
the name of the first vowel."):

ee
ea
oa
ai

Understands how contractions are formed:

can't
wouldn't
shouldn't
don't

Can read words that include silent letters:

gnome
know
wrap
*lam***b**

Can read the sounds of vowels when they are
controlled by the letter "r":

er as in her
ir as in sir
ur as in fur
Sometimes "or" as in worse

activities for play

Games for the development of the skills
necessary to sound out words are included in this section. *A
game for teaching the skill and another that tests the same
skill are presented together.* All children should be exposed first
to teaching materials before using test-games. The only time
test-games should be used first is when you are assessing a
child's knowledge of the skill being tested.

The activities parallel the skills listed
on pages 269 to 271.

<table>
<tr><td>

**activity 1:
teaching
final
consonant
sounds**

</td><td>

MATERIALS: Tagboard, a marker, pictures (cut from magazine) of objects whose names all end with the same consonant, and glue.

DIRECTIONS: Cut out the pictures of the objects whose names end with the same consonant sound. Select, for example, the letter "t" and cut out pictures of a foot, a hat, a pot, a rat, and a puppet. Paste these on the board (see Figure 6–10).

DIRECTIONS FOR USE: On a tape recorder, record the following: "Hi, I am going to name the things on this board. I will begin at the arrow and follow it along until I reach the end. Follow with your finger as I say the names of the objects. You say them when it's your turn. Ready? Go. Put your finger on the first picture. It is a foot. Read: Say, 'foot' (pause). Next—hat. Ready? Say, 'hat' (pause)." Continue in this fashion.

</td></tr>
<tr><td>

**activity 1a:
testing
final
consonant
sounds
(two players)**

</td><td>

MATERIALS: Tagboard cut into 5 × 7 inch cards, a marker, clear Contact paper, pictures of objects that end with the consonants "t," "d," "b," "k," "l," "p," and so on, and buttons.

DIRECTIONS: Rule the cards into sections and write a consonant in each section as shown in Figure 6–11. Place the pictures of objects in an envelope.

DIRECTIONS FOR THE CHILD: Pick a picture. Find the letter that ends the name of the object. Put a button on that letter. If

</td></tr>
</table>

Fig. 6–10

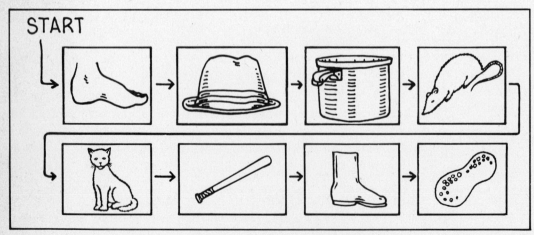

START

272

Fig. 6–11

d	k	l
s	p	b
r	z	g

more than one child plays, the first one to cover all the letters wins.

activity 2: teaching two-letter consonants (blends)

MATERIALS: 2 × 2 inch cards, a felt-tipped marker, and clear Contact paper.

DIRECTIONS FOR CONSTRUCTION: Write each of the letter combinations shown in Figure 6–12 on a series of 4 × 4 inch cards:

Make one card with "fl" written on it.

Put all of the cards except the "fl" card in one envelope. Place the "fl" card in a separate envelope marked with "fl." Put both envelopes in a large envelope with the following directions:

Make as many words as you can that begin with "fl." Copy them on a piece of paper. Repeat this activity with all the consonant blends (see checklist on page 269).

Fig. 6–12

ip	at	y	ap	op	it	ick	ock	/	fl

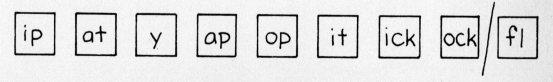

activity 2a: testing the ability to use blends (two-letter consonants)

MATERIALS: Small pieces of paper or cards (2 × 4 inches), a marker, and scissors.

DIRECTIONS FOR CONSTRUCTION: Print the following words on the cards:

sk/ip	fl/ip	cl/ap
gr/ab	fl/ag	tr/ace
st/ay	sl/ide	dr/ape
sk/ate	sm/ash	fr/y
sw/eep	cr/ash	pr/etty
gl/ass	br/aid	tr/ap
bl/ock	fl/y	gr/ow

Cut the cards after the blend as shown by the slash (/). Place all the cards in an envelope.

DIRECTIONS FOR CHILD: Make as many words as you can. Write them down if you like.

activity 3: learning to hear short vowel sounds in words (a teaching game)

MATERIALS: Tin cans or cylindrical plastic containers, paper, marker, masking tape, and pictures.

DIRECTIONS FOR CONSTRUCTION: Tape the paper to the can or plastic food container as illustrated in Figure 6–13. Cut out small pictures from a magazine of words that have short vowel sounds in them. Place these in the container. Cover the container.

Fig. 6–13

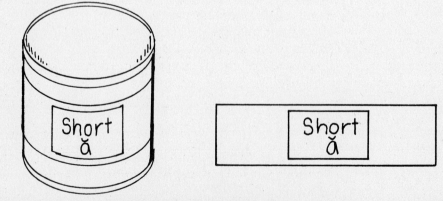

DIRECTIONS TO CHILDREN: "Look at the letter name on the front of the can. Name each of the pictures as you take one out at a time. Each object's name has a short 'a' in it." This can be done for each of the vowels. Suggested pictures include the following words:

Short "a"	Short "e"	Short "i"
hăt	bĕd	lĭp
măn	mĕn	pĭt
căt	slĕd	chĭp
răt	rĕd	chĭck
păn	nĕst	lĭd

Short "o"	Short "u"
hŏg	bŭg
blŏck	rŭg
dŏll	dŭck
pŏt	trŭck
bŏx	drŭm

**activity 3a:
testing short
vowel sounds
with words**

MATERIALS: Objects whose names contain a short vowel sound, a box, and the following objects: gum, a hat, a bell, a toy cat, a pen, rice, a small glass, a piece of paper, and a jar.

DIRECTIONS FOR CONSTRUCTION: Place all the objects in a box.

DIRECTIONS: Write the following on a card:

Make two piles from these objects. One pile should have things that have short vowels in their names. The other should **not** *have a short vowel sound in its name.*

**activity 4:
teaching
inflectional
endings ("s")**

MATERIALS: Tagboard cut into pieces 3 × 10 inches, a felt-tipped pen, pictures of objects (can and cans, shoe and shoes, doll and dolls, book and books).

DIRECTIONS: Draw or cut out pictures of the above objects. Paste them on pieces of tagboard. Place the single item on the left side of the card and the multiple items on the right side. Label the items as shown in Figure 6–14. Cut the cards down the middle. Place them in an envelope marked "An 'S' Puzzle Game."

Fig. 6–14

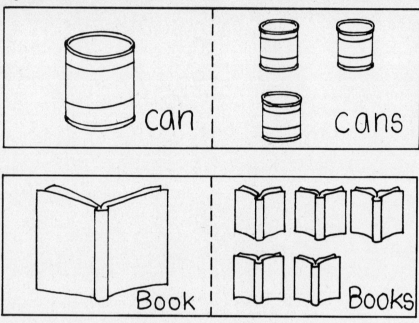

DIRECTIONS TO CHILDREN: Match the cards.

MATERIALS: Tagboard or corrugated board cut into a game board size (approximately 14 × 14 inches), markers, drawings of objects (many objects, such as animals, people, toys, automobiles, and others), dice, buttons, a small juice can, and small pieces of tagboard cut into playing card size, and two players.

DIRECTIONS FOR CONSTRUCTION: Paste pictures of objects (one per card) on each playing card made from tagboard. The cards should include objects like the following:

apple/apples   *top/tops*
pear/pears   *book/books*
toy/toys   *radio/radios*
orange/oranges   *skate/skates*
fork/forks

Make a game board as shown in Figure 6–15.

276

Fig. 6–15

boys	toy	skate	pots	toys
cards				ropes
pot		cards		radio
apples	top	card	books	Start

DIRECTIONS TO CHILDREN: Place dice in a can. Shake the can and spill the dice out. Begin at the square that says "Start." Move as many spaces as shown on the dice. Look at the word and find the picture in the pile of cards that represents the word. If the child cannot find the picture, the person who gets to the end of the board first wins.

**activity 5:
teaching
compound
words**

MATERIALS: Tagboard cut into squares 3 × 3 inches, marker, scissors, a box in which to store the game, and some blank pieces of paper.

DIRECTIONS FOR CONSTRUCTION: Draw the pictures shown in Figure 6–16 and 6–17, one on each card. Write the name of the object on the back of the card, as illustrated.

DIRECTIONS TO CHILDREN: Pick two cards. Put the pictures together and say the names of the objects in both pictures. Turn the cards over and place the two words together. Copy that

277

Fig. 6–16 and 6–17

word on a piece of paper and draw a picture of the object. Do this with as many cards as you can.

activity 5a: testing compound words

MATERIALS: The following compound words, each written on a 3 × 3 inch card: doghouse, basketball, toothpaste, afternoon, sunshine, bluebird, sidewalk, and driveway, along with some paper and pencils.

278

DIRECTIONS FOR CHILDREN: Look at each card. Find two words in the word you see and write down each of them.

activity 6: using word patterns to make new words (a teaching game)

MATERIALS: Tagboard cards (10 in all) cut into rectangular pieces 4 × 8 inches, a felt-tipped marker, picture of an object whose name has one syllable and ends with the word pattern being taught, clear contact paper, and a grease pencil (dark color).

DIRECTIONS FOR CONSTRUCTION: Write a pattern on top of each card (an, en, in, on, un, at, it, et, or ut). Next to that pattern, paste the picture of an object whose name ends with the pattern. Label the picture with its name. Draw in the rest of the cards as illustrated in Figure 6–18.

DIRECTIONS TO CHILDREN: Write as many words as you can by adding a letter in front of each pattern. Say the word.

activity 6a: testing word patterns

MATERIALS: Oak tag cut into two circles 6 and 8 inches in diameter, a paper fastener, a marker, and scissors.

DIRECTIONS FOR CONSTRUCTION: Fasten the two circles together at the center, placing the smaller one on top. Write one consonant on the edge of the inner circle. Write each of the ten word patterns on the outer circle, rotating the circle as you write (see Figure 6–19).

DIRECTIONS TO CHILDREN: "Spin the wheel and say the word that's created." The children might, at times, write words they say.

Fig. 6–18

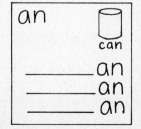

Fig. 6–19

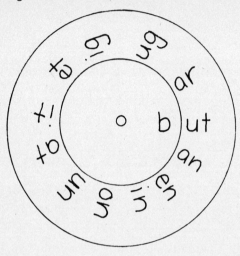

activity 7:
teaching
consonant
clusters

MATERIALS: Tagboard cut into 7 cards 6 × 6 inches and a marker.

DIRECTIONS: Divide each card as illustrated in Figures 6–20. Write one word in each box that begins with the same consonant cluster. Clusters include "scr," "shr," "spl," "spr," "str," "thr."

Fig. 6–20

splash	splat	scrap	screw	spring	sproat
splinter	split	scrub	scratch	spray	spruce

string	stripe	three	throne	shred	shrub
strut	strap	throw	thread	shrimp	shrink

280

Fig. 6–21

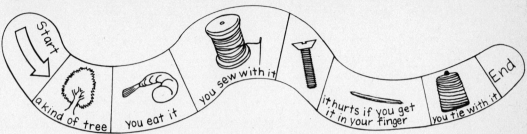

Put all the cards in an envelope with some blank divided cards and a few pencils.

DIRECTIONS TO CHILDREN: Pick a card. Take a piece of paper. Read each word and draw a picture of the object or activity. What do you notice about each word? What is the same? What is different?

activity 7a: testing consonant clusters

MATERIALS: Tagboard, felt-tipped markers, pictures of objects that begin with the consonant clusters, "spl," "scr," "shr," and "thr," dice, and two players.

DIRECTIONS: Cut the tagboard into a snake-like form. Divide it as shown in Figure 6–21 and paste a picture between each division.

DIRECTIONS FOR USE: Throw the dice. Move as many spaces as the dice indicate. Say the name of the object. Name the consonant cluster that begins the object's name. The first one to get to the end wins.

ALTERNATE DIRECTIONS: Same as above. When the child lands on the picture, he or she is to say another word that begins with the same consonant cluster.

activity 8: teaching different long vowel sounds (ai, ue, ea, ee, oa)

MATERIALS: A string about a yard long, tagboard cards cut into pieces 6 × 2½ inches, and a marker.

DIRECTIONS: Write one of the words shown in Figure 6–22 on each card.

DIRECTIONS TO CHILDREN: "Read each word. Write down all of the things that are the same for each. Look at the letters and the words and listen to the sounds." Children will realize that each word has two vowels in the middle and that the first one

Fig. 6–22

sleep	coat	sea	seam	stream	cloak
chain	team	creek	street	tea	
soap	meat	boat	pail	tail	
queen	sleeve	train	plain		

is heard. Rule: Two vowels go walking; the first one does the talking.

activity 8a: testing ability to read words with vowels in the middle

MATERIALS: A large paper bag, 3 × 5 inch index cards, and a Magic marker.

DIRECTIONS FOR CONSTRUCTION: Write the following words, one to a card:

sleep	street	train
stream	boat	seam
creek	sleeve	team
meat	sea	soap
queen	chain	tail
coat	tea	plain
cloak	pail	

Put all of the cards in the bag. Label the bag with the child's name (see Figure 6–23).

DIRECTIONS TO THE CHILD: Shake the bag. Take out a card. Say the word. Name the two vowels you hear in the middle of the word. Say another word with that same sound in the middle. After the child has selected words, tape them on a long card, as shown in Figure 6–24, and hang. This makes a lovely mobile.

282

Fig. 6-23 and 6-24

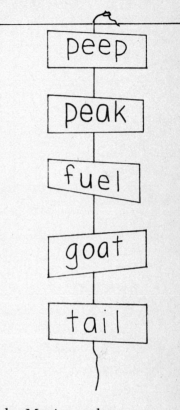

activity 9: teaching contractions	MATERIALS: Tagboard, scissors, and a Magic marker.

DIRECTIONS FOR CONSTRUCTION: Cut tagboard into four pieces, each 12 × 8 inches. Draw a line down the right side of the card and fold it over two inches as illustrated in Figure 6–25. Fold out again and divide the card into fifths by drawing vertical lines on the card.

Fold the right section of the card so that it covers the second word. Write the contracted part of the word on the back flap—"n't," "'re," "'s," and "'ve" words for each card include the following:

n't	're	's	've
can not	*they are*	*it is*	*I have*
would not	*we are*	*let us*	*I had*
could not	*you are*	*he is*	*We have*
do not		*she is*	*We had*
is not			*you have*

283

Fig. 6–25

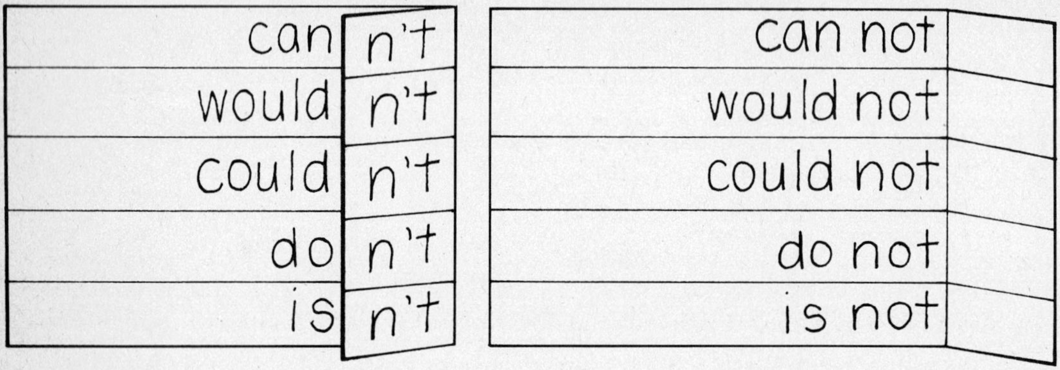

can	n't	
would	n't	
could	n't	
do	n't	
is	n't	

can not	
would not	
could not	
do not	
is not	

DIRECTIONS FOR USE: Pick a card. Read the two words. Fold in the flap. Now read the words. What has changed? How are they different?

activity 9a: contractions— a floor game for two people or more

MATERIALS: Oilcloth, preferably in bright colors, felt-tipped markers, scissors, and 3 × 5 inch index cards.

DIRECTIONS FOR CONSTRUCTION: Cut 16 feet. Make these by tracing around your bare foot (See Figure 6–26). Write one of the following on each foot:

can't	let's	I'm
don't	won't	wasn't
she'd		
he'd		

isn't	wouldn't	I've
hadn't	couldn't	he'll
		you've
		shouldn't

Write each one of the following on an index card:

can not	let us	I am	is not	would not
he will	you have	do not	would not	I have
had not	could not	should not	she had	was not
				he had

284

TO PLAY THE GAME: Lay the cut-outs of feet on the floor. Pile the cards face down on the floor next to the first foot. Player number one selects a card. The child is to step on the foot that represents the contraction. A group of people may play this, each rotating turns.

activity 10: teaching silent letters

MATERIALS: Tagboard, a Magic marker, scissors, and brown paper cut into long strips.

DIRECTIONS: Cut the tagboard into the shape of a television set. Cut two slits, one at the top and one at the bottom of the screen. Print the words from the following word list about three inches apart on a strip of paper. There should be approximately five to seven words on a strip. Insert the strip of paper into the television screen as shown in Figure 6–27.

gnome	know	wrap
gnat	knew	wring
gnaw	knock	wrinkle
	knife	wrapper
	knit	write
	knuckle	wrote
		wrist

DIRECTIONS TO THE CHILD: Read all of the words on the television set. What is the same about these words? What do you hear? What don't you hear?

activity 10a: testing the ability to use silent letters

MATERIALS: Writing paper, pencils, pictures of objects, people, and places cut out and placed in a box, and word lists.

DIRECTIONS FOR CHILDREN: Pick a picture, Pick a word list. Write a silly story, riddle, poem, or joke, using the words. Any list can be used with any picture.

List 1	List 2	List 3	List 4
gnome	knowledge	wrecked	wrinkle
knew	wrestle	wriggled	knee
knot	gnaw	gnat	knife
knuckle	lamb	knot	knit
wrote	gnashed	wring	knowing
wrong			

Fig. 6–26 and 6–27

let's

can't

she'd

I'm

cards

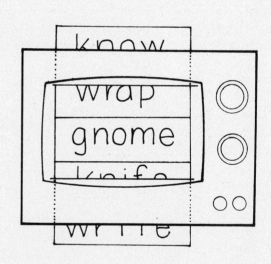

know

wrap

gnome

knife

write

activity 11: teaching "au" and "aw" sounds

MATERIALS: A felt-tipped marker and a large piece of poster paper.

DIRECTIONS: Act out the following for the child. Say, "I am going to do something. Watch as I do it." Then, crawl like a baby. The child will begin to yell out what you are acting. When the child says, "crawl," write it on the paper. Say, "I am going to do something again. Watch." Yawn with all of the body and facial activity you can use. Again, the child will offer words to describe the activity. When the child says, "yawn," write it on the paper. Say, "When I eat caramel, or taffy, or chewy foods, I chew and chew with this part of my mouth. Watch it work." Chew. Say, "Which part of my mouth do I use?" Children will offer suggestions. Write the word "jaw" when the child says it. Say, "A person has hands and feet. I have a pet dog and he walks on ──────." When the child offers the word "paw," write it on the paper. Now you have a list of words as follows:

crawl   jaw   yawn   paw

Say, "What do you notice about the words?" "How are they different?" Wait for suggestions. "How are they the same?" When children note that all the words have "aw" in the middle, ask if they know other words that have "aw" in their spellings. Make a list of these.

activity 11a: testing the use of words with "aw"

MATERIALS: 3 × 5 inch index cards, felt-tipped markers, and two or more players.

DIRECTIONS FOR CONSTRUCTION: Make small cubes from the cards. Paste six 3 × 5 cards together with tape to make a cube. Write one word on each side (see Figure 6–28). Make a number of these cubes. Write any of the following words on the cubes:

faucet	*brawl*	*pawn*	*crawl*	*thaw*
will	*salt*	*malt*	*wall*	*talk*
because	*caught*	*jaw*	*paw*	*halt*

DIRECTIONS FOR USE: Roll a block. Say the word that appears on the top. You get one point for each word you can say. Then make up a word that has the same vowel combination that

Fig. 6–28

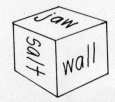

appears in the word. You get two points for this. Take turns and keep score. The first person to reach ten points wins.

This activity may be adopted to test all double vowels used in words.

activity 12: teaching the sounds of vowels controlled by the letter "r"

MATERIALS: The following poems, each posted on a wall or door, but only one poem at a time:

There was a nurse with a purse,
The purse was so full
It burst.

If you have a germ
I want it first
I'm dying of thirst
Said the girl as she twirled.

S. M. GLAZER

DIRECTIONS FOR USE: Read one poem to the child. Then say, "Read along with me." When you complete the poem, ask "What do you notice about the poem?" The child will notice that the words rhyme, that the poems are silly. The child will discover that many of the words, especially those that rhyme, have "er," "ir," or "ur," in them.

activity 12a: testing letters controlled by "r"

FOLLOW-UP GAME: Put cards in an envelope, each with one of the following words printed on it:

fur	sir	her	purse	verse	curl
turn	burn	perk	thirst	dirt	birth
perch	tern	serve	burst	hurt	nurse
curb	jerk				

Make bingo cards, filling in each space with one of the words. Leave one square free and write the word "free" in the space.

DIRECTIONS FOR PLAYING: Play bingo. Have a child read a word from a card and another player place a marker on the correct word if it appears.

the construction place

Construction encourages the development of vocabulary and helps children to develop independent learning habits necessary for reading. New experiences bring new words that involve new ideas. Children create objects and then find words to describe them. Getting an idea and making an object means making that idea come alive. When children construct, they are guiding their own behaviors and directing themselves to use materials and to work independently.

The constructing area can be in the kitchen, in a workroom, in a basement, or in a storeroom where the child can cook, sew, draw, or paste ideas together to make ideas into concrete objects.

materials for construction

Construction means cooking, planting and growing seeds, and taking care of home pets. These kinds of activities require some of the following or similar materials:

A hot plate, cooking utensils, food-wrapping materials, spices, and baking materials; fabric, needles, thread, and other materials for sewing; seeds of all kinds; house pets and outdoor insects that can be taken inside with care.

books that accompany construction

"How-to-do-it" books are wonderful for learning to read and follow directions. Cookbooks, sewing books, and books about planting and other construction activities will help to develop many of the reading skills important to 6- and 7-year-olds. The following list in Table 6–6 includes only a few of the books available for children's construction activities.

skills developed when constructing

Children develop comprehension skills when they construct. The following comprehension skills and

Table 6-6

AUTHOR	TITLE	PUBLISHING COMPANY
Baker, Jerry	*Plants Are Like Kids*	Grossett & Dunlap, 1978
Chernoff, Goldie T.	*Easy Costumes You Don't Have To Sew*	Scholastic Book Service, 1977
———.	*Clay Dough, Play Dough*	Walker, 1974
Deacon, Eileen	*It's Fun To Make Pictures*	Grosset & Dunlap, 1974
Gilbreath, Alice	*More Fun & Easy Things to Make*	Scholastic Book Service, 1977
Gilbreath, Alice	*Beginning Crafts for Beginning Readers*	Follett, 1972
Hoff, Syd	*How To Draw Cartoons*	Scholastic Book Service, 1975
Moore, Eva	*Seabury Cook Book for Boys and Girls*	Seabury, 1971
———.	*Lucky Cook Book for Boys and Girls*	Scholastic Book Service, 1970
Pountney, Kate	*Creative Crafts for Children*	Faber & Faber, 1977
———.	*Fun with Wool*	Grosset & Dunlap, 1974
Sokol, Camille	*Lucky Sew-It-Yourself Book*	Scholastic Book Service, 1971
Wyler, Rose, and Ames, Gerald	*Funny Magic: Easy Tricks for the Young Magician*	Scholastic Book Service, 1975

abilities used for reading throughout life are developed when children construct:

The ability to schedule events in order to complete a project.

The ability to locate answers to specific problems that occur (getting meaning).

The establishment of purpose for an activity.

The ability to record information (summarize and get details).

The ability to see the relationship between one idea and another.

The ability to show proof of facts.

The ability to use references (books and people).

The ability to follow written directions.

The ability to use graphic instruction (maps, charts, pictures, and diagrams).

290

guidelines for adult behavior when children construct

Adults must help children to become independent in their learning by providing assistance and materials when it is requested. The following checklist should provide information for appropriate adult behaviors that encourage children to learn when they construct. The desired response to all behaviors is "yes."

	YES	NO

I prepare sections of a room for construction.

I prepare materials for construction so that they are easily available to children.

All materials and instructions for use can be used independently by the child.

When a child asks for help, I direct his or her questions so that the child can see exactly where help is needed. For example, if the child says, "I need help," I might say one of the following:

> *"Tell me what you need help with."*

> *"How would you like me to help you?"*

> *"Show me exactly what is giving you problems!"*

The child and I have developed rules for behavior during construction. We have reviewed these at least three times.

Children know that they must clean up and put away all materials after construction.

Children know that they are to share some aspects of construction. They can tell, act, write, or draw it.

COOK WITHOUT COOKING:

**activity 1:
nut surprises**

MATERIALS: A large mixing bowl, 1½ cups of chopped nuts (walnuts, peanuts, or cashews), 1 cup seedless raisins, 1 cup pitted dates, 2 teaspoons of honey, butter or margarine (enough to butter hands), and a large plate.

THE BEGINNING OF FORMAL READING INSTRUCTION IN SCHOOL

ADULT ACTIVITY: Chop the nuts and place them in a bowl. Place a word card in front of the bowl that says "chopped nuts." Place raisins in another bowl and label in the same fashion. Do the same for the dates and the honey (see Figure 6–29). Place all of the ingredients on a table.

INSTRUCTIONS: Write these directions and post them for the child to see:

Pour everything in the big bowl.
Put butter all over your hands.
Mix everything with your buttered hands.
Take a little bit of the mix.
Roll it into a ball.
Make as many balls as you can.
Put the balls on the plate.

FOLLOW-UP ACTIVITY FOR RESPONSE: Have each child decide how to share the nut ball experience. Tell a friend how to make nut balls, draw a picture, or write about it.

EVALUATION: Your child is getting details, using new vocabulary, and getting "main ideas" about learning to summarize the most important passage of reading.

Fig. 6–29

activity 2: stuffed dates or prunes

MATERIALS: Pitted dates or prunes, peanut butter, a small spoon, and one large plate.

ADULT ACTIVITY: Take the pits out of the prunes or dates or buy pitted fruit. Place the fruit in a bowl. Place the peanut butter in a bowl. Set the spoon on the table next to the two ingredients. Label each item with a word card (see Figure 6–30).

INSTRUCTIONS FOR CHILDREN: Stuff peanut butter into the holes in the fruit. Put the stuffed fruit on the plate.

FOLLOW-UP ACTIVITIES: Ask children to respond in one of the following ways. Write the directions for making the stuffed fruit, tell how you made the fruit on a cassette tape, draw a picture of the fruit, or write when you think these would be good to eat.

EVALUATION: The child is organizing and finishing a project in order to learn to see a project to completion.

PLANTING ACTIVITIES:

activity 3: planting seeds

MATERIALS: Containers for planting, such as empty milk cartons, plastic food containers, or empty tin cans, soil kept in a bucket, and a watering can.

ADULT ACTIVITY: Supply a packet of seeds with a picture of the grown product on the package. If possible, have some grown plants available for the child to inspect. Try to use plants that have a fast germination period (radishes, marigolds, or lettuce).

Fig. 6–30

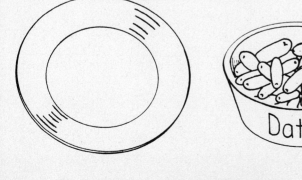

Children like to see things happen quickly. Place the planting materials in a corner of the room where there is workspace. Post a piece of tagboard near the area and hang a pencil from a string, as shown in Figure 6–31.

INSTRUCTIONS TO CHILDREN: Read the sign and do what it says. When you are finished planting, write what you see. Come back tomorrow and look at your plant. See if there is something new to describe. Write about how it look on a chart like the one shown in Figure 6–32. (For those who cannot write, encourage them to draw a picture of changes.)

EVALUATION: Children are encouraged to predict outcomes.

activity 4: comparing and planting

MATERIALS: Two containers for planting, seeds to plant in two containers, and a watering can.

ADULT ACTIVITY: Place lots of the same kind of seeds in a box. Be sure that the seeds are labeled with the name of the plant as well as with a picture. Place the seeds, soil, and planters near a window area. Post a large piece of paper or tagboard near the area and hang a string from a pencil next to the paper.

INSTRUCTIONS TO CHILDREN: Plant two groups of seeds. Put one near the window. Put one under the table so it does not get light. Water both each day. Write about what happens.

FOLLOW-UP ACTIVITIES: Children are to record the differences

Fig. 6–31 and 6–32

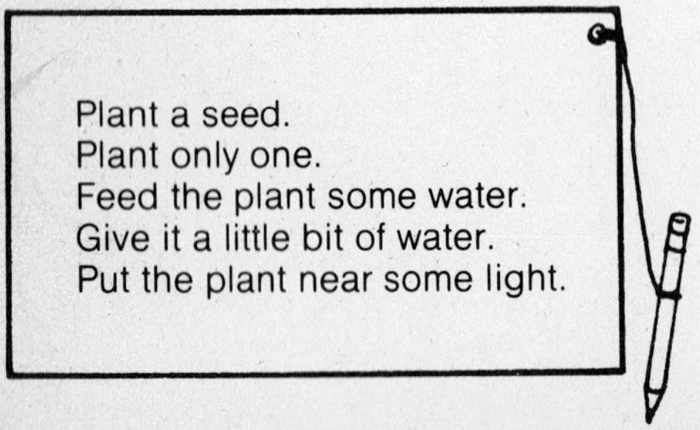

Plant a seed.
Plant only one.
Feed the plant some water.
Give it a little bit of water.
Put the plant near some light.

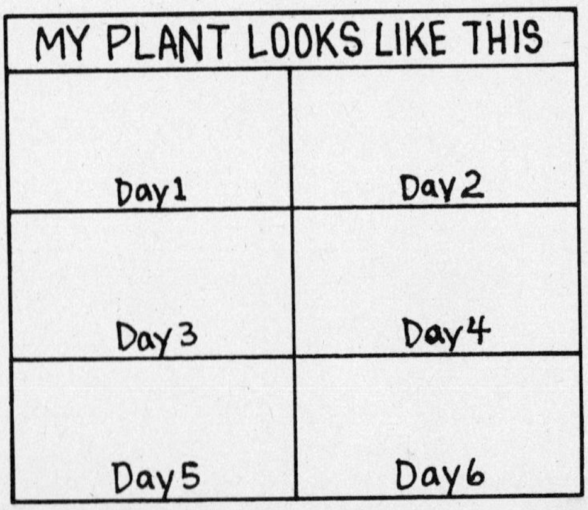

MY PLANT LOOKS LIKE THIS	
Day 1	Day 2
Day 3	Day 4
Day 5	Day 6

in plant growth. They may share these by telling the differences, reading the differences, or showing and telling the differences. EVALUATION: Children are learning to collect facts by locating information needed to plant the seeds.

activity 5: vegetables and planting

MATERIALS: Vegetables that root (potato, carrot, onion, turnip) a large glass, toothpicks, and water.

DIRECTIONS: Show your child how to place the toothpicks into one of the rooting vegetables, as illustrated in Figure 6–33.

DIRECTIONS TO CHILDREN: Root your vegetables in water. Watch them every day. Share by:

1. *Drawing a picture of the changes.*
2. *Writing about the changes you see every day.*
3. *Telling about the changes you see on a tape cassette.*
4. *Taking pictures of the changes with a camera and making a book from the pictures. Write about each picture.*

EVALUATION: Children are learning to recognize causes, predict outcomes, and explain predictions.

Fig. 6–33

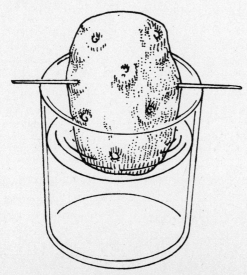

ANIMALS AND INSECTS ACTIVITIES:

**activity 6:
preparing
animal
houses**

MATERIALS: Determined by the animal. Rodents (hamster or gerbil), glass cage with wire cover, wood, cardboard tubes (paper towel or toilet paper rolls), and wood shavings or cut strips of newspaper.

DIRECTIONS FOR CONSTRUCTION: Put all of the materials on a table. The child's job will be to put the materials in the container and prepare it for the animal. Discussion is necessary and should include the following facts:

1. *Gerbils and hamsters chew things.*
2. *They like to get out of their cages when no one is looking.*
3. *They need exercise.*
4. *They like to be warm.*

INSTRUCTIONS: Begin a discussion. Offer the first fact and ask, "What do you suppose you must get for the animal so that it can chew?" Continue with the second fact and ask, "What must we do to keep them in the cage?" "Why is that important?"

A NOTE OF IMPORTANCE: It is important that children do the responding and that the adult ask the questions. Children are then involved in problem-solving situations.

When the discussion is completed—and it might take a few days—post the following near the materials:

Set up the cage.
Make it fun for your pet.
He wants to chew.
He wants to run.
He wants to hide.

EVALUATION: Children are learning to take responsibility.

**activity 7:
problem
solving
with junk**

MATERIALS: Pieces of sponge, pipe cleaners, pieces of styrofoam, pieces of wire, and scissors.

DIRECTIONS TO CHILDREN: Try creating something by pushing and twisting. Push things into other things.

FOLLOW-UP: Write about how you made your creation. Draw pictures of it.

EVALUATION: Children are using descriptive skills to illustrate their productions. This teaches the use of adjectives.

COOKING WITH HEAT:

Activities that involve using a stove, an oven, or a hot plate need careful rules. Cooking is an exciting experience that helps to develop much language. It can be hazardous, however, if used improperly.

activity 8: vegetable soup

MATERIALS: Select 3, 4, or more from the following: carrots, turnips, potatoes, onions, string beans, tomatoes, leeks. You will also need paring knives, a large pot, salt, and Anne McGovern's *Stone Soup* (Scholastic Press, 1971).

DIRECTIONS: Read the story together. Later, begin to make "stone soup." Lay all the vegetables on a table. Place a paring knife on the table. Children and adults together cut and pare the vegetables. During the paring, discussions about the vegetables can center around the following questions:

1. *How are these different?*
2. *How are they the same?*
3. *Describe the smell of the onion.*
4. *Describe the shape of the turnip.*
5. *Where do the vegetables come from?*

Place all the vegetables in water in a kettle. Simmer slowly for approximately two hours.

FOLLOW-UP ACTIVITIES: Make a list of the following words and post it:

Simmer
Vegetables
Onions
Carrots
Turnips
String beans
Tomatoes

The following activities can evolve:

1. *Have the child make a list of all of the vegetables according to color (or shape, or other uses, or likes and dislikes).*
2. *Ask the child to make a book describing his cooking experience.*
3. *When shopping at the market, ask the child to notice the vegetables. Note which ones are together.*

EVALUATION: Children are developing vocabulary, organizing information, and analyzing materials.

activity 9: eskimo cookies (no-bake)

MATERIALS: 1½ sticks of butter, ¾ cup of sugar, 1 teaspoon of water, ½ teaspoon of vanilla, 3 teaspoons of cocoa, 1½ teaspoons of wheat germ, 2 cups of oatmeal, bowls and spoons for measuring and mixing, confectioners' sugar, and a cookie sheet.

DIRECTIONS FOR ADULTS: Place all the materials on a table with the appropriate measuring utensils. Copy the following recipe on a large sheet of paper and place it on the table.

HOW TO MAKE COOKIES
Mix the butter; make it soft.
Add the sugar; mix again.
Add the water, vanilla, cocoa, and wheat germ. Mix.
Cover the bowl.
Put it into the refrigerator until tomorrow.

Label each ingredient with the appropriate quantity required for the recipe.

Place the following instructions on the cooking table the next day:

Get your cookie mix.
Take a little bit of the mix.
Roll it into a ball.
Put the ball in the sugar and roll it around.
Put the ball on a tray.

FOLLOW-UP ACTIVITIES:

1. *Write the recipe so that someone else can make the cookies.*
2. *Describe the taste of the cookie.*

EVALUATION: Children are learning to follow directions, to complete an activity, to use new vocabulary, to record information, to summarize the experience, and to work independently at a task.

a concluding remark
about construction

Construction activities also include magic tricks, art, games, holiday activities, sewing, cooking, puzzle making, and so on. Refer to the books listed in Table 6–6, on page 290. Children construct, and at the same time, they will be developing the skills necessary for becoming active, interested, and creative readers.

the thinking place: pulling
all experiences together

Children think in all learning places, so every area is a thinking place. It is important, now that the children are reading, to offer them some directed thinking/ reading activities. Directed activities give children specific instructions for proceeding with reading tasks. Children can be directed to read and find facts, details, or ideas. Directed activities that encourage free expression are also needed. Feelings, emotions, and personal challenges are expressed by children when they have been directed to read in order to find out how they feel about the events in a story. Guidance and direction help children to see purpose in language activity.

suggestions for directing
children in language
activities

Children can be guided in thinking and reading by having questions asked about their activities. Questions must encourage personal responses to reading and should be worded so that all of the child's answers will be covered. The following are a list of question starters that will encourage free thinking.

How would you feel if ——————————————————— ?
What do you suppose would happen if ——————————— ?
How would you have changed the story (recipe, trip, meal, and so

on) ——————————————————————— ?
How would you change the story (or event) to make it more exciting

(or happier or sadder) ————————————————— ?
Which part of the activity (or story, poem, trip) did you like best?
Which part of the story seemed true?
Which part of the story is like another story that you have read?
Which part of the trip (vacation, cooking event) is like the last trip
(vacation, cooking event) we took?

It is important to accept all responses to the questions. Adults must not place a value on the child's answers to questions. This will stop him or her from answering in a creative way. The child will put aside his or her own answers and develop the ability to answer as you want him or her to. This stifles thinking.

guiding children before
reading a selection

Often children have a difficult time getting into books. Some need a push to begin. An interesting question before reading a self-selected book might encourage the child who doesn't really care to read with some gusto. The following suggestions can be adapted to almost all literature read by children:

Read to find out which part you like best.
Read to find out why the story is called —————————— .
Read to find out who the main character is —————————— .
Read to find out certain facts. (Be specific.)

It is important to help children to love the language in books. They must be free to respond to language and literature in their own ways, without adult censorship. Children must be sure that adults really and truly accept their thoughts about their reading and language activities. Without this security, they will have problems being self-confident readers.

AN END TO A STRONG BEGINNING: A SUMMARY

Just as children's destinies for the desire to become literate lie in the hands of those adults who set up an exciting environment to stimulate that desire, so the true conclusion of this book lies in the minds of the readers. It is important, however, to tie together a few ideas in one last effort to convince parents and teachers that their role in children's learning to read is a crucial one and that their behaviors are the most significant variables in children's reading success.

The comprehensive process of learning to read begins long before the child sounds out the symbols from a page of print. It begins when the infant reacts to the world and to the language they use in the crib. Children learn from the first day of life to read adult reactions to their behaviors. Infants move about playfully as they manipulate their bodies in response to appropriate play materials provided by adults. These playful movements elicit favorable adult responses—a pat on the stomach or a soft rub on the cheek. These adult responses say, "Hey, I like you and your response to our environment." The child learns very quickly to move his or her body in order to get these adult responses once again, for they bring joyful satisfaction to the infant's life. As children gain the facilities necessary to manipulate the sounds of language, they receive adult responses as well. When Mother hears "Mama," for example, positive responses are awarded the baby.

302

So "Mama" is learned. Next time the baby says, "Mama," one of the child's purposes for making that sound will most probably be to receive a happy smile, a rubbing on the stomach, or a lift into the air from Mother or Father.

Babies play with objects, hear sounds, smell good things, taste exciting flavors, and see new worlds each day they grow. They learn the language that describes the sensations offered by activities that stimulate learning through the senses and that are offered in the adult-prepared environments. Children are provided with the incentives (the activities and objects) for learning language, and their instinctive curiosities help to provide a desire for the purposeful explorations they must engage in in order to find out about things in their worlds. They discover the nature of the materials in their special places, and they learn the language that describes the wonders of their environment. As they learn language, children are building the foundations necessary for formal reading. They are collecting words that represent ideas, situations, happy times, and sad times, and they are organizing these recollections in order to respond to these same kinds of situations once they read about them in books.

Children summarize the ideas from language experiences all through their early years into "mind collections." When they read words, they will recall these summarized collections, which help to tell what words in print describe. These mind collections, which have resulted from the manipulation of materials and events prepared by adults in environments conductive to learning, are the foundations—the incentives—that help the child to set personal purposes for reading. Children know about the events and objects in life and can relate to them. The knowledge of things in life will permit the child to deal with the written symbols that represent these ideas and events because they have personal, purposeful meaning.

Activities and materials have helped the child to construct the purposes for learning to read words, for they have had experiences in constructing purposes for responding to and reading the environment from their first days of life in the crib. This last statement is almost paradoxical in nature, for it has been the adult who has had the purpose or incentive to teach the child to read, to rear the child, and to help the child learn. However, when adults set out to teach reading, the adult goal must be viewed first and foremost as making learning to read a child-centered behavior through which children teach themselves in the presence of learning facilitators, adults, materials, and environments that have been carefully and meticulously created by adults in order to help youngsters to create their own incentives for language and reading learning. Once the natural desire for learning to read is created, the battle of literacy is almost accomplished. Language has become an exciting experience, for it has been learned delightfully in conjunction with art, music, literature, and drama as well as through daily love and conversation from those in the home environments. Just as a ski slope provides a firm, solid base to support the powdered snow for skiing, so children's language experiences in exciting environments from the first day of life support the learning of reading skills that children are expected to master once they are in school.

Children's physical growth, language growth, writing growth, and reading growth are parallel in development. The body, the sounds of language, and the scribbles on pages—all first experiences for the child—are clumsy in nature. The infant body moves all together, without differentiated muscle control. Infant speech sounds are also haphazard, without any seemingly meaningful message. The child's scribbles are uncontrolled and meaningless. These unrefined movements become controlled as children grow into the ability to take control of the variables that they encounter in the world. When children begin to learn to read, they sometimes hold the book right side up and sometimes upside down, turning globs of pages without any direction. With time and muscle growth, they will hold the book correctly and turn one page at a time. Experiences in thier minds give them information so that they can make believe and tell a story about pictures before they read the words. With time and involvement with varied experiences that use language—action and spoken, written, and artistic language—children will build the foundations, the resources that are needed for direct reading instruction. Once the skills are acquired through purposeful interactions with these exciting experiences, the rest of the child's reading life will be full of adventures, feelings, and facts. Reading will become the activity through which youngsters learn and think about things in their worlds. Reading will be an active process where one human manipulates or organizes the ideas of another human to add to the ones already existing in the reader's mind.

Not all children will make their lives in a world of books, but there is no reason for books and reading to be alien to any youngster. Because the gift of literacy is unique only to the human species, it is one of our means of survival in a perplexing world. Books and the ideas in them are the world's investments in future success—the coat-of-arms, so to speak, that preserves the legacy of human ideas through the ages. Books are the maps of mental navigation through all content worlds, fact or fancy. Books offer prescriptions for remedying the confusions of a constantly changing universe. Books serve as human sources of mental relief in times of emotional searching.

The more competent children are with language, the more competent they will be when reading. Just as a language base builds the foundation for competent readers, so competent readers build a foundation for a society that has the capacity to keep itself healthy and productive. Children's destinies for literacy are in the hands of the adults who rear them into learning. **Wake up to the world of reading, adults, and children will be happier for it!**

FURTHER READING: BIBLIOGRAPHICAL NOTES

Many of the ideas in this book have come from the works of outstanding psychiatrists, educators, linguists, and psychologists. Listed below are their works. Listed also are other useful writings currently available concerning the young child's total growth and development. Of course, this list is incomplete, since there are many resource books that I am not familiar with. There are books on child development and rearing as well as on the reading/language process, many with varying points of view. The following annotated bibliography is recommended for professionals as well as interested laypersons.

general growth and development

Elkind, David. *A Sympathetic Understanding of the Child: Birth to Sixteen*. Boston: Allyn & Bacon, 1975. The author presents a brief and informal discussion of the major aspects of child and adolescent development. Development is viewed in the context of the social relationships in which the child lives and learns. Mental development is discussed, relating it to Jean Piaget's theory. The author gives year-by-year descriptions of developmental changes from birth to sixteen consistent with the research of Arnold Gesell.

Gessell, Arnold and Frances L. Ilg. *Child Development.* New York: Harper & Row, 1949. The forerunners of Drs. Spock and Burton White, Gesell and Ilg provide remarkably useful information concerned with expected preschool behaviors. Although old (1949) and in many ways contradictory to the ideas that early experiences influence development, the information concerned with maturation and child rearing is interesting.

Stone, J. and J. Church. *Childhood and Adolescence: A Psychology of the Growing Person.* New York: Random House, 1964. This widely used introductory textbook in child development looks at human growth in a humanistic way. It presents an excellent general assessment of the young child.

White, Burton L. *The First Three Years of Life.* Englewood Cliffs, N.J.: Prentice-Hall, 1975. After a lifetime of research, Dr. White has written this book emphasizing that infancy and toddlerhood are the years that form the foundation for all later development. The book offers valuable insights into the effects of parents and the environment on young children.

All of these books were used as sources of information to develop the growth and development charts in Chapters 3, 4, 5, and 6. Descriptions of behavior throughout the book are gleaned in part from the works of these outstanding scholars.

intellectual and social growth

Ault, Ruth. *Children's Cognitive Development.* New York: Oxford University Press, 1977. A simplified version of Jean Piaget's theory of cognitive growth as well as the research efforts of experimental child psychologists who have ideas different from those of Piaget are presented in a useful and enjoyable way. Although not a layman's guide to child rearing, it is helpful to anyone who has contact with young children.

Buhler, Karl. *The Mental Development Of The Child.* New

York: Arno Press, 1975. Growth and development are discussed in relationship to progress in the forms of child activity—in speech, in thinking, in play, in drawing, and in social behavior. This book is highly recommended for professionals as well as for educated laypersons.

Elkind, David. *Child Development and Education: A Piagetian Perspective.* New York: Oxford University Press, 1976. Sections two and three of this book are most helpful in understanding the child and his intellectual growth. Section three helps in the application of the theory of cognitive (intellectual) growth—what to do to help its maximum development.

Linstrom, Miriam. *Children's Art.* Berkeley, Calif. University of California Press, 1970. Realizing the fact that the art of children discloses their characteristic mode of understanding—their visual realization in imagery at different stages of their development—the author has written a wonderful book from which we can learn much about children's intellectual growth. The underlying assumption taken by the author is that children have a native ability to express themselves in visual terms—symbols—just as they have an ability to express themselves verbally. The book traces the development of visualization in children between the ages of 2 and 15 from the earliest scribbles to pictures that show evidence of organization.

Lowenfeld, Viktor and W. Dambert Brittain. *Creative and Mental Growth.* Sixth Edition. New York: Macmillan, 1975. This book traces the development of children's art and creative expression, viewing these in the context of cognitive and social growth. The study of children's art from age 1 through age 12 is fascinating and sheds much light on the development of written language. This text served as a guide for developing the sections of this book concerned with writing activities and for the growth of written expression charts. It is an outstanding volume.

Piaget, Jean. *The Language and Thought of the Child.* New York: Harcourt Brace Jovanovich, 1926. This classic work is the basis on which other books in this section were written. It should be read by all professionals who are concerned with child rearing and education.

language development

Chomsky, Carol. *The Acquisition of Syntax in Children from Five to Ten.* Cambridge, Mass. M.I.T. Press, 1969. This classic study served as a guide for the development of language activities. The expected use of grammatical patterns in children's speech, as indicated by this research, is the basis for many of the activities in this book, particularly those in Chapters 5 and 6.

Chomsky, Noam. *Syntactic Structures.* The Hague: Mouton, 1957. This monumental work is reflected through each section of this book that deals with language acquisition. It is, in a sense, the bible of language theorists. In this book, Chomsky explains his theory of transformational generative grammar. This is an extremely difficult text to understand. It is suggested that those interested in understanding Chomsky's theory read Frank Smith's *Comprehension and Learning: A Conceptual Framework for Teachers* (Holt, Rinehart and Winston, 1975), for an exceptionally well-done simplification of this theory.

————. *Reflections on Language.* New York: Pantheon, 1975. For those interested in further study of the deriviations of language, this is an excellent reference.

Dale, Philip S. *Language Development.* Second Edition. New York: Holt, Rinehart and Winston, 1976. This book presents the syntactic, semantic, and phonological developmental patterns of language. Included are discussions of language development and its relationship to learning reading and writing skills. Sociological differences in language are touched upon. Technical in nature, this book is an excellent resource and was used as a reference for the language development charts included in this book.

Menyuk, Paula. *The Acquisition and Development of Language.* Englewood Cliffs, N.J.: Prentice-Hall, 1971. This pioneer in transformational grammar research as it relates to language acquisition has written a very fine technical representation of language acquisition. This work is based on the research performed by Dr. Menyuk and her colleagues.

————. *Language and Maturation.* Cambridge, Mass. The M.I.T. Press, 1977. This book offers an overview of the current literature in language development from birth to adulthood. The text includes discussions of language throughout life and hypothesizes the causes of the developmental changes. The book summarizes, in a well-organized way, some current discoveries on language development. It is a fine guide for the language educator.

Robinson, Violet B., Dorothy S. Strickland, and Bernice Cullinan, "The Child: Ready or Not?" in Lloyd O. Ollila. Editor, *The Kindergarten Child and Reading.* Newark, Del. International Reading Association, 1977, pp. 13–39. This article is concerned with reading readiness. Much of the information dealing with reading readiness mentioned in Chapters 5 and 6 is referred to in some way in this scholarly work.

Smith, Frank and George A. Miller. *The Genesis of Language.* Cambridge, Mass.: M.I.T. Press, 1966. This important book for professionals is concerned with language acquisition. It offers a complete description of children's language development. It was used to develop most of the sections concerned with language learning and its relationship to reading.

Weir, R. H. *Language in the Crib.* The Hague: Mouton, 1962. The studies of language development provided in this book served as a strong influence supporting the "playing with language" activities, especially those in Chapters 2 and 3.

historical, psychological, and pedagogical aspects of the reading/language process

Arbuthnot, May Hill. *The Arbuthnot Anthology of Children's Literature.* 4th Edition, revised by Zena Sutherland. Glenview, Ill.: Scott, Foresman, 1976. This anthology of children's literature is an excellent source for teachers and parents. It offers an array of good poetry, folk tales, fables, myths, epics, hero tales, and modern fantasy as well as realistic stories, including historical fiction, biography, and informational selections. Adults who care about children will find this reference book excellent for identifying good authors and illustrators for them. An excellent group of professionals, led by Dr. Zena Sutherland, has helped to revise this mammoth volume.

Bettelheim, Bruno. *The Uses of Enchantment.* New York: Knopf, 1976. Dr. Bettelheim, in this enchanting book, shows how fairy tales—Cinderella, Jack and the Beanstalk, The Three Little Pigs, and others—work in supporting children's emotional growth needs. It is through the characters in the tales, this world-renowned psychologist believes, that children begin to sense for themselves feelings of love, courage, hate, envy, and more. This is an essential book for everyone who cares about guiding children's emotional growth through literature.

Durkin, Dolores, "What Classroom Observations Reveal About Reading Comprehension Instruction," *Reading Research Quarterly* 14:4, 1978-1979, pp. 481–533. This major contribution to the field of teaching reading examines whether reading comprehension is being taught in classrooms. The study clearly demonstrates the distressing fact that very little is known about teaching for reading comprehension. The implication from this study, most meaningful to this text, is the fact that those teaching reading to children must work together to find solutions for teaching comprehension.

Gans, Roma. *Common Sense in Teaching Reading.* New York: Bobbs-Merrill, 1963. Dr. Gans, one of the most exciting figures in the reading profession, has written a sensitive book in which reading and its explanation is based on a "common sense" approach to life. The how and why of reading are carefully and academically presented.

Gelb, I. J. *Study of Writing.* Second Edition. Chicago: University of Chicago Press, 1963. The history and evolution of writing are presented. Writing is discussed as an expressive form of communication, and its future in relationship to speech, art, and religion is reviewed. This is an important book for understanding the relationship and importance of writing to reading.

Goodman, Kenneth S., "Reading A Psycholinguistic Guessing Game," in Harry Singer and Robert B. Ruddell, Editors, *Theoretical Models and Processes of Reading.* Second Edition. Newark, Delaware: International Reading Association, 1976, pp. 497–508. This major article discusses the reading process, considering the psychological as well as the linguistic aspects. Goodman offers a model of the reading process that has been used and accepted widely. It is an article that all in the field should read.

Huey, Edmund Burk. *The Psychology and Pedagogy of Reading.* Reprint, 1908. Cambridge, Mass.: M.I.T. Press, 1968. A classic in the psychology of reading, this book still serves as a resource to those interested in understanding the reading process. Huey attempts to describe one of the most complex operations of the human mind—the reading process. The information in this book is still, after 72 years, in the front line of current research. Although the information is somewhat dated and incomplete, Huey also reviews the development of written language.

Jennings, Frank. *This Is Reading.* New York: Teachers College, Columbia University Press, 1965. The book is concerned with the quality and function of reading in childhood and adult life. The historical, sociological, and educational settings of reading are developed. Reading is treated as a family-centered and community-wide activity as well as a school matter. This book is a must for parents, teachers, and educators.

Larrick, Nancy. *A Parent's Guide to Children's Reading.* New York: Bantam Books, 1975. This popular book is an inclusive guide offering activities and good books for young children. It belongs in every library.

Mathews, Mitford M. *Teaching To Read: Historically Considered.* Chicago, Ill.: University of Chicago Press, 1966. The author deals with what a child normally does when he reads—only with respect to the letters of an alphabet. The content focuses on the significant historical events of teaching children to read English, with the hope that the information will shed light on a "natural method" by which children learn to read.

Moffett, James. *Teaching The Universe Of Discourse.* Boston: Houghton Mifflin, 1968. In this new classic, language learning is treated in a realistic fashion, with emphasis on the young student's native ability to manipulate grammatical variables. An integration of all the language arts—

writing, reading, and dramatic dialogue—in a naturalistic way is the basis for a curriculum that helps youngsters "to play freely with the whole symbolic scale." The theoretical aspects of this book served as a guide for some of the writing activities in this book.

Olson, David R., "From Utterance To Text: The Bias of Language in Speech and Writing," *Harvard Educational Review* 47:3 (August, 1977), pp. 257–281. This very technical articles traces the history and impact of conventional explicit language from the invention of the Greek alphabet through the use of the British essayist technique. The article concludes with a discussion of the resulting conception of language and the implications for linguistic and psychological issues raised by language in society.

Reber, Arthur S. and Don L. Scarborough, Editors. *Toward A Psychology Of Reading: The Proceedings of the CUNY Conferences.* Lawrence Erlbaum Associates, 1977. Distributed by the Halsted Press Division of John Wiley and Sons, New York. The book attempts to span some of the differences between research and practice in the area of human perceptual, cognitive, and motor abilities. The papers are concerned with the relationship of reading to these abilities. The underlaying notion in all of the essays is that all are concerned with the constant pursuit of the goal for universal literacy. The volume's authors see reading as a collection of cognitive and linguistic skills, with all of the complexities that accompany the process.

Sartre, Jean-Paul. *The Words.* Translated from the French by Bernard Frechtman. New York: Braziller, 1964. Sartre's childhood joy in words and his lifetime commitment to literacy are portrayed in this moving autobiography. In the book, he explores the human experiences of language and communication. The moving rhetoric will convince all that literacy is the most gratifying human experience.

Singer, Harry and Robert Ruddell, eds. *Theoretical Models and Processes of Reading.* Revised second edition. Newark, Del.: International Reading Association, 1976. For those pursuing further understanding and alternate viewpoints of the reading/language process, this text has the answer.

Included are many models of the reading/language process. The text is very technical, but it is informative.

Smith, Frank. *Comprehension and Learning: A Conceptual Framework for Teachers.* New York: Holt, Rinehart and Winston, 1975. This book is written from the cognitive psychologist's viewpoint. The complex facts of human thought processes are discussed in such a way that those who teach children will find it extremely helpful in gaining insight into how children learn, particularly in those areas relating to language and reading. This, along with Smith's other works, served as a theoretical framework for the philosophical basis of my book.

————. "Making Sense of Reading—And of Reading Instruction," *Harvard Educational Review* 47: 3 (August 1977), pp. 386–395. Smith discusses the fact that one understands that (1) written language is meaning and that (2) written langauge is different from spoken language before he or she reads. The importance of each of these insights and how children learn them are discussed. These insights underlie the environmental preparations in Chapters 3, 4, 5, and 6 of this text.

————. *Understanding Reading: A Psycholinguistic Analysis of Reading and Learning to Read.* Second edition. New York: Holt, Rinehart and Winston, 1978. The author does an excellent job in explaining the complex skill particular only to humans—reading from linguistic, psychological, and physiological points of view.

Wolf, Thomas, "Reading Reconsidered," *Harvard Educational Review* 47: 3 (August, 1977), pp. 411–429. Wolf uses the historical definition of "read" and the results of current psychological research to reveal the narrowness of the definition of the term. He emphasizes the new ideas about the process and stresses the remarkable similarities found in the processes underlying memory, perception, reasoning, and problem solving. Wolf makes a strong case for looking at reading in connection with these cognitive capacities. The article served as support for this book's view of reading as an integral part of all cognitive behavior.

INDEX